AN IRISH TAIL

NICK ALBERT

A hilarious tale of an English couple and their unruly dogs,
searching for a new life in rural Ireland

ISBN-13: 978-1481823692

ISBN-10: 1481823698

I have tried to recreate events, locales and conversations from my memories of them. In order to maintain their anonymity in some instances I have changed the names of individuals and places, I may have changed some identifying characteristics and details such as physical properties, occupations and places of residence.

For Lesley

We must be mad!

Acknowledgments

Lesley, my beautiful intelligent and supportive wife, who gave me the time and space to finish this book, thank you for accompanying me on this search for a better life – and for all the cakes.

Joanne, our daughter, who gave her unflinching support to each of our nutty ideas; she politely pointed out my mistakes and gave me the motivation to continue writing.

Mark, thanks for you keen eye and honest opinion.

Many thanks to Gabrielle Warnock, for your exceptional help with the editing; now you can get back to your golf!

My love and thanks also to my good friends Joyce, Michelle and Michael – you all know what you did for me.

Thanks to our dogs, past and present, you make our lives richer and more interesting.

Finally thanks to the good people of Ireland, who have made us feel welcome and at home in a foreign land.

AN IRISH TAIL

Chapter 1 – In which we start a new life

"Carry on like this and you'll be dead in six months – or at best, in a padded cell with nothing but a packet of crayons to keep you entertained," my doctor said with a thin smile. "Sort your life out, Nick – or else." He gave me a cheeky wink, "Now, come outside and see my new car!" This is where it all started.

At work, the lunatic accountants had taken over the asylum, constantly changing departments, reassigning responsibilities and outsourcing customer support, I.T. functions and the office of spectacular cock-ups to some city in India, where all the telesales staff have more qualifications than an astronaut, but cost less to keep than an anorexic hamster. I loved my work; I was passionate about it – totally committed to the cause and proud of my contribution. However, in the last six years my workload had increased substantially, along with a more demanding travel schedule and too many nights away from home. Staffing levels were being slashed repeatedly, but on each occasion I had successfully fought for one of the few remaining positions. Now the stress was finally getting to me. At that moment, sitting with my doctor after a massive stress event that was cleverly disguised as a heart attack, I was one of only six survivors from the original staff in my division. At times, it seemed like I was the last man standing on the battlefield, just waiting for the sniper's bullet. I could feel that red dot itching at the back of my neck, as the accountants identified the next cost saving required to create the illusion of more profits, at the expense of decent hard working people – and perhaps me. Ironically, I had recently admitted defeat and offered my resignation, only to be told that I was indispensable to the business. I am confident that this assessment had more to do with my proportionately low pay rate, than my excellent transferable skill set and record of consistently making bonuses.

In any event, as I sat on a low wall at the back of the surgery with my doctor, looking at his new car, we agreed that I really needed to get a new life.

"Honestly Nick," my doctor said, "There's no point in working so hard and putting up with all that shit, if it means that you're going to drop dead before you are forty."

"But I'm already forty-five."

"Are you? Christ! You look well for a dead man! What's the point of having all that money, if you're dead anyway?"

"But I don't have any money, Dave; it's no more than a house of cards. I feel like I'm in debt up to my flipping eyeballs. I seem to be running all the time, just to keep up – I can't even afford a day off."

"Me neither, mate. This car cost me a ruddy fortune and I'm always running around seeing patients at all hours. I never seem to get time off." He pulled a handkerchief out of his jacket pocket and wiped an invisible speck from his windscreen, "Still –over 40 mpg and it goes like stink!"

"You need a break, you know! All that work is bad for you," I joked.

"Don't start! Anyway, we're talking about you here. What are you going to do about it?"

"I'm not sure yet. I've been talking about change recently with Lesley. We think that, provided we can sell the house for a decent price, I could jack my job in. Then we might be able to buy a place somewhere for cash and start a new life – simple living, without any debts or credit cards."

"Where would you go?" he asked.

"We were considering Scotland, perhaps Skye, or Portugal or maybe Spain. We even looked at France; prices look pretty attractive there at the moment. If we can sell the house, we might afford a small holding with a few acres; maybe we could get some goats."

My doctor leaned back on the wall, ran his fingers through his unruly blond hair and gave a big sigh. "It sounds idyllic. Can I come?"

"Nah! You've got all those people in the waiting room to see to. Get back to work – this car won't pay for itself you know."

"Piss off," he said, "Anyway, they're all a bunch of old farts with piles and boils. Such a waste of my enormous talent!" Then, with a smile, "Good luck, I hope it goes well for you. If it helps, tell your boss that if he doesn't let you go, you'll probably go nuts within six months."

I shook his hand, "Thanks mate – I think!"

"Hey," he shouted, "Don't forget – it's never too late to be who you could have been." He crossed his eyes and gave me a Vulcan salute, "Live long and prosper!"

So we went our separate ways, he reluctantly to his waiting room full of coughs and sneezes and I towards the prospect of starting a new life, with a slightly tentative spring in my step.

A lot of things had happened during the previous few years to bring my beautiful wife Lesley and me to this place in our lives. Our equally beautiful daughter, Joanne, was suddenly all grown up and already buying her own house, as she rocketed towards spectacular success in her career. My father had died recently, after a slow decline into dementia followed by a massive stroke. He was always a big influence in my life and, like many sons, I would subconsciously seek his approval for everything I did. His passing, along with the pointless and tragic death of my closest friend in a car crash, and then the recent news that another friend had just been diagnosed with brain and bowel cancer, left me feeling that I should be doing more (or perhaps less) with my life. Finally, Lesley had given up work recently and was now enjoying being what she liked to refer to as "a lady of leisure."

Retrospectively, I think that in some ways we had become like emotional nomads, travelling from challenge to challenge as if they were waterholes in the desert. We were at our most comfortable when we were fully engaged in a task that had a clear path to an obvious conclusion. Even the seemingly pointless exercise of doing jigsaw puzzles could help to fill the void between projects. A puzzle, after all, is a simple challenge, with a clear goal, that can be achieved with obvious steps. If the challenge seems too large, then you can break it down into interim steps, by first finding the corners and then connecting the edges and so on, until the picture is completed. You may feel some sense of achievement once the jigsaw is finished, but this will be followed by a feeling of emptiness – until you start the next. As young parents, the demands of everyday life provided some measure of simplicity to our lives, where each day was planned around our daughter; the need to put food on the table and pay the bills – like most people. Once Joanne was old enough to be more independent, Lesley and I instinctively started to look for new challenges, changing jobs, taking evening classes to learn new skills and renovating our Victorian terraced house. A few years later, when the renovations were complete and around the time when Joanne was getting old enough to move out, we got into the habit of "window shopping" for houses during the weekends. I don't think we actually had any serious intention of moving, but I had recently been promoted again and the housing markets were buoyant, so we were curious about what was available. One day we spotted a delightful, but derelict cottage, in a pretty village just outside Colchester, in Essex, England. It contained one elderly resident, a friend of the lately deceased original owner. The family who had recently inherited the cottage wanted to sell – as quickly as possible – but because the current and previous residents were so old and frail, the entire property had remained untouched, without maintenance or repair, for almost thirty years. With everything but the roof and walls needing replacing or repair, it was going to be a major renovation project. The state of the cottage would have put a lot of people off, but we were instantly in love with the property and committed to becoming the new owners; with Joanne's enthusiastic support and a huge bridging loan from my bank, three months later we were. Unfortunately it took another four months before we could sell our first house, which was a considerable additional strain on our nerves and finances. My employer joined in the fun by announcing a 50% cut in staff nationwide – and then giving me a new project requiring trips to every corner of the country and hundreds of nights away from home. Undaunted, we got our heads down and started the process of creating a new home. The garden was a wall of impenetrable bramble that would take three months to clear, there was no heating, all the electrics were pre-war (1939), there was significant woodworm damage in the floors and all of the windows were rotten. The kitchen was unbelievably filthy and caked in grease, but not as foul as the toilet, which showed significant signs of impatience and inaccuracy from the elderly male residents. Curiously, the bathroom was fitted with a top quality corner bath, although with mismatched, second-hand taps. Also, there was a new double garage with remote-controlled doors, but no sign of there ever having been a car. A search of the outbuildings and accessible parts of the garden revealed thirty years of collected junk, including seven hundred sheets of glass and dozens of old window frames, presumably taken from skips and building sites around the village. Disposing of all the rubbish would eventually fill twelve large skips and cost thousands. Almost five years later, all of the renovations were complete and the house looked superb – beautifully presented with real "curb appeal". Lesley's mighty efforts had produced a magnificent garden that was the envy of many visitors, especially during the recent open gardens day in the village. After so much hard work, renovating the house and gardens while still working full time, we had a real sense of achievement. But at the same time we were both getting restless, perhaps subconsciously feeling the need to get on to the next project. Also, I was also starting to feel the effects of the stress I had been under.

In another life, I might have been diagnosed with "a mid-life crisis" and given a prescription for a motorbike and an illicit affair with a nineteen-year-old blonde Latvian girl. While one cure would have been fun, the other would surely have killed me – you may decide which. In any event, money was tight and neither stress treatment was available free on the National Health Service in England. Money, or the lack of it, was a constant worry for me, even though we were not spending wildly, nor living the high life beyond our means. In common with most middle-class families at that time, our only debts were a reasonable mortgage, a small bank loan and a few credit cards. Although we were able to meet the repayments at that time and even add a little to our savings account each month, I was acutely aware of how tenuous the situation was. If I were to suffer even a small drop in pay, or, worse, lose my job, then we were only a few weeks away from financial disaster. Just eighteen months after we were married, a cruel twist of fate during an overseas contract left Lesley and me out of step with our financial commitments and potentially facing homelessness. It was shocking how quickly the reversal of fortune had occurred, with seemingly insignificant events turning into major stumbling blocks. In the end we worked our way out of the mess and the experience made us stronger, but the memory of that time is like an icicle driving into my heart. The fear of a repetition now weighed heavily on my mind and I had recently started having premonitions of disaster, waking in the night, panting, with the sheets soaked in my sweat. Even though every day the post brought further offers of new credit cards and cheaper bank loans, I felt strongly motivated to find a way out from under the burden of debt. I can understand now why some desperate people rob banks, or even consider going into politics, to make a quick buck. In any event, towards the end of 2003 the housing market seemed to be at a peak, local demand was substantial and it was obvious that, through selling the house, we could more than double our investment.

My own career, in training and coaching, was obviously at its peak and likely to demand more commitment, for fewer rewards, along with the eventual and inevitable certainty of redundancy and unemployment. Although still a comparatively young man, I was starting to feel like an old dog, no longer able to keep up with the pack. Perhaps this ridiculous feeling of vulnerability was leading me towards unrealistic expectations of my own performance and adding to the pressure I was feeling. My employer was also contributing substantially to my stress, setting higher targets, demanding longer working hours, frequent nights away from home and creating a general air of anxiety. The tension around me was palpable; I had fallen into the trap of allowing my work to dominate my life, to the detriment of my family and my health. Many people who work in management within large organisations become institutionalised, living in a sort of "corporate bubble," where the unacceptable and even the unthinkable can almost become company policy. Large organisations can develop rules and working practices that evolve dangerously, because of how the employees are rewarded. If you want to stay inside the bubble and continue to draw a salary, you must think and act as the others do. In its most benign form, you may miss out on promotion by wearing a tie on "dress down Fridays," or by taking your full holiday entitlement. At its worst, these corporate lemmings can knowingly destroy families, economies and environments in the pursuit of bigger profits. I loved my job, I was passionate about my work and proud of my achievements, but at what cost? I had started to question whether the rewards were worth the cost to my physical and emotional health; after all was said and done, were a few "exceptional" performance reviews and a cash bonus going to be adequate compensation if I ended up a physical, emotional and matrimonial wreck? To add to the fun, I was frequently dragged halfway across the country for meetings that did little but add to our workload and frustration; commuting in England was a daily nightmare of stress and delay. The trains are expensive and unreliable, and the London underground can be horribly hot and overcrowded. There are few less pleasant ways of not getting around London, than standing for two hours on a stationary underground train, with your face jammed into some fat guy's sweaty armpit, all the time wondering how long it is medically safe to hold on to a fart. The M25 London outer ring road and the terminally constricted coronary artery that allegedly connects it to Heathrow Airport, under the cheeky name of the M4, were rumoured to be the inspiration for Chris Rea to pen "Road to Hell." Every painful minute of delay in your daily commute is irreplaceable time, callously stolen from your family. Little wonder then, that people are so depressed and that road rage is becoming more violent.

When working within a large company, life can be hard and sometimes impossible to justify to those on the outside, who may live by other (more sensible) rules. One colleague proudly evidenced the commitment of his management team, by how almost all of them were now divorced. On another occasion, disaster was only narrowly averted, after a manager deliberately disabled the alarm system so he and an assistant could fight a fire without disruption to the business. Sadly, three years later, similar actions cost the life of a dear friend and almost one hundred others, in an office fire in Indonesia. Large corporations are particularly adept at destroying the souls of their employees, by simply moving the goal posts, so that those things that were almost "life and death" yesterday, become irrelevant and unimportant tomorrow. I have personal experiences of sweating blood and disregarding my family to meet some arbitrary deadline, only to find the project has been cancelled at the last minute, as the corporate eye lost interest. At times I have screamed, cried and punched the seats of my shiny new BMW because of the frustrations of outrageous business targets and inter-department wrangling. "Business as usual" and "the show must go on" are clichés that are frequently overused in an attempt to justify the indefensible. I am ashamed to say that I wasn't there to hold my father's hand as he slipped from a coma into death, because I was preparing slides for a crucial presentation – and what for? In the end, the meeting never took place. I am sure that many of the good people who worked at Lehman brothers before the crash, also gave their all – right up to the last day, when they packed their meagre belongings into a cardboard box and joined the dole queue.

Perhaps even more damaging to the spirit these days is the constant threat of unemployment or redundancy, brought about, not by the failings of loyal, hardworking employees, but by the financial manipulations of faceless executives in their ivory towers. Previously I had seen many of my friends and colleagues pointlessly lose their jobs almost overnight, to achieve a temporary "blip" in the share price in support of a failed attempt at a merger with an American company. Now it was evident that my job would probably cease to exist again, probably within six months and that I could either fight for another position, as I had done several times before, or simply accept redundancy and try to get on with a new life. After much discussion, Lesley and I had decided it was time for me to leave, and we started to plan accordingly. The previous week I had even discussed my options and opinions with my boss and his boss also, only to be told that I was too valuable to lose. For some reason, this well-meaning vote of confidence only added to my stress; I imagined that on my boss's desk, my photograph was sitting in a personnel file marked, "Must keep! Will work for peanuts and is reasonably unlikely to really screw up." Lesley and I were very conscious of a shared desire for a different and better life, and the possibility of starting anew was a regular topic of conversation; particularly when we were out walking our dogs.

At that time we had two dogs, named Brandy and Romany. Brandy is a pedigree Lhasa Apsos bitch, one of a pair we had purchased from a local breeder some ten years previously. Her sister "Tammy" had sadly died after a long illness when aged just seven. Brandy has a thick coat the colour of warm honey and "love me" eyes, which were like looking into her heart and seeing melted chocolate. If you are unfamiliar with the breed, the Lhasa Apsos originates from Tibet where the name means "Barking Lion or Little Lion," depending on which book you read. They are loyal, intelligent, playful and inquisitive dogs with a warning bark that is twice their diminutive size. On the day that I secretly collected our new puppies from the breeder while on my journey home from work, I walked into the house clutching a small cardboard box and a few items of paperwork from my office. Our daughter Joanne was still a young girl, as pretty as her mother, tall for her age and athletically slim, with short brown hair, sparkling blue eyes, and a cheeky smile displaying the silver braces on her teeth. Although normally a diligent student, she had recently become a teenager and on this day she was keen to avoid her homework, by reprimanding me for my own.

"Aw Dad!" She groaned, "Have you brought loads of work home again? I thought we were going to the cinema – you promised."

"This isn't my work; it's something for you to do." I countered, dropping the box onto her lap.

She was quick to respond. "I can't help you, I've got loads of homework to do – I've just remembered."

"Tuff luck," I said with mock sternness.

Lesley was in on the gag and added from the doorway, "You should do as your father says!"

Joanne fixed a full teenage pout onto her face and was about to launch into another objection, when the box on her lap started to move and whimper. Open mouthed she looked at our beaming smiles and then opened the box and gave a yelp of delight. Inside were two squiggly little balls of fur, one brown and white and the other white and brown, both were desperately scrabbling for her attention. Like miniature overstuffed caricatures of the perfect puppy, covered in velvety soft fur and equipped with beautiful deep brown eyes, each was no larger than her hand. They became her constant companions, happy to lie at her side while she did her homework, or trot along proudly when she took them for long walks in the park. With Joanne's enthusiastic encouragement

Tammy learned to use the slide at the park, patiently waiting in line with the children, before climbing the stairs and sliding down the shoot and into Joanne's waiting arms. Brandy even learned how to run after a ball, but she considered the process of pursuit and retrieval to be somewhat pointless and would usually drop the ball and wander off at the first distraction. As far as she was concerned, if you wanted the ball then you shouldn't have thrown it away in the first place.

After we bred Brandy and Tammy, and mostly at the behest of our daughter, we decided to keep the runt of the litter, who was eventually given the name Romany. She was a delightful puppy, playful and full of beans, until she was old enough to have her first proper walk... Along with her mother and aunt, Romany confidently and proudly trotted along with her nose and tail held high in the air, like a princess in a white fur coat. Once we reached the field and were away from the main road, I let all three dogs off their leads. Brandy and Tammy bounded away along the usual route and Romany trotted along behind, confidently mimicking her mother's every move. When they ran, she ran, when they walked, she walked and when they peed, so did Romany. At the bottom of the hill, the footpath was bisected by a narrow ditch, filled with stagnant water, slime, and the usual garbage generated by most fast food eating, beer swilling populations in town centres these days. In line astern first Brandy, and then Tammy, jumped across the three foot gap with an athletic spring. Last in line, Romany attempted to replicate their aerial acrobatics, but because she was half the size of her mother, she only covered half the distance. Like a scene from a "Road Runner" cartoon, Romany hung in the air for what seemed like several seconds, with her legs paddling desperately, before plopping like a fluffy stone into the filthy water below. The poor little thing went in looking like the latest celebrity fashion accessory and emerged, a few seconds later, looking like an oily rag. With head down and tail between her legs, she turned dejectedly for home, her confidence shattered forever.

Because she was always the smallest doggy in the room, competing with the other two for a fuss from somebody with only two hands, Romany quickly discovered that she could become the tallest by balancing on her bottom, in a begging position. She wasn't particularly adept at this mildly acrobatic feat, wobbling precariously back and forth like a drunken Scottish sailor until she received a fuss, or rolled over backwards. When she was a young dog, as skinny as a racing snake, she would instantly spring up again and resume her begging position, but as a more rotund dog in later life, she would remain stranded on her back, turtle-like, until the inevitable rescue. Should you decide to subject the helpless dog to a tummy tickle, she would squirm and giggle in delight, like a child. As prissy as a teenage prom queen and reluctant to even step in a muddy puddle, she once amazed us by spontaneously inventing the game of "mud surfing" while we were walking on the mud flats of the River Severn estuary in high summer. While Brandy sunbathed in the baking heat alongside Lesley on a sandy embankment, Joanne and I decided to walk Romany out across the cool muddy sands of the estuary, in search of seashells and interesting pebbles. Suddenly the little dog ran ahead, perhaps intending to chase after a nearby wading bird, but moments later she lost her footing and slid sideways into a shallow puddle. The resulting splash of cooling water seemed to delight her and she immediately jumped up and repeated the slide into the next puddle. For almost an hour Romany raced about madly, ignoring our ever more desperate calls to return, leaning over like a bike racer and using her shoulders to surf along the mud. Each "surf" sprayed water, and stinking estuary mud, several feet into the air and all along each flank of her previously white coat. In due course, she tired of this never to be repeated game and trotted back with a huge grin on her otherwise mud smeared face. For some reason, Lesley refused to believe that Romany had invented this game without any input from me, although how she thought I had explained the rules and techniques of "mud surfing" remained unexplained. In punishment I was sentenced to find a hosepipe and wash the stinking mud off our little prima donna. By the time we had walked back to the camp site in the hot sun, the mud had dried to a dull grey, prompting a passing pensioner to comment on the unusual colour of our pretty dog! Later in life Romany was plagued with infected eyes and the canine equivalent of Crohn's disease, which caused cramps and a bleeding bowel – both afflictions are unfortunately quite common in the breed, although Brandy remained in excellent health.

During the previous few months, we had endlessly chewed over the numbers and options for moving, spending hours on the internet, looking at houses, businesses and jobs, both at home and abroad. If everything worked out in our favour, it would be possible to start a new life, free of debt and stress, where the air is clean, the sky blue and the water sweet. There were hundreds of interesting and exciting properties available in Scotland, Wales, Portugal, Spain and the north of England, but painfully few job opportunities. A year previously, I had even set up my own limited company and started building up a small bank of private clients that I could see in the evenings and at weekends, but the income was still a long way from replacing that of my employed position. I had also placed my C.V. with several local recruitment agencies in an effort to keep my options open. Although I had an excellent work history with several notable awards and achievements and consistently high performance review scores, I had been unsuccessful in all of my job interviews. While I presented very well on each occasion, either the package on offer for my grade was well below my current basic salary, or I was deemed to be too experienced to fit into any alternative career. Put simply, I was over-aged and over-paid. The prospect of being without a regular income was starting to frighten me. On paper the figures added up, but for everything to work out, allowing Lesley and I to start a new life successfully, a lot of ducks needed to get in line and the first "duck" in line was probably quitting my job. This was an alarming step, because there was no guarantee of any of the other ducks joining in, but I felt it needed to happen first and it needed to happen quickly. In an ideal world we would have first sold our house and perhaps rented for a while, as we organised the move abroad. Then the final step would be to quit work and jump on the next flight out; it all sounds so easy. However, our experience was that the dream of starting again, in a simpler, less stressful life, would remain a dream unless we jumped in with both feet. If I carried on working we wouldn't have the time or freedom to do the house-hunting and there would be no incentive to sell the house. On the other hand, even if I continued to see clients privately, if I left my job first, we would have to sell the house and cash in our investments, to clear any outstanding debts before my severance pay and savings ran out. We would need to buy another house in some (yet to be selected) country, move and then probably try to find some work. In the unlikely event that we couldn't sell the house, I would be forced to try and find work locally at a similar, or better salary – and this seemed doubtful, at age forty-five, in a changing and competitive job market. It was a tricky conundrum. We both needed the motivation to start things moving; otherwise we would end up carrying on, out of habit, as we had in the past.

Then on Sunday morning, while I was meeting with a private client, I started to feel unwell. At first I felt a little dizzy and flushed, and then I noticed that I was distracted and unable to concentrate. Thinking that I might just be coming down with a head cold, I did my best to carry on working. However, within an hour I was feeling considerably worse, with a sharp pain in my chest and back, cold sweats and a racing heart. Obviously, something was wrong, so I apologised to my client and set off for home. Lesley was surprised to see me home so early, but immediately noticed that I was looking very pale in the face and unwell. Despite my protests, she called the out of hours medical helpline who advised us to go immediately to a nearby clinic. Within minutes I was on a heart monitor while a nice Indian doctor was checking my blood pressure and shaking his head. I wasn't worried or scared, but I could see that Lesley was very concerned, despite her attempt at "gallows humour" by asking about my level of life cover and funeral preferences. Initially I was quite pragmatic and practical in my thinking – I was after all a comparatively young and fit non-smoker, a former karate instructor who enjoyed running most days; I had been vegetarian for twenty years and didn't drink much alcohol. My feeling was that if something was wrong with my machine, the doctors would fix it. Although I wasn't happy, I didn't see any need to worry. After about an hour, our local GP Dave Harrison popped his head around the door; he was about my age and we were friends.

"Hey Nick, Hi Lesley," he waved and smiled. "I heard you were here – I thought I would pop in."

"Thanks Dave. No need to worry though, I'm feeling a good bit better now. It's all a big fuss over nothing. I only came here because Lesley was worried."

"Well you're not dead yet, I suppose."

"Do you have any idea what's going on?" asked Lesley.

"I was thinking we might send you home in an hour or so, if nothing changes. It looks like you had a bad reaction to all the stress you've been under. I have been warning you about this for months." He looked at my chart. "Come and see me at the surgery tomorrow morning – I should have all the test results by then." Then more sternly, "Nick, we need to talk about this – it's important."

The following morning Dave explained his diagnosis.

"Listen Nick, the human body is a wondrous machine; it can absorb all manner of punishment and yet heal itself. With poisons and toxins it can even build up a resistance, like with alcohol. When you first drink, you are under the table after a couple of glasses. But if you continue drinking regularly, you discover that you can drink all night and hardly feel the effects."

"So you didn't waste your time at medical school then?" I quipped.

"Not at all, it was all serious research. Lots of hangovers, but it had to be done."

"What's all this got to do with me?" I asked.

"Well – here's the thing. Stress is different. It seems like the body and mind can absorb almost any amount of stress without any negative side effects. In fact, some people, like you, almost seem to thrive on it. Then one day – bang! You can't take any more. Worse than that, you suddenly can't take any stress at all. That's what I think has happened to you."

I sat quietly for a moment. "So what does all this mean, how do I get better?"

"Well, at the end of the day you need to get away from all this stress. Your body just can't take it any longer. There are some drugs we could try temporarily, but that would merely be postponing the inevitable. Yesterday you had a big warning, next time it could be a lot worse."

I put my head in my hands and we fell silent for a while. Dave was being very clever, he wanted me to think seriously about what had happened. I wasn't frightened, but I was angry. Angry with my employer for exposing me and my colleagues to such unnecessary stress. Angry with myself for allowing it to happen, for being too weak and selfish to stand up and say, "Enough!" and angry with my body for failing me. It had always seemed to me that, provided I looked after my body, it would look after me. If I had a good diet, didn't drink excessively and kept fit, it was reasonable to expect that I would stay fairly healthy. That was the deal. In my limited experience of ill health, most things that broke could be fixed, with the application of a little medicine and time. I had never considered that my body would let me down. Breaking a leg, getting cancer or catching some virus was acceptable and manly. It seemed to me that there was nothing "macho" about being a victim of stress. I wasn't a coward, I was a karate black belt and I had faced up to my fears in the past, except for big spiders – I'm not that stupid! But now I was being told I couldn't handle stress anymore. I wondered how I could fix this; I was starting to feel like a heavyweight boxer, who had just been told that the next punch would be fatal. Finally I looked up.

"Okay. What do you suggest I do?" I asked.

"Well that's up to you my friend, but I think you've got some important decisions to make, and quickly." I noticed he changed his posture, leaning forward to emphasise his point. "Carry on like this and you'll be dead in six months – or at best, in a padded cell with nothing but a packet of crayons to keep you entertained." He patted my knee and gave me a thin smile. "Sort your life out, or else. Now, come outside and see my new car!"

It was a cold and frosty morning, but the sun warmed us as we sat on the wall admiring Dave's new car. I was grateful that he had taken the time and trouble to help me find a cure. We chatted about nothing in particular, for twenty minutes and then he sent me on my way to get my life back in balance. Lesley and I had discussed the options extensively, but ultimately the decision was a "no brainer." Something had to change. At lunchtime on Monday I called my boss and informed him that I wanted out, and two hours later he called me back and my wish was granted. I was to be made redundant. At that moment, I felt as if a great weight was lifted from my shoulders. At the same time a cold hand seemed to grip my bowel.

I thought, "That's it. No going back now."

Chapter 2 – In which we begin our search

From that point, things seemed to happen quite quickly. I was only required to work for a few days, to clear my desk, before being placed on garden leave until my official termination date. I carried on seeing my private clients and looked at ways of finding new clients through referrals and advertising. After a little research we put the house up for sale with a "posh" estate agent, on the clear understanding that we would also be trying to sell privately. It was first advertised the following week in a glossy "House and Garden" magazine. The advertisement and pictures made the property look so attractive that we almost put in an offer ourselves.

Over the next few days, we spent hours on the internet, looking at houses in Scotland, Wales, Portugal, Spain and the North of England. There were quite a number of nice looking properties within our budget, but at the same time each presented some issues or concerns, either running costs, location and size, or, for the overseas properties, language and taxation. We soon started to realize that shopping for a house that was hundreds of miles away, and possibly in a country where English was not a first language, was going to be a challenge. Even some basic research produced several horror stories of well-informed house hunters losing everything by buying homes in Spain and Cyprus. It seemed that there was a potential minefield of legal loopholes and planning disasters, waiting for inexperienced house hunters. We needed to tread very carefully. Secondly, I was concerned about the possible levels of income tax, inheritance tax, property tax, social security and healthcare. Although we were about to have a much healthier bank account, the overall plan was to reduce our overheads and survive on a lower income. Any small miscalculation in the planning stage could have major repercussions further down the line. For example, in at least one country we looked at, inheritance tax was paid on all of the joint assets after the first death in a married couple, whereas, in Britain, inheritance tax was only due on part of the estate, after the second death. The result, if we got it wrong, would be either carrying additional and expensive life assurance, or needing to sell the house to pay taxes in the event of a death.

We drew up a wish list of things we wanted or needed from our new home and, although it wasn't comprehensive, it gave us some rules to work to. Starting with the location, we decided that we wanted to be close enough to travel and visit our families in Norfolk and Essex, within a day. By travelling by road for six hours, we could consider houses on the south coast of England, as far west as Devon and Wales and north to the Lake District. If we included rail travel, then Cornwall and the Scottish borders came into range, while if we added budget air travel, then Ireland, Scotland, France, Spain and Portugal were also possibilities, provided the house was reasonably near the correct airport. The type of property we wanted was always going to be limited by budget and availability, but there were a few things we both agreed on. Our dream property would probably not be a newly built house; we both preferred homes with some personality – even if it was slightly eccentric. It would have some land, perhaps several acres, giving enough room to grow plenty of vegetable and enough space for our dogs to run free. Ideally the house would be remote enough to provide a sense of freedom and privacy, but close enough to shops and essential services to remain feasible. It needed to be big enough to accommodate all of our oak dining room furniture and several display cabinets, as well as having a large kitchen and at least three bedrooms. We also wanted to be able to add a separate wing or building, should we need to care for our elderly parents, or start a B&B at some point. We were happy to consider a renovation project, even something requiring substantial work – provided that there was sufficient budget left over to pay someone else to do the bulk of the work. Lesley declined to describe her dream house any further, saying only that she would "know it when she saw it."

As for the availability of work, this again depended on our budget resulting from the house purchase. I was positive that I did not want to end up, as an over-stressed manager, doing the same job as before, just in a different country. If necessary, I would be quite happy working as a delivery driver or filling shelves at a local supermarket – good honest work that I could easily cope with and still be able to sleep at night. On the other hand, if our income requirements were low enough, I would love to be able to do the work I was trained to do, the thing I am best at, but on a freelance basis. To do that, we needed a house with low running costs and a location that gave me ample access to clients who spoke English.

"I've been thinking," is a phrase that sends chills down my spine, as it is usually followed with a request from Lesley to relocate the newly erected greenhouse, knock down a wall, build a taller house, or move the planet a bit to the left. I usually counter humorously…

"Now dear, I thought we discussed this and decided that you were going to stop thinking for a while." To which she traditionally responds by delivering a loving punch to my arm – worthy of a heavyweight boxer.

One evening, about a week into the house hunting process, Lesley sidled up to me in the small room that I used as my office.

"Nick?" She said as sweetly as a little girl, about to ask her father for a pony, "I've been thinking."

I glanced away from the computer and eyed my wife suspiciously over the top of my reading glasses. In the weeks leading up to my "stress event", she had become equally gloomy and tired, almost bordering on depression. Now as I looked into her pretty blue eyes, I could see a new sparkle of enthusiasm and hope. Her long brown hair was tied up with a frilly band, exposing the soft curve of her neck and she was wearing a white blouse and beige hipsters that accentuated her trim figure. Moments earlier Lesley had returned from a trip to town to get some shopping and now she was holding a copy of the "Smallholder" magazine. I noticed that our two dogs were happily dancing around her heels, perhaps sensing her excitement. Suspecting that something big was coming my way; I turned and gave her my full attention. Lesley drew herself up to her full height, took a deep breath and with a huge smile, delivered the punch line, like a magician pulling an elephant out of a hat.

"I-R-E-L-A-N-D!"

"Ireland? What about Ireland?" I asked.

"We could move to Ireland!"

"We could?"

"Yes!" She said triumphantly.

"Really?" I asked sceptically.

"Yes!" She replied with exasperation.

"But why Ireland, doesn't it always rain there?"

"Not all the time – silly! Anyway, I wouldn't mind."

Remembering how she had "felt a bit cold" in the fifty degree midday heat, during a recent trip to Egypt, I raised my eyebrows until they got to within a few inches of my receding hairline.

"Are you sure?"

She gave a big sigh. "Look, forget that for a minute. It's a good idea. I've been looking at houses from all over in here," she waved the magazine at me, "and Ireland is the best. It's cheaper than France, closer than Scotland and the economy is doing well. They call it the Celtic Tiger."

Her enthusiasm was infectious. I nodded at the magazine. "Go on then, I'll bite."

She gave me another beaming smile and leaning over, pointed to an advertisement in the magazine; it showed a small cottage without a roof, overlooking a beautiful valley. The text read, "Pile of stones on 2 acres with optional donkey, outline planning permission for a 4 bedroom house – €58,000." The honesty and humour of the advertisement was immediately very attractive, there was a web address and we felt compelled to investigate further.

Alan Sykes is English, a quirky fellow and an estate agent (or auctioneer, to apply the correct local title) in County Clare, in the west of Ireland. He has won awards for his honesty as an estate agent although presumably not from other estate agents – some of whom might view such dubious values as a breach of a secret code. To the naive house buyer, it can sometimes seem that an honest estate agent is as rare as a delivery arriving on time or a politician admitting to an affair, or a computer security patch actually patching security. Work out the odds yourself. In any event, we were intrigued enough to look at the website. There appeared to be hundreds of properties on offer, from small plots of soggy earth with little prospect of ever being anything but small plots of soggy earth, to huge mansions with swimming pools and helicopter landing pads. The website was conveniently arranged by price, so it was easy to review every property within our budget. It quickly became clear that Lesley was correct. Compared to the other countries we had looked at, there were considerably more properties available in Ireland within the price range and of the style we were looking for. Although neither of us had ever visited Ireland, I had lived in Scotland for a few years as a child and had later holidayed there with Lesley. Although not quite the same, Ireland at least offered the prospect of being reasonably similar and therefore potentially familiar. A small amount of research revealed that, since the end of the "troubles," Ireland had developed a healthy and expanding economy. It also boasted a very low crime rate and slightly better weather than some of the alternatives like Wales and Scotland. Additionally, Ireland was very much a part of Europe, using the euro and because the sterling exchange rate was excellent, the houses we liked seemed even cheaper and a potential move more plausible. We decided that our next step should be to combine a short holiday with a house hunting expedition. This would give us the opportunity to see and experience Ireland for ourselves, view some houses and decide if we liked what we saw – a bit like a blind date.

Over the next few days, we booked flights to Ireland and a hire car and then arranged accommodation at a B&B near Ennis, in County Clare. We were encouraged to discover that Ryanair had three daily return flights from London Stansted directly to Shannon Airport, which was just a short drive from Ennis. As both our daughter and Lesley's mother lived close to Stansted, should we decide to move, with a flight time of around an hour we could visit "door to door" far quicker than we could have driven from Wales, Scotland or Cornwall. So that was another positive for the move to Ireland.

When we had started married life twenty-two years before, Lesley and I had a Victorian terraced house with one hundred and twenty feet of garden, and then we progressed to a village cottage with three quarters of an acre. So the prospect of owning a smallholding of up to five acres, with a renovation project, was becoming extremely attractive. We had created a primary list of "must see" properties, from three different auctioneers, and then had agreed dates for the viewings; we also kept a back-up list of some houses that appeared to be less attractive. All of the properties had at least an acre of land and all but one were what the Irish call "second-hand houses," properties that have been lived in before. We were surprised to discover that, because of the wealth being created by the "Celtic Tiger" economy, many Irish people would only consider buying new products; this resulted in many second-hand items, including cars and houses, being more difficult to sell. A high proportion of the houses being sold at the time were going to overseas buyers from England, Germany and America, with many of the properties being "banked" for future sale at a higher price. Bizarrely, those Irish people who decided to invest in property were mostly buying overseas in Bulgaria and Spain, although some did borrow heavily to engage in the lucrative "buy to let" market at home. The house that we finally bought almost didn't get on the list at all. It was presented as the feature property on the Clare Valley website and was totally ignored by us, on fifty or sixty visits to the site. The photographs made it look so beautiful that we assumed it was either hugely expensive, or just an advert for the site, rather than a house for sale. Fortunately, one day Lesley clicked on the link to the property and we were instantly interested. It was secluded, with four acres of land and a beautiful house with four bedrooms and outbuildings, all in need of some renovation but well within our budget. We put it at number three on the "must see" list. Now it was time to visit Ireland for the first time.

One morning near the end of 2003, we booked our two Lhasa Apsos dogs into the kennels, arranged for a friend to feed our chickens and were just loading our bags into the car before setting off for the airport, when our new neighbour walked by. We only knew him to smile, wave and chat with. He seemed like a nice chap, but as they had only moved in recently and both he and I worked odd hours, we hadn't had much social contact. I was aware that he and all of his family were members of a religious sect called the Plymouth Brethren, most obviously because the wives all wore headscarves and walked two paces behind their husbands; I was also aware that several members of his extended family had recently bought houses in the village. He stopped to say hello and then asked if we were going away on holiday. We told him that we were planning to move abroad and that the house was up for sale although no sign had been erected at that time. Immediately, he started looking over my shoulder at the house and then asked what the sale price was.

"Why do you ask, Richard?" I questioned jokingly, "Do you want to buy it?"

"Well, you never know. I would like to buy a house for my parents, something closer to our house, and you can't get much closer than this." he said with a very serious face.

As we had a little time to spare before our flight, I asked him if he wanted to come in to have a look around. He and his wife toured the house for about thirty minutes, making all the right noises about knocking down walls and adding toilets and chairlifts. Finally, they viewed the garden and even asked if we would be interested in leaving the chickens, as they had always wanted to have fresh eggs in the morning; which I took as a positive sign. Although it was nice to chat, our time on that day was limited, so we agreed that we had to move on, or we were going to miss our flight. Richard thanked us for our time and wished us well on our trip. In a perfect world they would have bought the house right then, but it wasn't to be. Still – at worst we had wasted thirty minutes and gained a little confidence about just how saleable and well-presented our house was.

Despite what most people seem to think about Ryanair, I have always found then to be quick and efficient – but then anything is an improvement after flying with Nigerian airways! The flight to Ireland was smooth and quick, we arrived on time, alive and with some of our luggage. Who could ask for more? I love flying, and so I spent most of the flight looking out of the window. We flew North West out of Stansted, turned left near Birmingham, crossed the coast between Anglesey and the Isle of Man, then out over the Irish Sea. Through breaks in the cloud I could see the ferries below, looking like toy boats, sailing between Holyhead and Dublin. I wondered if we would be making the same trip soon, with our furniture and dogs. The sky started to clear as we passed over Dublin and almost immediately the pilot set the aircraft on a gradual descent towards Shannon Airport. I was struck by how lush and beautiful the land looked, with each tiny field separated from the next by dry stone walls, and by how much space there appeared to be between each village and town. In no time, we were passing the spectacular Slieve Bloom Mountains and then Lough Derg at the base of the River Shannon. As we flew over empty looking roads, I could see Limerick to our left and some houses and industrial estates. Then, just as it seemed that we were going to land in a field, the runway appeared and we were down. The spoilers deployed, the engines roared in full reverse thrust and the breaks groaned as the pilot attempted to leave the runway at the first available exit. This must be a ploy to help the hard pressed cabin crew achieve their "five minute turnaround" I thought, as all the rubbish in the plane, along with a few coats, two passports and a bag of fresh vomit, slid to the front for easy collection. The stewardess welcomed us all to Ireland and asked that we "remain in our seats until the plane had stopped and the captain had switched off the fasten seatbelts sign," an instruction that is completely ignored by almost every passenger worldwide. After passing through the delightfully quiet arrivals hall, we collected our hire car and set off towards our B&B, which was situated just north of Ennis, the county town of Clare. Within minutes we had passed out of the airport and were enjoying our first view of Ireland.

Chapter 3 – In which we discover Ireland

My initial impression of Ireland, during the drive to Ennis, was that it was green, clean and wonderfully quiet. For the majority of our visit, we saw no graffiti, hardly any rubbish and only 10% of the traffic we were accustomed to seeing in England. In fact, there was so little traffic that, on one trip of around fifty miles later that week, we realised that we could have pulled out of every junction we encountered, without looking, and we wouldn't have been hit by another car. It seems that some Irish drivers drive that way anyway! On the fifteen mile trip up the N18 dual-carriageway from Shannon Airport to Ennis, we saw only six cars, and yet on two occasions I saw one car travelling, on an otherwise deserted motorway, with a second car no more than inches behind. "Tailgating" of this sort, in most civilized countries, would quickly lead to fist waving, shouting and physical violence, but in Ireland it was completely ignored; perhaps there is an exception in their highway code. I did wonder if the same rules applied when standing in a queue of two people, in a bank or shop. Should I stand one inch behind the lady in front (who had just tailgated my car for the last ten miles) and if I did, would she comment?

Local quirks aside, I found driving in Ireland to be most pleasurable, both then and now. Most of the larger roads have space on the left to help slow farm traffic (and nervous tourists) to keep out of the way, allowing faster traffic to pass. Most drivers are courteous, quick to give way and happy to let you pull out of side roads. The road signage is similar to that of most European countries and easy enough to follow, although you need to allow a little flexibility with regard to the distances shown. At the time, the country was changing from miles to kilometres on all road signs and to the casual observer it seemed that the local council staff just went out with a crayon, crossed out miles and wrote kilometres. On Monday, one sign near us showed "Ennis 14 miles" and by Tuesday the new sign, in exactly the same spot, read "Ennis 14 km"! Many directional signs seem to point in entirely random directions and in some places the number of signs on each post seemed to challenge the laws of gravity. However, we found one particular road safety sign to be downright dangerous. When leaving the N18 near Limerick, we approached a sharp bend and saw the word "Slow" written on the road – one hundred yards later the bend tightened still further and as helpful advice to obstinate drivers the word "Slower" was written across the road – we laughed so hard that I almost put the car in the ditch!

After a short search we found our B&B accommodation, where we were warmly welcomed and shown to a quaint bedroom, in which the walls were covered with pictures of Jesus and a huge crucifix at the head of the bed threatened the risk of crushing injuries, even death, should the headboard move too violently for any non-sleeping reason. At least we had a nice view of the road, carpets and an en-suite bathroom with a mouldy shower. Although it was well into winter, there was no heating in the bedrooms and every night we slept almost fully clothed in an effort to stay warm under the damp sheet and threadbare blanket. I even wore a woolly hat to warm my threadbare head. The guest lounge, however, always had a roaring peat fire, which gave off a lovely smell and enough heat to warm anyone who could manage to sit within three or four feet. The lack of heat didn't really matter anyway, as the lady of the house seemed to be going through "the change" and had every window open, even when it was snowing. Nevertheless, we enjoyed some lovely late evenings in the lounge, chatting aimlessly with our host and the other guests, who were mostly travelling students and American tourists. After all the stresses of the last few months, it was delightful to sit in such an oasis of calm and converse about nothing in particular, for no apparent reason. One night, the strangest thing happened. As we all sat by the fire talking, I noticed a butterfly flapping about near the ceiling and a few moments later it was joined by a second – and then a third. Within twenty minutes, there were perhaps thirty butterflies flying around, all having appeared from thin air – or so it seemed. After some discussion, we decided the butterflies had taken refuge for the winter, through the open windows, and had then been temporarily woken by the heat from the fire. Since then, I have seen the occasional butterfly woken in similar circumstances, but never nearly so many – it was a truly magical and beautiful moment. In retrospect, although we had yet to find our dream property, I believe that it was on that evening, sitting by the fire, enjoying the easy company of strangers and laughing at the dancing butterflies, that we decided we would move to Ireland.

Each evening we drove into Ennis to eat, either at a pub or restaurant. As a vegetarian, I was pleasantly surprised by the quality of the food on offer, along with the delightful flavour of the local Guinness. Lesley is almost teetotal and I don't drink much alcohol either, although I was sometimes partial to a decent glass of red wine with a meal; drinking this Guinness was a new experience for me. The flavour in Ireland is quite different to the pint that is served in England – much smoother and nuttier; I understand that the flavour of Guinness in Ireland can even vary from county to county. Perhaps it was my age, or the wonderful fresh air, but after a good meal and just two pints of "the black stuff," a few moments relaxation by the fire was guaranteed to send me off to sleep. Buying my first pint was slightly embarrassing because I was unaware that there is a special technique to pouring the perfect pint, which involves half-filling the glass and then leaving it to settle, whilst serving several other customers and apparently ignoring me and my outthrust handful of cash, before returning to finish the job a few minutes later. As I was reasonably familiar with the British system, where one attracts the attention of the barperson by waving money and then maintains "ownership" through eye contact or conversation until the transaction is complete, I was flummoxed when I ordered my pint and the barman seemed to just walk away. My protests exposed my inexperience and the lovely patient barkeeper explained the process with a smile, before delivering my first pint with a perfect shamrock drawn in the foam head – it was delicious and well worth the wait. On another occasion, our local knowledge and cultural differences created a glut of liquid. We visited a pub near Bunratty Castle (both the pub and castle are well worth a visit) and, being quite thirsty, Lesley asked for a pint of orange juice and lemonade and a few moments later she was duly presented with a pint of lemonade, called "white" lemonade, and then a separate pint of orange juice. Later we discovered that we should have asked for something called a "55". It was all good fun and greeted with a smile, from us both.

Lesley and I have always been "early to bed and early to rise" people and we had plans to start early each day on our house hunting expedition, so we were amazed to discover that breakfast at the B&B was not served until nine o'clock. Most mornings we were awake, washed and dressed by six thirty and sitting in our freezing bedroom, hungry and desperate for our morning "cuppa". There was no kettle in the room, but by the third morning we had hidden away a secret stock of biscuits and orange juice, to see us through the long dark morning hours. At the other end of the day, things were a little different. One night at around eleven o'clock, our hostess came into the lounge with a huge pile of thick cut ham sandwiches. It seems that ham is deemed suitable food for vegetarians in Ireland, along with fish and chicken. As we were already full to the gills after our earlier pub meal and I don't eat ham, chicken or fish, Lesley was faced with the prospect of eating the entire plate, or creating a regrettable international incident. Luckily, just as all hope seemed lost, the Americans saved Britain again, when two hungry female backpackers arrived and gratefully cleared the plate. On another occasion, we were both woken from a deep sleep, at half past midnight, by a violent banging on the door. I leapt out of bed, heart thumping and expecting to have to fight a fire or grapple with a burglar, only to discover our sweet hostess had taken it upon herself to bring us tea and biscuits. It was a lovely thought, but would have been more welcome six hours later. On the other hand, breakfast was a magnificent affair. I would stock up on porridge, then eggs on thick slices of toast dripping in butter, washed down with gallons of strong Barry's tea. Lesley looked forward to her coffee and a "full Irish breakfast," which was a large plate heaving with bacon, sausages, black and white puddings, fried eggs, tomatoes, mushrooms, fried potatoes, baked beans and toast or wheaten bread. On holiday in Ireland during the winter, I guarantee there is no better way to start the day.

Walking around Ennis late at night was unusual, but pleasing, after living in South East England for so many years. Late at night in many British town and cities, you would see a heavy police presence, public drunkenness and be aware of the constant anticipation of violence. Daylight would reveal streets littered with discarded takeaway containers, broken glass, vomit and the signs of pointless vandalism. In Ennis by comparison, the streets were safe, clean and entirely devoid of any signs of rubbish or graffiti. It seemed that everyone we passed made eye contact, along with a smile, and they were willing to stop and chat at the slightest provocation. Initially, we were convinced that we were being mistaken for someone else (perhaps someone famous, richer and better looking), but it was soon clear that people were just more open and sociable than we were accustomed to. In many parts of Ireland, and in County Clare in particular, people still have the inclination, and time, to stop and talk to passing friends and strangers. Try making eye contact with random strangers in most British cities and you will be treated as an escaped mental patient, or end up having a conversation with one. I think that, along with the natural affability of the rural Irish, this tendency to acknowledge the presence of other people comes from the proportionally lower population. Obviously two English people meeting in the middle of the desert and unable to ignore each other any longer, will find themselves striking up a conversation about the weather, or the nearest waterhole – but progress through a crowded London shopping centre is still best achieved by keeping your eyes on the prize.

This uncontrollable urge to acknowledge the presence of other people as they pass also applies while driving, although there appear to be local and regional variations that cannot be explained. In general, in rural parts of County Clare, passing drivers will subtly raise the right index finger, no more than two inches, but without removing the hand from the steering wheel, to say "Hi" to other motorists or pedestrians. It does become a habit and you find yourself looking for a "finger" to respond to, and even getting annoyed when you miss a late presentation from a passing driver. On one occasion the habit got the better of me and I accidentally waved to a horse that was leaning over a gate, only to be delighted when the lovely beast waved its head in reply! Of course, not all motorists will comply as some may be visitors from the city, or tourists who can get confused and stare blankly, or panic and wave their entire hand – which is only acceptable when returning an identical wave from the first generation of your immediate family.

Strangely, as you drive across the county, the practice of "giving the finger" to passing strangers will suddenly stop and then resume a few miles later, without any perceptible logic or reason. I am convinced that the weekly parish notices secretly contain messages like, "This week, random waving at passing strangers will be conducted in Corofin, Kilfenora and Kinvarra on Tuesday, Wednesday and Friday. Drivers through Tulla and Scarriff will continue to wave at every third vehicle and those in Flagmount will wave at everyone except Paddy Malone, as his fecking cows were on my land again last week!"

Another peculiarity to parts of Clare comes from the fact that the introduction of the horseless carriage has not changed people's desire to stop and chat. It is quite ordinary and acceptable to find two cars facing in opposite directions, completely blocking the road as their occupants talk through the open windows. If you are delayed on your next visit to Ireland, please do not toot your horn or enquire as to the cause of the delay. On encountering such an obstacle, it is deemed best practice to switch off your engine and wait patiently, while perhaps reading the paper or learning to play the tin whistle – I know someone who carries one in his car for this reason alone. Strange then, when there is clear evidence that the pace of life is slower in Ireland, that some of the driving can be so unsettlingly fast.

For many years, it seemed that Ireland had a very relaxed attitude to things like learning to drive, road safety, speed limits, vehicle maintenance and drink driving. Before 2010, it seemed that passing a driving test was optional and unrelated to whether you owned and operated a car or a 40 ton lorry. In the UK, drivers can practice driving on a provisional license, provided they are insured and accompanied by an experienced driver. As I understand it, at one time in the past in Ireland, the department of transport decided that it would be nice if all drivers proved that they could drive by passing a test. Shortly after, they realized that they were woefully short of test centres, testers and instructors. So they issued the existing drivers with licenses immediately and required that any new drivers pass the test. However, still short of test centres, they decided that provisional driver should be accompanied at all times when driving, but should they take a test and fail, they would be issued with a second provisional license, which would allow them to drive unaccompanied indefinitely, provided they continued to display an "L" plate. I am sure that the department of transport expected drivers to return diligently to be retested at their earliest convenience, but few, if any, ever did. Before the latest initiative in 2010 to force all drivers to become qualified, it was rumoured that some 200,000 drivers in Ireland had not passed their test, out of a total population of fewer than 4.5 million. Adherence to driving laws appears to be equally balanced with the need for flair and style, particularly in the more rural areas, where it is entirely acceptable to drive at speed using a mobile phone, whilst map reading, applying makeup, drinking coffee and eating a breakfast roll all at the same time! By the way, a "breakfast roll" is required morning sustenance for all commercial drivers; it is a full Irish breakfast, with all the trimmings, including runny eggs, loosely contained within a French stick.

In an attempt to try and see further around corners, rather than slowing down, some of the locals have a disturbing habit of driving on the wrong side of the road, which can make life interesting if you are travelling in the opposite direction and on the correct side of the road. On two such occasions, I noticed that the other vehicle was a very large tractor, being driven by a dwarf or "little person", who had to drive standing up in order to reach the steering wheel. Another local quirk is driving at breakneck speeds along single track country roads, warning oncoming traffic of your presence by madly tooting your horn; this ploy works in theory, until you meet someone travelling in the opposite direction doing exactly the same thing. I have also seen a car towing an animal trailer being used to transport seven wildly waving children to school. One of our own cars, conversely, was obviously used at some time to transport and store pigs and retains a unique fragrance, regardless of the amount of chemicals we apply. Probably the most unusual thing I have seen on the roads in Ireland, is a man riding a bicycle with a three-seater sofa strapped "rucksack style" on his back, as he wobbled his way along a single track lane. In any event, driving in Ireland is relatively safe, and I am happy to report that the speeding driver of the large red 4x4 that ran my wife and her little car into a ditch, took a moment away from his mobile phone conversation to raise his index finger in subtle acknowledgement of her presence although, sadly, he did not see the need to stop and hold a conversation.

Chapter 4 – In which we go house hunting

On our first full morning in Ireland, we met with our estate agent Alan Sykes to discuss our selection of properties and arrange the viewings. He is a tall, slim fellow, aged about forty, casually dressed, with an equally casual manner that could easily be mistaken for indifference. In between numerous interruptions to take telephone calls, from clients in America and Germany, he reviewed our selection and marked them on the map. Most were local to his office in East Clare, but one from his portfolio and a two from another agent were miles away towards the west coast. Alan agreed to show us several properties the following day and suggested we set off for this day on our own to "discover" Ireland, view some houses, and have a pub lunch. He also suggested that we buy some ordnance survey maps of the areas we were going to be visiting because, "House hunting in Ireland is really hunting for houses." So, equipped with some maps, property details, basic directions and borrowed wellington boots (yes – we really were that naive.), we set off in search of our new home in Ireland.

On a map, the outline of the island of Ireland looks a little like the craggy face of an old man, facing to the left. Dublin sits at the back of the head and the unruly mop of hair at the top is the northern counties, from Dundalk in the east to Strabane in the north. The eyes are below Donegal, and to the south is a bulbous nose running from Sligo to Galway. The Loop Head peninsula is the top lip, the mighty River Shannon the mouth, and the Dingle peninsula the chin and beard. Most of our house hunting took place in the area of the top lip, which is mostly County Clare, and along the north side of the River Shannon, from Loop Head, past Kilrush, Ennis, Shannon Airport, Limerick, and inland to the spectacular Lough Derg. This part of Ireland has a delightful rural quality that is similar in feel to the England I grew up in during the 1960s, with sparse housing and long, narrow country lanes, overarched with trees. The people seemed untouched by the fears of theft, vandalism, violence which seemed so obvious in other countries and blissfully unaware of the recent spate of dreadful child abductions and murders in the UK. Miles from any obvious habitation, we saw young ladies powerwalking and children playing by the roadside – they always smiled and waved enthusiastically. The lack of crime was obvious; shops, garden centres and building sites were fronted with piles of valuable, unguarded stock. At that time in England, a pallet of potting compost left outside overnight would miraculously disappear, entire landscaped gardens were being stolen to order and any empty builders' skip was guaranteed to be filled, with someone else's rubbish, as soon as you turned your back.

The ordnance survey map of County Clare is covered with a mind-blowing mass of little squiggly lines, almost like a Victorian maze, which on closer inspection is revealed to actually be the rural road network. Only a few roads travelled across the map with any sign of confident purpose and these major roads were coloured red and given numbers, although the actual roads seemed unaware they were expected to be major thoroughfares, or display numbers. More numerous than the red roads on the map were yellow ones. These jolly little lines travelled in all directions, like a spilled packet of spaghetti, occasionally connecting two red lines for no visible reason. Whereas the red lines indicated "A" class regional roads, the yellow lines represented "B" roads and they were usually around four metres wide, or less, and resisted all attempts at identification. After some discussion we decided that the "B" was actually an abbreviation of "Bloody hell! We are lost again." Branching off from the "B" roads were hundreds of grey lines that the map key indicated as "other roads" and in our experience these were usually barely passable, impassable or non-existent. The grey lines were usually subdivided, sometimes several times, into branch roads, becoming ever more difficult to find and navigate. Inevitably nearly all of the properties we had selected were hidden at the end of one of these branches.

Another delightful feature of rural Ireland is that there are no post codes (called zip codes in the USA) and the roads have no names or numbers. The individual houses are named, but many of the houses seem to carry the same name as others in the same area. Confused? You will be; we certainly were. Actually, it's quite simple, once you know how the system works. Each area has a "townland" which is the local name in Irish for a particular hill, valley, road, bog etc. So your house is named after the local townland, along with twenty or so others. Second to that, your address will also carry the name of the local post office, even if it closed twelve years ago and your post is now handled by another post office. Then you show the county that the house was in when it was built, but not necessarily the county it is in now, even if the borders of the county were changed a few years ago. And finally you would announce that you definitely live in Ireland, or The Republic of Ireland, or Eire. To save any confusion, when you first take ownership of your new home, you should seek out the local postmaster and inform him which of the twenty or so identically named houses you now live in. Now your post and packages can be correctly delivered, although only on the odd days when the post van happens to be passing near. So your postal address may read, "Joe Smith, Knockdrumleague, Tulla, Co. Clare, Ireland," and your post will find you easily. In fact, the system is so efficient that in our case, a letter posted from England and addressed to "Lesley, Feakle, Ireland," arrived safely the next day. However, owning and paying for your house may not make it yours in the eyes of the locals; after eight years in our home, it is still known locally as "Harris' house," which is an Irish peculiarity as Mr Harris himself was actually English, the second of five owners, and only lived in the house for a few years. In conclusion, I can report that house hunting in Clare is best conducted using the combined skills of explorers, cartographers and clairvoyants. How DHL and FedEx manage, is a mystery. I have never seen the same driver twice – I wonder sometimes if perhaps they go out on a delivery and just never come back.

The first house on our list for the day was in the townland of Derryshaan, to the west, halfway between Ennis and the port town of Kilrush. As we had some time in hand before our appointment, we decided to take the scenic coast road, through Killadysert and along the northern bank of the Shannon estuary to Kilmurry McMahon and then ask for directions. It was a very typical Irish winter morning, frosty and calm with a crystal clear blue sky. The air, flowing in from the west over thousands of miles of the Atlantic

Ocean, was so pure and clean that breathing suddenly seemed like a forgotten pleasure. The coast road is relatively unused and we only saw two other cars during the forty mile drive, which was fortunate, because the views were so spectacular that we both spent most of our time looking out of the side windows. Our breakfast tea soon started to take effect and we switched our attention to searching for a service station, with a toilet. There are none. There may now be one in Dublin somewhere, but there are no public toilets in Clare, so over the wall we went. Inevitably, both of the cars that we saw during that morning's trip arrived while we were having a pee. In due course, we found the village of Kilmurry McMahon and headed to the post office to ask for directions.

The first person that I encountered was an ancient and weather beaten woman, in an equally ancient and weather beaten car of indeterminate manufacture. She had on three coats, fingerless gloves and was wearing a knitted hat that may, at one time, have been a tea cosy. As I approached, I noticed that she appeared to be trying to reattach her car door with a piece of baling twine and, assuming that she was the victim of some recent automotive disaster, I offered my assistance.

"Ah, you're grand," she replied. "The fecking thing falls off every time I open it. It's been like it for years; I just stick my arm out of the window and hang on till I get home."

Peering through the mould on the cracked windshield, I could see two bottles of holy water and statues of Jesus and the Virgin Mary on the dashboard. There also appeared to be a bale of hay and a goat on the back seat.

"Have you far to go before you get home?" I asked.

"Only a few miles, but I'll be shopping in Ennis first. Are ye lost?"

I explained that we were looking for a house that was for sale locally and showed her the property details, in the hope she could provide directions.

"Don't know it," she said and pointed to a nearby building. "Try the postmaster."

After much clanking and the issuing of alarming quantities of oily smoke, she started her car and, still holding her door, drove off at a terrifying speed. Feeling slightly shell-shocked, I entered the post office and, proffering the property details, asked for directions.

"I don't recognise that house," the friendly postmaster said. "Whose house is it?"

I shrugged, "No idea. All I know is we are to meet Mary or John there, in half an hour. I don't even have a phone number for them."

"That's a bit of a problem," he said scratching his head. Then he called to a man by the door, "Here Paddy, do you know where this is?"

Paddy also asked who the house belonged to and then recruited the support of a third person. Within a few minutes, no fewer than eight people were involved in the discussion, all of them animated and excited by the challenge. After some animated discussion, they decided that the property was McNamara's house and then they coerced another local into giving me directions.

"Here, Seamus. Tell this feller how to get to McNamara's house. You know – where John Kelly lives."

Seamus seemed delighted with his newfound responsibility and, after pulling up his trousers and squaring his shoulders, he began his directions.

"Right – you go down this road and then you go that way, right?" he said, pointing left. "Then you go on a ways, until you can't go no further, then you go that way, right?" Pointing left again.

"You mean left" I offered helpfully.

He went quiet for a moment, "Yea, that's right, left – right?"

"Err, yes I think so," I said.

"Right then," he said with renewed confidence. "Now when you get to the crossroads you go that way – right?" He waved his hand to the right. "Kelly's place is up the end of that lane, you can't miss it – ten minutes tops." He smiled confidently and the others joined in smiling and nodding. We thanked our new friend for his help and, armed with our directions, set off on the short trip to the house. About forty-five minutes later we arrived at the crossroads, which turned out to be a six way junction with each road looking identical to the others. All were helpfully devoid of any road signs.

"I think we are supposed to turn right here," I said scratching my head.

Lesley shrugged, "All roads lead to Rome," she said helpfully.

"We may go there next," I quipped. "Perhaps they can give us better directions."

Lesley squinted at the map, "It's up that road," she said confidently, waving vaguely somewhere to our right.

I chose a lane at random and astonishingly we arrived at the correct house two minutes later, and half an hour late.

At that time in the UK, prospective house sellers were being subjected to an avalanche of television programmes, providing advice on the best ways to present your property for sale. Much was being made of the importance of clearing personal clutter, painting everything with neutral colours, completing maintenance projects, tidying the garden and making the kitchen smell of coffee and fresh bread. Ireland had yet to catch up with this trend, so it would be fair to say that we were slightly taken aback with the first house we visited. It was a fairly large bungalow, sitting in seven acres of meadow at the top of a gentle rise which provided panoramic views south to the Shannon estuary. We parked at the rear of the bungalow, by some outbuildings and cowsheds and then sloshed our way through three inches of mud and dung to the back door, where a portly lady wearing an overcoat and an apron was waiting.

"You 'ere to see around?" she enquired, "Better come in then," she said without waiting for a reply. We stepped into a back kitchen area that contained an ancient oil burning range, a dining table and an enormous picture window. We stood looking out towards the estuary and the smoke from a distant power station.

"Lovely view," Lesley said politely. "I see the house comes with seven acres; is this the land at the front?"

"My husband deals with all of that, and he ain't here. But in any event, it's twenty-nine acres now."

"Twenty-nine acres!" I squealed, "but this says seven!" I flapped the property details at her.

"We been and decided that we don't want the other land no more, so it's got to go with the house – or we won't be selling." She brazenly told us the new asking price, which was almost double the original price, and edging dangerously close to the top of our budget.

After some prompting from Lesley, the lady then led us through the house on a quick tour. By the time we reached the back bedrooms, I was beginning to ponder if they had recently been burgled, or the victim of a mini tornado, as most of their belongings appeared to be on the floor, with the discarded clothing being several inches deep in places.

"That's my daughter's room – she don't clean up much," she observed, helpfully.

The dear lady took us around the house and garden for the next half hour, before setting us loose to explore the mud and rushes which made up the remainder of the twenty-nine acres. Overall, it was a nice property and had the potential to become a pleasant home. There were three obvious problems. First, the new asking price would be pushing our budget to the limit. Secondly twenty-nine acres is a lot of land particularly when you are used to owning no more than a large garden, but it wasn't a deal-breaker. Finally, as you travel west in County Clare towards the coast, the land flattens and the trees thin out, leaving a rather barren and wild outlook. We both suspected that the area could be "hard living," particularly during the winter months. Nevertheless, we had a positive feeling about the property and even returned for a second visit within days. After that trip, we were chased along the road by a car with madly flashing lights. Initially, I thought the driver just wanted to get past to attend some farming emergency, or beat the lunchtime rush at the pub. It transpired that he was, in fact, our prospective neighbour. He took a few minutes to grill us on our opinion of the property, the area and how much we were willing to pay, before getting to the point.

"If you buy it, can I keep grazing my cows on the land?" he asked.

"I expect so – if we buy it."

"That's grand," he smiled, and then as an afterthought, "for free, mind you." He gave my hand a mighty shake and then waved us off towards the next house on our list.

After much discussion with the auctioneer, we made a generous offer, at slightly below the asking price. It was firmly refused. We then made a counter offer on the asking price and this was accepted, with one proviso. We had made it abundantly clear that we would be selling our house and moving to Ireland and would probably require the sale to be completed, and the property vacated by May 2004, or even earlier if possible. The vendors said that they were quite happy to complete the sale by March, as they needed the money to buy a plot of land and build their new house, but would expect to remain in the property, rent free, for a year or so, until they were ready to move. According to Alan Sykes, even though their suggestion was not common practice, it was not considered unusual in west Clare. We politely withdrew our offer.

Our next prospect was a 1970s bungalow, just outside the pretty village of Corofin. It was a decent enough property, with an acre of land at the back and views to the front over Inchiquin Lough. I am sure that it had a lot going for it, but for some reason I couldn't warm to it. To me it was never going to feel like home, our home. It had walls and windows and a roof and all the other things you would expect, but it felt dead – no more than a pile of bricks. Somehow it was always going to seem like we were living in someone else's house. So we cut our losses and took the afternoon off. We had a delightful early lunch in a local pub, run by a friendly English couple. They told us that they had taken over the pub recently, after many hard years running pubs in the tough east end of London. Used to regular knife fights, and even gun battles, between warring gangs, they overreacted spectacularly when faced with their first drunken brawl in Corofin. In most village pubs in the west, a bar fight can usually be stopped by someone shouting, "Ah! Paddy, would you cut that out – here, have another pint!"

Whereas, our dear English friends launched themselves across the bar, brandishing baseball bats and screaming blue murder. Lessons learned all around, I expect.

After lunch, we set off north, in an anticlockwise loop, pausing for a short walk in the Burren National Park, before driving on towards the spectacular "Cliffs of Moher." The word "Burren" comes from an Irish word "Boíreann" meaning a rocky place, which is very apt as much of the area is made up of exposed natural limestone pavement formed around 350 million years ago, from sediment, when a tropical sea covered most of Ireland. The initial impression is of a barren landscape, looking as if some mighty hand had swept away all of the soil and trees, leaving behind only the bedrock, for as far as the eye can see. The mighty hand was probably a glacier, during the last ice age, which initially scoured away much of the top soil and the process was completed by thousands of years by rain, snow and ice. However, nature abhors a vacuum. So every crack and crevice in the limestone is now alive with a dazzling array of flora and fauna. The area is also rich in wild birds, insects, feral goats and wandering tourists. It's a great place to visit, with breath-taking views from the bald hill tops of the green pasture below and the mysterious "disappearing lakes," which fill and drain into underground rivers at random intervals. In 1651 an officer, in Oliver Cromwell's army observed of the Burren, "There is not water enough to drown a man, wood enough to hang one, nor earth enough to bury them." Today we would add, "and there is no broadband or mobile phone access." One exciting sport you can play when driving through the low lying areas of the Burren, is counting the number of bizarrely designed houses, which have obviously been constructed without any consultation with the planning authority. Many parts of the National Park are now heavily wooded, and hidden within are frequently to be found oddly constructed dwellings, parts of which may once have been wooden caravans. These delightful follies are usually coloured purple, blue and red, and then decorated with "new age" medallions and wind chimes. Some may also have a tethered goat at the front and a small vegetable garden at the rear, with a child's swing hanging from a tree. Additional points can be scored in the game, if you can correctly spot the cannabis plants, being grown for local consumption.

The Cliffs of Moher are one of Ireland's busiest tourist attractions; they run for about five miles along the Atlantic coastline of County Clare, and are over seven hundred feet high at the highest point. The name Moher (pronounced Moo-har by an American tourist) comes from the word "Mothar," after a promontory fort which was demolished during the Napoleonic wars, to make room for the signal tower, called O'Brien's Tower, which is now on the high point of the cliffs. On a clear day, the views are spectacular.

Looking north you can see the Aran Islands, Galway Bay, into Connemara and, to the South, Loop Head. On a less than clear day, the wind will flail the skin from your face and the crashing waves will send salt spray all the way to the top of the cliffs.

When we first visited the Cliffs of Moher, there was just a small car park, staffed by a pleasant gent in a garden shed, and an ancient wooden shack, selling refreshments and the usual range of trinkets for the tourists. The food was good, the service friendly and the toilets were spotlessly clean, regardless of the number of coach parties through that day. The entrance fee was €5 and, once parked, you were free to roam the cliffs without any restriction or interference. The walk up to the cliffs was interspaced with local traders and musicians, all earning a crust with honest work, in what can be very difficult conditions. On one memorable occasion we saw a young girl in traditional Irish costume, playing a full sized harp, in a blizzard of sleet and snow. I couldn't feel my toes with two pairs of socks on, so how she was able to play the harp so beautifully was a mystery to me. She earned every penny that day! Along the cliff edge there had been a few half-hearted attempts at erecting safety fencing, but these were roundly ignored. The drop from the cliffs is sheer, with rocks and the crashing Atlantic waves seven hundred feet below. The edges of the cliff are worn and unstable, and yet thousands of visitors could be observed each day, defying certain death in the pursuit of the perfect photograph. There was also a flat sandstone ledge, about one hundred and fifty by fifty feet, which hung out above the water, accessible by an unofficial path. It sat twenty feet or so below the cliff top. On wild days you could feel the ledge "jump" as the waves hit the cliffs below, while on quieter days, the ledge seems to be reserved for family picnics and ad hoc soccer matches. Most disturbing to those of us with vertigo and vivid imaginations, was the row of unsupervised children dangling their legs off the edge, while eating their sandwiches. Access to the sandstone ledge is a little more difficult today, because a few years ago it fell into the ocean, pretty much without any warning. I present this fact purely as evidence in my defence; it seems that I am not such a snivelling coward after all and was right not to go to the very edge – that ledge really was dangerous! However, despite the obvious risks, or perhaps because of them, people loved to visit the Cliffs of Moher. I understand that occasionally a single car would remain in the car park at the end of the day, like a lonely suitcase at the airport luggage retrieval, indicating that perhaps someone had wandered too close the edge and would not be returning. These incidents were fortunately rare, but perhaps not always accidental. Sadly, these days there is a shiny new high tech visitor centre, only authorised musicians are permitted to busk and access to the cliffs is thoroughly discouraged by the health and safety Nazis.

Chapter 5 – In which we find Shangri-La

Our next property hunting expedition took us inland into East Clare. There is a beautiful and wide valley running from Ennis and the river Fergus, slightly northeast for around thirty miles, to Mountshannon, on the north shore of Lough Derg. The valley is bordered by Gappaghabaun Mountain to the north and Slieve Bearnagh to the south, which rise to some five hundred metres above the valley floor. The valley is green, fertile and yet sparsely populated, containing only a dozen or so small villages, interspaced with farms and the occasional cottage. During the warm summers the lush grass provides excellent grazing for many sheep and cattle, and in the winter months the mountains are usually topped with snow, although the valley can still remain largely clear. The valley is characteristic of the beautiful scenery of East Clare. We had several likely properties lined up to see, and we had arranged for Alan Sykes to show us the houses in the north of the valley in the morning, while we would again "go solo" in the afternoon, to see those in the south.

It was another beautiful frosty Irish morning when we met up with Alan, outside a famous local pub. I climbed out of the car and chatted with him about our itinerary for a few moments and then, after agreeing that I should follow him in our rental car, he shot off in a cloud of blue smoke, before I even had a chance to climb back into our car. Like most men, I consider myself to be a decent driver, but on the narrow, icy lanes, in an underpowered rental car, it took all of my driving skill just to keep him in sight. For a while we lost contact, but I pressed on regardless, and a few miles later we found him taking photographs of an ancient rusty tractor. It was a delightful example of vintage local farm machinery and yet obviously still in daily use, even though the cab was missing, there was a plastic bag acting as an air filter and an old wooden kitchen stool had been attached with baling twine, to seat the driver. A few miles further up the road, we viewed the first property. After our previous experiences with estate agents in England, where descriptions like "convenient for commuters" actually means that locals know a short-cut through your back garden to get to the railway station, and "scope for improvement" would turn out to be a derelict cow shed, Alan's approach was a breath of fresh air.

"You won't like this one, it's horrible – been on the market for ages," he said as he introduced the first property of the day.

He was correct. It was a nasty, dank little cottage, balanced precariously on the side of a hill so steep that we almost needed ropes and crampons on the approach. We quickly agreed with his assessment and moved on to the next house, all the time wondering how that house had ever got on our list. The next two visits were equally depressing, both being muddy fields that had no services and just outline planning permission for a "jelly-mould house," an apt description for houses of a standard design plopped like jelly-moulds, at random, across the countryside. Just as we were starting to despair that our entire trip might have been wasted, Alan pulled to a stop at the crest of a hill and we climbed out of our cars. Although it wasn't obvious to us while driving, we had climbed to a height of around eight hundred feet and there before us was the spectacular view looking south, down across the valley. Even though our viewpoint was not particularly high, the slope was steep and the valley floor below so flat as to give the impression that we were much higher and able to see for hundreds of miles. It was utterly breath-taking. The sun was in our faces, low in the sky behind Slieve Bearnagh Mountain, which one could imagine being the aged remains of an exploded volcano. Ten miles to our extreme left we could see part of Lough Derg and the village of Scarriff, where a single column of white smoke rose vertically into the morning sky. The valley floor was predominately green, occasionally obscured with patches of light mist, and dotted with lakes glistening in the sunlight. To our right the land was flat for thirty miles, leading out towards Limerick city. Just visible in the haze was the Shannon estuary and some distant smoke arising from Money Point power station, the only visible sign of any industrialisation. We stood in silent awe for a few moments until Alan broke our reverie.

"Some view, hey?"

"Spectacular," we both agreed.

"Can you imagine waking up to that every morning?" he asked, as his sales instincts finally kicked in.

It was immediately obvious that the next house was much closer to what we were seeking, albeit rather more basic than we had hoped for. It sat in a dip at the base of a hill, by the side of a stream and surrounded by mature trees. The property had around half an acre of vegetable garden to the front of the buildings and, up the very steep hill at the back, another six acres of pasture. There was a house, a barn and a new garage that had been partially converted into a two-storey accommodation. The house was typically Irish – concrete built and about eighty years old, with two downstairs rooms divided by a single wall containing the chimney and fireplaces. The room on the left was a living room that contained the stairs and the other room was the kitchen and eating area. The floors were dry bare mud with some straw sprinkled around, and overhead you could see rafters and the bare floorboards of the rooms above. The upstairs was a copy of the rooms below, being two rooms divided by a central chimney and lateral wall. One of the rooms contained a bath, sink and toilet, enclosed by a curtain to create the illusion of privacy; the other room seemed to be the only bedroom. Electricity was provided to lights and sockets, through a series of disturbingly antique wires that hung precariously from nails along the walls and rafters. The only obvious source of heating was a few peat briquettes burning on the hearth below the chimney, which stubbornly refused to accept any of the smoke. We gave this house careful consideration, as we felt it had the potential to become a very nice home, which it did – in the hands of some friends of ours. On the upside it seemed that although the renovations were obviously going to be substantial, they would be reasonably straightforward. The main house needed to be gutted and extended, or simply demolished and replaced; in the meantime we could live in the converted garage. The downside was that it was obviously going to be a long job and living in a garage, or perhaps renting a mobile home, was not an attractive long-term prospect. Secondly, there was nowhere to store our possessions and furniture securely during the renovations, which realistically could take more than a year. We wanted to keep them close, for security and to avoid paying twice for removals; we suspected that the nearest storage facility was probably thirty miles away and that the alternative of renting an onsite container would undoubtedly eat in to our precious savings. In the end we decided, "close, but no banana!" and moved on to the next house.

After a short drive we arrived at the final property of the morning. "Glenmadrie" was the house that would eventually become our new home. This was the house that we had almost excluded from our list, mistakenly believing it was either just an advertisement on the website, or that it would be priced well beyond our pocket. Viewing Glenmadrie for the first time was like seeing Audrey Hepburn dressed as Eliza Doolittle, the tramp flower girl at the start of "My Fair Lady," whilst all the time knowing how elegant she would look by the end of the film. To us the potential was immediately obvious, provided you could look past the flaws. Alan described it as an "English" house, meaning that because of the unconventional layout, it would not appeal to most Irish people and would probably only ever be owned by an English or perhaps a German family. At that time most of the Irish were riding the wave of the Celtic Tiger years and only interested in new houses that had the best of everything. Years of high wages, freely available credit and mortgages of over five times earnings and 100% of the purchase price, had fuelled the illusion of wealth. It was entirely understandable that people in that position would want to buy the biggest and best they could, whether it was televisions, cars or houses. The obvious benefit to others, like ourselves, was that second-hand and non-standard properties, of the type that we wanted, became much cheaper, particularly compared to the current prices in England. Another interesting difference was that houses in England generally became more expensive as you moved away from the town centres, but in Ireland the opposite applied. It seemed that the Irish were so keen to get away from their farming past, that they would pay a premium price for the privilege of living in a cramped house, on a busy street with no parking or garden. For example, in 2004 a four bedroom house in Ireland, on an acre of land, situated in the countryside about thirty miles from two cities and an international airport, could sell for €250,000. The same house in England, thirty miles from Colchester, Chelmsford and London

Stansted Airport, would probably sell for €1,000,000. Of course, this also meant that our move to Ireland was probably going to be a one-way trip; there would be no going back while that price differential remained.

Through the years I have established a potted history of how Glenmadrie was developed as a property. This may help to describe what could easily have been called a "higgledy-piggledy house," the end product of the incomplete thoughts and unfinished ideas of several underfunded owners. The original house faced west, towards a farm track that was once the main road; it was probably a stone built, single storey farmhouse, about twenty feet deep and forty feet wide in ten acres of poor quality meadow. The two first floor rooms had only bare mud floors covered with straw. The building was divided by a chimney and there would have been two sleeping platforms at either end of the thatched roof, accessed by rudimentary ladders. In early 1900 the walls were extended upwards to create a second storey, with two bedrooms, and at the same time a large barn and hayloft was added to the north end. Because of the high incidence of lung infections caused by living in such damp and mouldy conditions, with the assistance of a government grant and perhaps an accidental fire, the thatch was replaced with a corrugated metal roof, and sometime later this was changed to slate tiles. In 1977, the chimney and centre wall was removed and replaced with an open fireplace on the west wall, connected to a new external chimney. This was a very significant date as it also marked the introduction of some rudimentary indoor ablutions, along with running water, pumped from a shallow well. To achieve this, the north wall was opened into the barn, which was converted into a kitchen, below a bedroom and open-plan bathroom, all on separate floors and connected by a purpose built spiral staircase. Several years later, when the metal roof was replaced with slate tiles, the upper part of the main house was then divided into a bedroom and a bathroom with a lockable door, and the original open-plan bathroom was changed to become an additional bedroom with a sleeping platform above. In 1980, a second extension was added to the south end of the property, with the upper floor bedroom accessible from the main house and the lower floor possibly being used as a garage or store room, before it was converted into a music studio by the current vendor who was a musician. At some time a new road had been constructed, running one hundred feet to the rear of the house, and with the cutting of a new driveway, the front of the house became the back. To trap the sun, somebody added a series of arches at the back of the house creating a covered walkway and private courtyard, with a distinctly Spanish feel. The final touches of luxury were added in late 1990 when the existing windows, which were just sheets of glass cemented into holes in the walls, were replaced with a variety of decidedly second-hand, wood framed, double-glazed windows, and part of the walkway was covered to create a conservatory.

You may be picturing a well-constructed, beautifully presented and tastefully decorated house – but think again. Sadly, the lack of any significant maintenance for the past fifteen years had permitted the Irish weather to destroy many of the outbuildings. Internally, most of the construction materials that had been used were recycled; this would have been acceptable and commendable, had they not mostly been comprised of waste wood that was infected with woodworm and rot. Furthermore, although the walls and roof were sturdy, all of the floors and dividing walls were beyond repair. It was possible to see right through the upper floors, which creaked alarmingly when walked on, and produced a shower of woodworm dust onto anyone sitting below. Finally, the most recent attempts at decoration had a distinctly "new age" feel, with rainbows, fire serpents, half-moons and peace signs covering the walls, both inside and out. Nevertheless, the building clearly had the potential to become a delightful home with the application of money, work and time. Furthermore, because of its size and layout, it would be conceivable to live in one part of the house while the work was underway in another, and the music studio would provide ample and secure storage space for all of our possessions.

Whereas the property showed potential, the land and location really delivered the "wow factor" we were hoping for. Set high in the hills to the south of Lough Graney and several miles from significant habitation or any neighbours, the house sat in four acres of land and was truly remote. There were one hundred acres of forest to the rear and to the front, unrestricted views across miles of moorland dotted with huge glacial boulders, like discarded toys in a giant child's bedroom. Although it obviously had not been cultivated for years, the land was of decent quality and fertile, having once been used as a goat farm. There were hundreds of trees and a small wood, an acre of garden, two acres of pasture and a small disused quarry. At one time in the distant past, limestone had been quarried here and turned into quicklime, by baking for days in a furnace called a lime kiln, which was still visible above the quarry. Quicklime and slaked lime (which is produced in reaction with water) were important chemicals used in farming, agriculture, the manufacturing of iron and steel, in medicine and as an ingredient in cement. Some lime kilns were still in use as late as 1950, when they stopped being commercially workable. The quarry was shaped like a horseshoe with the open end facing the setting sun, which was presumably why the base had recently been levelled to allow the construction of a fifty foot high oak pyramid. To my practical mind, this wooden monstrosity spoiled a spectacular view and the money could have been spent far more wisely by treating the house for woodworm – but that was only my opinion. Many times in the years to come, I would sit at the top of the quarry and marvel at the peace and beauty before me, as the sun set spectacularly in the west.

Because the house was vacant, with the owner working abroad, the keys were hidden behind a loose rock in an outside wall and we were given permission to revisit as often as we pleased. On one visit we met with Jim, a local farmer who was in the habit of grazing his cows on the pasture attached to the property. He was a delightful man, with a ready smile, twinkling blue eyes and a tendency to call everyone "Sir." Today, he was wearing boots, jeans and a mud smeared jacket that may once have been green; a faded baseball cap partially covered his tousled dark hair. Like an eight year old boy, his pockets overflowed with bits of twine, pocket-knives, apples and cattle feed. Next to him was an immaculately dressed actual eight year old boy, standing politely to attention and shyly watching us from under the brim of his Munster rugby baseball cap. After introducing ourselves, I said we were seriously considering buying the house and asked his opinion of what it would be like to live there.

"Well Sir, you will find it's grand – apart from the midgets," he said.

"Midgets?" I queried, thinking of the dwarf I had seen twice, driving a tractor while standing up, "What about them?"

"I fecking hate them. Bastards – Sir!" he replied.

I knew that some people had a prejudice against those that they considered outside of the norm and while I understood that everybody is entitled to their own opinion, I felt very uncomfortable with Jim's venom. However, I was conscious that this man could soon become my distant neighbour and I didn't want to get off on the wrong foot.

"Really? That seems a little harsh," I offered in pacification.

"Harsh?" He seemed almost shocked, "Harsh is it, Sir? Them little bastards cum up here in their 'undreds. They's after me cows they is. Well, you ask my opinion, they should feck off to Scotland, where they cum from," he spat.

I looked out over the hills and pictured a missing scene from the movie "Braveheart," with hundreds of kilted dwarfs, belonging to some secret cattle rustling clan, charging across the moor like slightly taller versions of Mel Gibson. It seemed a little far-fetched, but I was new to the area.

"Well, I'll have to try and keep out of their way, I suppose," I offered.

"You can try, Sir, but it won't work. The girl midgets are the worst. When it's time for them to breed, they can smell you out for miles, so I've heard."

"Good gracious – how extraordinary! You learn something new every day." I was now picturing a miniature version of an Essex girl's hen night. "Perhaps they are attracted to the smell of Guinness."

"Oy don't know about that," he said, and then, changing tack like a drunken taxi driver, "Can I graze me cows on yer field, Sir?" he asked.

"Yes Jim, I don't see why not."

Nine months later, I was mixing some cement when I became aware of tiny hot pinpricks of pain on my neck and face and several small lumps were already growing on the backs of my hands. In the sunlight I could see a cloud of dancing dust that seemed to follow my every move.

"Oh! MIDGES!" I said slapping my forehead, physically and figuratively. I quickly made my escape indoors in search of the antihistamine cream, and then told Lesley that the puzzle of the "midgets" was now solved.

The Americans call them "no-see-ums" the British call them "gnats" and some Irish people call them midgets, although the correct name is "the Scottish biting midge." Midges are tiny biting flies that are active from May to October in Ireland, particularly when the weather is calm, humid and overcast. It is only the pregnant female that bites and they are most active at dawn and dusk, but are happy to come out and play whenever the conditions are right, or you need to work outside. Standing in one place for any length of time is guaranteed to attract a large cloud of midges. Our midge hats have an all over net, similar to a beekeepers hat, and are very effective at providing protection, for those days when you have no alternative to being outside. Although there is no known disease transmitted by midge bites, most people find the repeated bites intolerable, as they usually result in itchy lumps. On "midgy" days, the best advice is to stay indoors or wear a space suit.

Even though we had fallen in love with Glenmadrie, there were several more properties on the list to be viewed that day, so we had to get on. We waved goodbye to Alan as his car roared off in a cloud of blue smoke, and then made our way toward Scarriff for some lunch. We stopped at a dark little pub in the village of Tuamgraney and had a pot of Irish tea, two bucket sized bowls of delicious thick vegetable soup and wonderful fresh soda bread. Refreshed and reinvigorated, we set off in search of the last few properties on our list. Although there are now several decent alternatives, the radio in our hire car refused to listen to any station other than Clare FM, the local station. We were at first amused by the truly awful cover versions of popular songs, which they seemed to play regularly, and then mortified by the dreadful "Irish country music," which even Lesley couldn't stomach, although she is a long-time country music fan. However, all of this paled into insignificance when we heard the local radio "Death Notices" for the first time. Ireland is obviously a religious country with a long heritage; most families still have strong traditional associations to their local church, even if they are no longer believers. Perhaps in an effort to appear more holy than everyone else, each tiny village we passed seemed to have built an even larger church than the last, so much so that some village churches we saw were larger than many city cathedrals in Britain. Even atheists, it seems, must choose to be either Catholic atheists or Protestant atheists – but never a Methodist atheist. We were, of course, used to seeing the occasional obituary in English newspapers, paying respectful acknowledgement to the passing of some local gentry. In my travels I have witnessed organised wailing and mass browbeating at funerals in Africa, and even joyous dancing and drinking combined with genuine sadness celebrating the life and loss of a loved one. But the "Death Notices" being read, like soccer results, left us totally gobsmacked. For several minutes twice a day, a flat voice will recite the list of those recently departed, including descriptions of how they passed like, "suddenly, quietly, peacefully or unexpectedly." We speculated that these descriptions were code for, car crash, drunk, drunk and asleep and died without leaving a will.

Back to the house hunt and, over the next four hours, we visited a field with outline planning permission for a small "jelly-mould house," a field with full planning permission for a large "jelly-mould house," and a field with no planning permission at all, but several scrap cars. Next we visited a newly built "jelly-mould house," on the standard three-quarter acre plot, in a row of identical jelly-moulds, on a busy main road. Although it was completed and ready for sale, there were no kitchen or bathroom fittings and the build quality seemed very poor for the price being asked. We demonstrated our displeasure by emptying our bladders behind the garage before setting off to see the next house. The most likely alternative property to Glenmadrie that we saw was in the possession of a delightful eccentric elderly Dutch widow. We arrived by appointment, dead on time at three o'clock, to find her amiably drunk and by the time we left at four thirty she could barely stand. She had a nice house, built on several levels, full of character and quirky rooms. There was also a second house, a few yards away, which would provide immediate revenue through rental income. While this was financially attractive, we felt that moving so far to get away from it all and then living so close to your neighbour and tenants, somewhat defeated the purpose. In the end, we discovered that the second house was originally the only house, and that the new house had been built entirely without planning permission, and was going to present many legal obstacles before a purchase could safely be made. We left our smiling host in her cloud of gin, as she slowly slid from her kitchen chair towards the floor, and happily made our way towards England and home.

When we arrived at Shannon Airport we joined a bizarre ritual that we were to witness many times over the next few years, until it stopped without explanation. At the entrance gate to the airport was a small glass sided cubicle, similar to a toll booth, and sitting inside was an airport policeman who was tasked with challenging the intentions of each driver. This poor unfortunate soul, or an equally unwilling colleague, was present in all weathers and around the clock, presumably as some form of cruel and unusual punishment for a hideous crime. The road, guarded by the checkpoint, had only two possible destinations, the airport, or Shannon Golf Club. On every occasion we flew from the airport, or collected visitors, the unfortunate policeman would step out into the wind, rain, sleet or snow, to ask us, "Where are you going?" The answer was always the same. "The airport," while pointing at the big place behind him, full of terminal buildings and shiny flying machines. The poor blue faced policeman would then look over his shoulder in surprise, as if noticing the airport for the first time, and say, "Oh – that's okay then," and on we would go. I am unsure what the real intention of the checkpoint was; perhaps they hoped that some fiendish master-plan to blow up the pro shop at Shannon Golf Club would be thwarted when the terrorist accidentally announced his intentions to the lonely policeman. Of course the villainous evil-doer could have simply put the bomb in a wheelbarrow and walked past the checkpoint unchallenged, on the opposite side of the road.

We successfully navigated the checkpoint, only to discover that Stansted Airport was closed by a blizzard, and our flight was cancelled. Luckily, I guessed that the long delayed flight was going to be cancelled and jumped the crowd to secure seats on the morning flight for the next day, as well as the last room at the airport hotel. While others, less fortunate than us, had to sleep on cold hard plastic seating in the airport departure hall, we ate well and, despite our best efforts to resist, became quite drunk, in the company of a generous businessman from Manchester. Anesthetised by our libations we slept deeply in a warm comfortable bed, to wake refreshed and a little hung-over, in good time for our flight home.

Back in England, the snow had turned to beige slush, so our journey to the kennel to collect the dogs, and then onward to our house, was uneventful. After acclimatising to the pace of life in Ireland, I was struck by how busy and bad tempered everyone seemed to be. We stopped at a local supermarket for some milk and bread and, as we waited to pay, I foolishly tried to pass the time of day with a lady in the queue, only to be cut short with the comment, "I'm sorry, I don't know you." It was not surprising then, that Lesley, who had not smoked a single cigarette in the ten days since we had set off for Ireland, was back on the evil weed just moments after we set foot back in Britain. However, arriving home was not without is benefits. Our two dogs were delighted to see us and alternated between barking madly, running around in circles and leaping up like they were on springs, in an effort to give us "welcome home kisses."

Once we were settled and drinking tea, I was sorting through a pile of junk mail and utility bills when I noticed an unstamped envelope of high quality vellum. Inside was news of another "duck," joining the line-up. It seemed that our neighbour wanted to buy our house.

"Well," Lesley said with a big smile, "It looks like we had better start packing."

Chapter 6 – In which we become homeless

Richard, our neighbour, was offering to buy our house as an immediate cash sale with no chain, for the full asking price, less only the estate agent fees we would be saving. The only provisos to his offer were that our asking price needed to be assessed as being fair, by three independent valuations, and that the sale then be completed without a forward chain. In other words, we were to take his money and get out! The following day I met with Richard and accepted his offer for the house. We immediately contacted our respective solicitors to start the ball rolling and I also informed the estate agent that we had sold the house privately. The reason Richard wanted to complete the purchase so quickly was so they could make an early start on the structural changes necessary to prepare the house for two elderly relatives. Whereas this was excellent news for us in moving the project forwards, it created a logistical challenge, as we had to pack our lives into boxes and arrange safe storage with a firm that could deliver to Ireland, at a reasonable cost. Over the next few weeks, all of the necessary inspections and property searches were completed, contracts were drawn up and signed and the deposit was lodged with our solicitor. Barring any last minute hitches, we would move out on March 12th, 2004.

I found a removals firm who could store our belongings and then deliver them safely to our new home, at a cost that was only slightly more than that of the first moon landing. Next we acquired dozens of one metre triple-ply cardboard boxes and started packing. Each box needed to be labelled and the contents listed separately, or so we were advised, in case the lorry was inspected by customs when arriving in Ireland. Lesley did a magnificent job of packing the boxes, although the task was made a little easier because we still had several boxes in the garage, yet to be unpacked from our previous house move, several years before. Once she had packed and taped the first box, Lesley asked me to move it to the dining room at the front of the house, where all of the completed boxes were to be assembled. I grabbed the box and went "Ooff!" but it didn't move. Next I spread my legs, bent my knees and with a straight back made an "eeeffe" sound, but to no avail. Finally I tried going blue in the face and heaving with all my might, until the veins in my neck looked like hosepipes and sweat dripped down my back, but the box stubbornly refused to budge.

"What the hell did you put in it?" I asked, lying on the floor, watching little white dots dancing before my eyes.

"Just the records and a few books," Lesley replied.

"Not all of the records?" I asked in horror. We still had our vinyl collection of over 100 albums.

"And a few books to fill up the box," she explained in a matter of fact tone.

"But I can't even move it," I complained. "It must weigh a ton."

"Oops!" She shrugged and gave me that little girl smile that I love her for.

After that we redistributed the weight more manageably, across three boxes, and then agreed that just because she could lift a box herself, it didn't follow that two strapping removals men could also lift it. Within a week the packing was completed, except for the items we required each day for cooking, eating, dressing and so on.

While the house sale and packing was progressing, we had also been in regular contact with Alan Sykes, the estate agent in Ireland. After a few false starts, we had decided to put in an offer on Glenmadrie, but things were moving even more slowly than one might expect in Ireland. The vendor was off travelling somewhere in South America and was only communicating with Alan by fax once a week. So Alan would forward our offer, and a week later we would get a reply refusing the offer. Then we would increase our offer, adding comments about the condition of the property, Alan would fax it off, and the entire sorry process would start over. On occasions, the vendor would reply to a question via his solicitor and we would miss the communication completely or, as on one occasion, believe that the response referred to a different question. The process was long, laborious and very frustrating as, apart from the price, there were dozens of things that needed to be resolved before we could safely complete the sale. Our experience gained from the purchase of our current house, was that confusion over the ownership of certain fixtures and fittings can create tension, if they are not clearly recorded. Although this was then standard practice for property sales in England, things were a little less regulated in Ireland. Also, after we moved into our house in England, we were shocked when it had cost us more than £2,500 to remove rubbish, glass and asbestos from the garden and outbuildings; an unbudgeted expense we were keen to avoid in future. We were conscious of the likely cost of a similar exercise in Ireland, given the remoteness and lack of local waste and recycling services, so we pushed for the site to be cleared before we moved in. I am sure that the vendor was probably a nice chap; I have never heard a bad word said about him, but as our frustration grew at the lethargic communication process, I found myself loathing the man. I created mental images of him sitting on some sunny beach in Mexico, drinking his afternoon cocktails and laughing heartlessly, like a pantomime pirate, at our latest desperate request for essential information. As ridiculous as it sounds, I think that if we had met back then, God forgive me, I would have punched his lights out. Of course he was probably equally frustrated by the poor communications and our seemingly ever more asinine questions and demands. However, all's well that ends well, and in the end we reached a stage where we could push on with the purchase – or so we thought.

We had appointed a solicitor in Ennis to act on our behalf in the purchase, and although he had our best interests at heart, he seemed determined to present every possible reason he could find to stop us from buying Glenmadrie. Although he had some good points to make, we decided the problem was that he simply couldn't understand why two nutty English people would want to waste their money buying an old farmhouse, when we could buy a shiny new jelly mould, just like his house. In the end we acknowledged each of his objections, politely dismissed them and moved on. Our surveyor (or engineer as they are called in Ireland) had a more refreshing approach. After delivering his largely negative official report, laced with damming observations like, "the guttering is a thriving habitat for all forms of wildlife," and "much of the flooring is rotten and requires replacement," his unofficial comments were more positive. As we sat together one sunny day on the hill overlooking the house, he remarked, "Gosh, what a beautiful spot this is. Nick. You and Lesley would be fools to miss the opportunity of living here."

As we pressed on with the purchase, the next step required signing papers with the solicitor, applying for our PPS numbers, which were necessary to pay stamp duty on the purchase and opening an Irish bank account. Our presence was required for most things, so we collected together all of the required documents, like old bank statements, utility bills and other forms of identification, and jumped on the next Ryanair flight to Shannon. After meeting with our solicitor and yet again assuring him that we were indeed willing to deliberately waste our money on a derelict hovel, when much nicer new houses were readily available, we pushed on to the bank.

In England we banked with NatWest, and have over thirty years of excellent history with them, but there are no NatWest branches in the Republic of Ireland. Oddly, they seemed unaware that Ulster Bank was part of the same group and advised us instead to try AIB for all of our banking in Ireland. At the time, banks in Ireland were reminiscent of those in England during the 1950s – as large as churches and of similar architecture. There were no security cameras, guards or walls of bullet-proof glass – only a counter piled high with money and a kindly old lady to give it out. Once the sale in England was completed, we expected to deposit a substantial amount of cash – much more cash than I had ever had in one place. I therefore had a reasonable expectation of some courteous treatment, or at least some respect on a par with NatWest, where I had an account called "Platinum with Nobs on" or something similar, but it was not to be. After being shunted repeatedly from one employee to another, we found ourselves talking to a particularly sour young maiden, as we stood at an old school desk in the centre of the banking floor. Around us, queuing customers were able to hear our every word, and probably read our old bank statements at the same time. The clerk treated us with obvious suspicion and ill-concealed contempt, as we attempted to entrust her and her employer with all of our money. Nevertheless, we pressed on regardless; we were after all, foreigners in a foreign land, but things started to become tense when we reached the subject of our wanting a joint bank account. Apparently it was, and may still be, normal practice for men in Ireland to keep control of their bank account and money, even if their wives work as well. Unaware of this snippet of local trivia, as we stood there side by side, facing the schoolmistress's desk and surrounded by curious customers, I began to feel a bit like Oliver, asking for more gruel.

"Are you sure you really want a joint bank account?" the clerk asked me conspiratorially.

"Yes, we would," I replied pointedly.

"Are you really sure?" she asked again, as I imagined her stabbing frantically at an alarm button concealed beneath the desk.

"Yes, I – I mean, we – are sure, thank you."

"Well, if you're sure, I suppose it's ok," she said, looking at the application form with a frown.

I glanced to my right at Lesley, who stood stiffly, staring at the desk. I thought she looked a little pink in the face.

The clerk continued to fill out the application form. As she approached the section requiring details from Lesley, I took half a step back, to allow her better access.

"Now, Sir, what is your wife's name?" she asked, looking at me, over Lesley's shoulder.

"She," I said pointing at Lesley, "is called Lesley."

"Yes, Sir, thank you, Sir. And what is her date of birth?"

I answered, and again did the pointing thing. Lesley had now gone a nasty red colour.

"And what was her maiden name?"

Lesley stepped forwards and answered, through tightly clenched teeth. I noticed she was now rather purple around the neck.

"How are you spelling that, Sir?" the clerk asked.

I was about to answer, when Lesley placed both hands on the desk and leaned forwards, until she was nose to nose with the unfortunate clerk.

"I – AM – RIGHT – HERE!!!" she said slowly and rather loudly, by way of confirmation. As if a gunslinger had just walked into a Wild West bar; all conversations stopped and several people turned to look in our direction. There was an awkward moment of silence, and I imagined the two women facing off in the street and preparing to draw their weapons, as a tumbleweed blew by in the background. Finally the clerk pulled a face, rather like someone whose finger had just gone through the lavatory paper, and then, with a stiff smile she pretended to notice Lesley for the first time.

After that, the form filling continued splendidly, although my finer senses detected some air of tension between the two women, as they circled each other like feral cats. I wisely avoided standing between them. By three o'clock, the bank appeared to be closing; the curious onlookers had been shooed out and there was a man guarding the door. Once our clerk had finished filling the forms, which we had both signed, she added copies of all of our documents and then pointedly wished me good day. Lesley and I laughed together as we made for the exit.

"We're lucky she didn't call in the police to arrest me." Lesley joked as we stepped through the door. Outside, the street was empty except for an armoured personnel carrier, two jeeps and about twenty soldiers, all fiercely brandishing rifles.

"Christ! Perhaps she did!" I said in shock as we slowly raised our hands. There was a moment of tense silence combined with some extreme stillness. Then the officer, who was bravely standing behind his men, gave an exasperated sigh and spoke loudly but clearly, as if he was addressing a group of school children.

"Excuse me, would you please move out of the way?"

Compared to Britain, the security inside many Irish banks was still very relaxed, but following a recent spate of security van robberies, cash collections were now being conducted under armed guard – or so we had just learned. The heavily armed soldiers watched us suspiciously as we sidestepped our way cautiously along the front of the bank for twenty yards, before bursting into giggles and running towards the car park.

With our administration visit completed in record time, we had a spare night and day before our flight back to England, and so after a meal in Ennis and another freezing night at our regular B&B, we revisited Glenmadrie with a camera and tape measure. I had in mind the majority of the structural changes that I wanted to do at the house, but I needed to take some more accurate measurements, so that I could draw up plans and get a decent idea of the kind of budget we would need. Also, Lesley wanted to measure up the windows, so that she could buy curtains, or material, for those windows that our current curtains wouldn't fit. We had only recently bought posh new drapes for our house in England, but with twenty windows in Glenmadrie to cover, we could be damaging our limited budget quite quickly. Luckily Lesley is such a dab hand at sewing that most of the curtains would be altered to fit the new house, with the rest being made from material bought in the sales. We spent a couple of hours quietly walking around the house and grounds, getting a feel for the place and noticing little things that would pass unseen in other circumstances. It was another lovely day, quite warm for the time of year with a crystal clear sky. Again we were struck by the beauty of the location. The hill to the rear was recently planted with fir trees, which gave the house a sheltered backdrop and provided a safe haven for red deer, goats, badgers, foxes, pine martens and polecats, but not always all at the same time. To the front there were unrestricted views across the moor, where a rocky, fifty-foot cliff face sharply dissected the hills and gave nesting for a pair of rare Hen Harriers. Looking a little more to the right, the moorland gives way to the heavily forested slopes of Maghera Mountain, which rises steeply to over four hundred metres and is one of the highest points in County Clare. Once we had completed our photographs and measurements and finished imagining all of the things we wanted to do with the property, we decided that it was time to move on. It was obvious that we were both falling in love with Glenmadrie, and we were at risk of becoming seriously disappointed and upset should the sale fall through unexpectedly. We needed to make an effort to maintain some emotional distance, at least until the house was ours.

As I was thinking that this could be the last time we ever saw Glenmadrie, I was suddenly struck with an overwhelming urge to test the plumbing, so Lesley said she would have a final walk around, while she waited for me. Wondering if perhaps I was subconsciously trying to mark my territory, or simply the victim of a bad vegetable curry, I made a dash for the bathroom. The toilet was balanced precariously on a block of wood, presumably because the waste pipe was fitted at the wrong height. I found myself needing to hold onto the bath and brace my feet to the floor, so that my efforts to hurry the ablutions didn't topple the toilet. Enjoying these few moments of solitude, I opened the bathroom window and looked out onto the courtyard. I was struck by how quiet it was, and yet how noisy. The wind was rustling the trees, water was running in a stream below, thousands of birds were chattering, and in the distance I could hear the roar of a mighty waterfall. In my experience, wherever I went in Britain, one could always hear indications of civilization; the noises of trains, cars, people or music were always present. But in the fifty square kilometres around Glenmadrie there were just ten other houses, all but one were on the road to the next village. Here, perhaps for the first time in many years, I was experiencing real solitude. But what was that noise at the periphery of my hearing? Is it the squeak of a rusty gate swinging in the wind, the baying of a feral goat, or the call of a rare eagle? No, it is my lovely wife distantly calling for my help. My brave dash to provide assistance was immediately foiled by the sight of an empty toilet roll holder. In desperation, I was just contemplating putting my remaining stock of five euro notes to good use, when I luckily spied half a roll of lavatory paper, hiding behind the cistern. Once outside I tried to locate the source of her agitated cries, repeatedly shouting her name, but without success. Each time she called, the sound was whipped away by the wind, or bounced back from the distant cliffs, confusing the direction and source. Suddenly I was certain that she had accidentally fallen into the quarry and was at that moment lying injured and bleeding, pathetically cry out for my help. I turned left and ran across the meadow towards the quarry, but after a hundred paces I noticed that her voice seemed more distant. Was I heading in the wrong direction, or was Lesley just getting weaker? A mighty bellow of "N-I-I-I-CK?" from the rear, confirmed that I was indeed on the incorrect track. I turned back towards the house shouting for Lesley, but without receiving a response. Still unable to locate my wife and unsure of what to do next, I stood in the driveway scratching my head in frustration. Just then I heard another shout, this time from much closer. I yelled back and finally received an immediate response. Homing in on Lesley's calls, I had to walk for several yards further before spotting where she was standing; forty feet away and fifteen feet below me, hidden amongst the trees on the edge of the wood.

"Where have you been?" She demanded sharply. "I've been shouting for ages."

"I was looking for you." I replied. "I couldn't figure out where you were. Anyway, what are you doing down there?"

"I wanted to see what the wood was like. I went in over there," she said pointing far to her left, "and walked through that bit, then down that bank and over that log – until I got to here."

"Oh, Okay." I said. "What's it like then?"

"Rather muddy actually." Lesley replied with a smile, looking down. "Especially this bit."

I stood, hands on hips and searched the terrain for a moment. "I think that you're standing in the percolation area for the septic tank. That's probably why it's so muddy."

"Yes, that would explain it." She said tersely. "Anyway, can you help me please? I seem to be rather stuck."

As she was slightly hidden by a small tree, I moved a little to one side for a better view. Finally I could see the full scope of her predicament. The intrepid explorer was holding a low branch and balancing precariously on one foot, with the other wellington boot firmly stuck in the mud, just out of reach. A bright pink sock was gangling limply from the toes of her other foot, like a slightly effeminate warning flag.

"Stay right where you are," I said, not being one to miss an opportunity. "I'll get the camera."

Unfortunately, she had the camera in her pocket and refused to repeat the pose after being rescued. It seems that she had decided to explore the wood and had stumbled into the "muddy bit," but pressed on manfully until her wellington boots became stuck in the mud. We cleaned our boots as best we could and then set off for a leisurely drive towards Shannon and our flight home again. We drove passed Lough Cullaunyheeda and paused for a few moments to take in the peace and beauty, and marvel at the solitude. I was struck by the lack of boats, yachts or fishermen. There are several similar lakes near to our house in England, and on most days it is difficult to see much of the water because of the number of people skiing, swimming, fishing and roaring around on any number of motorised boys' toys. Ireland may have been missing out on a large chunk of the recreational water hobbyist market, but that was absolutely fine with us. A few miles later we stopped at the village of Sixmilebridge, to look at the stone bridge (which must be six miles from somewhere) and to feed the ducks by the pink pub. There is a small duck pond next to the pub and on it floats a beautifully crafted duck house which is an exact replica of the pink pub. I am not sure if the ducks appreciate the effort that had gone in to providing their accommodation, but we certainly did.

While driving around over the last few days, two particular things had struck us about the houses alongside the roads. During the day, it was obvious to see that the residents of County Clare had finally discovered coloured masonry paint. Although many traditional Irish stone cottages were protected with a white lime wash, I understand that for many years, new houses were constructed of concrete blocks and then covered with cement render, leaving them a depressing, dull grey – perhaps to match the depressingly dull grey skies. Recently, however, the locals had discovered the power of coloured masonry paint to brighten up their homes. "But what colours should we use?" they ask. Not for them the mid-tones and pastel shades of those town folks in Dublin and Cork (locally pronounced Cwork). No: the brave people of Clare chose unflinchingly the most audacious colours imaginable, colours previously only reserved for safety jackets, warning signs and perhaps hot air balloons. Then, presumably because they were not satisfied with that singular insult to the eyes, on some houses, two colours, which cannot naturally exist together in nature, are combined on the same building to produce a mind-numbing effect that can only be safely replicated by hyperventilating, whilst snorting fresh lemon juice. On seeing one of these ocular monstrosities for the first time, the only appropriate response was to inadvertently stamp on the brake pedal and shout, "Holy crap – look at that!" Driving at night, one could imagine that many people in Ireland had the benefit of free electricity, or immense surplus incomes, and a total disregard for the effect on the environment, at least judging by the number of lights most houses displayed. One grandiose house that we frequently passed on the road to Shannon was a typical example. Set in about an acre of garden, there were carriage lights on the gates, twenty lampposts lining both sides of the driveway and six massive flood lights illuminating both the front and back gardens. To add to the effect, there were yards of outdoor Christmas lights hanging from the roof eaves and on every tree in the front garden, and although the entire family was probably sat in front of the fifty inch television, every indoor light was also shining brightly. In recent years, the decline in the economy can be measured by how few excess lights are now visible at night.

The day after we arrived back at our home in England, I was out walking with our two dogs, when I realised there was a problem; one of them was clearly unwell. Brandy had been with us for about ten years; she was usually fit and healthy and loved her daily walks with her niece Romany, but now she seemed to be getting out of breath and was unusually unwilling to walk, and so I arranged to take her to the local vet. Jane Finch was a professional and knowledgeable vet, who knew our dogs well. As we were planning to move abroad, both of our dogs had just had a full check-up with updated inoculations, as well as being micro chipped; so this sudden onset of illness was unexpected. Although she wasn't overly worried about Brandy, Jane decided to keep her at the clinic overnight, as a precaution. Perhaps she was mindful of Brandy's sister dog Tammy, who had suffered a long and painfully slow decline in health, because of a mystery lung condition that finally took her life, in the summer of 2000. This same vet had previously spent a considerable amount of our money, in unsuccessfully treating Tammy, and I think she wanted to take early action, to ensure that Brandy was kept healthy. Despite what had happened to Tammy in the past, we were confident that Brandy was in excellent hands and we both went to sleep that night without worrying. But when I telephoned the following morning, Jane told me in a tear filled voice that our darling Brandy was dead!

Jane explained that she suspected that Brandy had suffered a heart attack during the night and that she may have been having an allergic reaction to the microchip, or the inoculations. As often seems to be the case when bad news needed to be delivered, it fell to me to tell Lesley that Brandy had died; I was of course deeply upset by the loss of our beautiful dog, but it seemed that my heart would break for Lesley, as she sobbed uncontrollably onto my chest while I hugged her as tightly as I could. After I had collected Brandy from the vet and tearfully driven my way home, we laid her body on the dog's bed in the conservatory. Poor Romany seemed genuinely confused that Brandy wouldn't wake up, and in an effort to ease their mutual sadness, Lesley sat alongside Romany and the body of her friend, while I prepared a grave in the garden. Later that evening we wrapped Brandy in a blanket and, along with her favourite toy, buried her next to where her sister Tammy lay. Romany sat by the grave in the pouring rain for over an hour, then with obvious sadness, she finally answered our calls to come indoors. The loss of such a close companion can be very difficult for some people to get over. Brandy was so central to our lives that it sometimes felt that we had lost a close family member. I was deeply upset that Brandy had died, but a dreadful pain boiled up in my chest whenever I saw the terrible sadness in my wife's eyes. Lesley seemed particularly affected, perhaps because Brandy's death was so sudden and unexpected, but also because she knew we would be moving away so soon.

Moving house is allegedly one of the most stressful things you can experience; add to it sudden unemployment and the sadness caused by the death of our furry close companion, and you could be heading for the "Perfect Storm." Strangely, I was feeling less stress than one may imagine. Although I was still experiencing a few minor stress events, which usually presented as a sudden sensation of falling, along with palpitations and a cold sweat, by carefully controlling my breathing, I had learned to manage these incidents better. Also, the fact that we were now so focused on such a positive future seemed to help diminish any stress I may have been feeling. On the other hand, everybody in Ireland who was even remotely connected to our house purchase, seemed hell bent on sending me to an early grave. The sale of our house in England was finalised and we would have to move out within a few days, my company car had gone back and I was now out of work. However, the purchase of Glenmadrie was stalled, with no sign of progressing; it looked like we were soon going to be homeless, as well as unemployed. There was no other option; I had to fly back to Ireland and try to push things along. We decided that if it became clear the purchase of Glenmadrie was going to drag on for weeks, I should arrange to rent a cottage somewhere near Ennis where I could be on hand to resolve any issues. Lesley would then remain in England, at her mother's house, and as soon as Glenmadrie was ours and our furniture had arrived, she could drive over, along with our car sick dog Romany.

So I went back to Ireland yet again, on the next available flight, all the time worrying that we would never buy our Irish home, and thinking, "What a shame Ryanair don't do frequent flyer miles." At least "Jules," the outrageously camp flight attendant, recognised me and immediately left me in peace, abandoning any attempt to sell me the most expensive sandwiches in Europe. After another smooth flight at the steady hand of our fifteen-year old pilot, and his twelve-year old friend, we landed ahead of time and I bade a relieved farewell to Jules and his two Latvian beauty queen assistants. The girl at the car hire firm also remembered me and provided a free upgrade from my base model car, to a monstrous V8 4X4, which was great fun to drive, but seemed to drink petrol faster than a rugby team can drink beer. An hour later, I booked myself into a hotel on the outskirts of Ennis, which smelled vaguely of damp, dust and garlic, a curious mix of aromas, which made me question what the kitchen was cooking. After I had dumped my luggage, I stopped in Ennis for a delicious lunch of vegetable soup and a sandwich, before setting off to meet with the people who I was ostensibly paying to not sell me a house. In the end there was little more I could do, and no amount of ranting and pleading was going to progress the sale any faster. I decided that with time, patience and a watchful eye, the purchase would proceed; but clearly I needed to be on hand to deal with any issues and to keep things moving along. On the assumption that it could take another month or more to complete the purchase, we were going to waste a lot of money if I stayed in a hotel; surely there had to be a more realistic alternative. Before flying over I had even looked into the possibility of buying a caravan and camping until the house was ready; but most caravan sites were closed for the winter and I certainly didn't want to end up parked at the side of the road and be accidentally mistaken for a "Traveller," as these local Gypsies seemed to be hated and mistrusted by most people in Ireland. In the end, through a local pub, I found a traditional Irish thatched cottage in Corofin that I could rent weekly for a reasonable off-season rate. I paid the deposit and made my plans to move to Ireland on March 13th, 2004.

On the up side, for some time I had been looking at the possibility of working freelance in Ireland, rather than trying to go back into formal employment, but I needed a base to work from that offered a good customer demographic. A little internet research had shown that there was a ready market for my skills in Clare, and I was confident that my offering would quickly draw customers. So, before this trip, I had arranged to meet with three suitable local businesses, to discuss my idea. One lovely married couple was immediately very keen on the proposal and they recognised that my business could be complimentary to theirs, adding value and bringing in some extra customers – or perhaps they simply felt sorry for me. In any event, after some discussion, we agreed terms, and as quick as that I was back in business. In my head I imagined that another of our "ducks" had just stepped into line.

Before my trip was over, I decided to visit the house once again. The key was still under the usual stone and everything else was as we had left it. Despite a specific agreement with the vendor, no effort had been made to remove the rubbish in the out buildings, or the junked cars in the driveway. Inside the house, the half completed decorating and building work remained untouched, under a thick layer of dust and cobwebs. Although I could see that someone had been keeping an eye on the place; the heating had been on and there was a new toilet roll in the bathroom. Because of the communication difficulties we were having between two different solicitors in Ireland, and someone living in the heart of Brazil who was infrequently accessible by fax, things were moving slower than a glacier before global warming and becoming more acrimonious than a celebrity divorce. As I walked around to the quarry I was unsurprised to discover that the fifty-foot wooden pyramid was still obscuring what was otherwise a beautiful view. I would have been happy for the pyramid to have remained, as it would have been a welcome source of much needed firewood, but the vendor was clearly very attached to his folly. As part of the contract of sale, he had insisted that the pyramid remained in situ for the next six years, to be maintained by us, although he wanted the right to remove it at his convenience, without any prior notice. It was a crazy idea and we refused point blank, indicating that this issue had now become a ridiculous "deal breaker"; in the end he agreed to remove it before the sale was complete, or donate it to us as firewood. In retrospect, I think that the illusion of animosity went both ways. Soon after my visit, the pyramid was removed by a local couple, who ended up feeding it to their fire, rather than mine.

Although I had no rock climbing experience or equipment, for some reason I took it into my head to try and climb the rock face at the highest part of the quarry. I could say that in the spirit of a mountain climber, I attempted the east face of Glenmadrie quarry, "just because it was there," but actually it was "just because I'm an idiot!" Nobody was about and I was wearing wellington boots and a long cashmere coat; the rock face is about fifty feet high, almost vertical, slick with ice and crumbly with loose shale. About halfway up I thought, "nobody is about and I am wearing wellington boots and a long cashmere coat." I found myself stuck, unable to go back down and unwilling to climb further up, because of the risk of falling. In my mind I was transported back to a time when, as a child playing alone in the woods near our house, I had climbed a high embankment and become stuck. Now again I found myself similarly paralysed, not by fear but by my analysis of the situation; if I tried to climb down when unsure of a decent foothold, I might slip; conversely climbing higher increased the risk of damage should I tumble. The safer option seemed to be staying put and waiting for help, but the quarry is very remote and help from a random passing stranger seemed unlikely. In the end I remembered what I had done as a child; I climbed upwards, focusing only on the next handhold, one step at a time. When I reached the top of the quarry, I laughed out loud at the absurdity of the situation. Although the quarry wall was not particularly high by climbing standards, it would be a high enough fall to break a leg or knock my silly head off. In the middle of winter, an injured person lying at the foot of that cliff would have died of exposure and shock within an hour. Perhaps I learned an important lesson that day, that sometimes when things seem hopeless, focusing steadily on the next step will keep you moving forwards, or, as the SAS say, "proper planning prevents a piss poor performance." If I did learn anything, it didn't stop me from being an idiot during the next eight years by falling off ladders, getting electrocuted, climbing the quarry again, or just taking long walks across the moor, without telling anyone where I was going.

Strangely elated and convinced that everything was going to be okay now, I set off towards Shannon Airport and another Ryanair flight home. Near Spancelhill cross, a few miles from Ennis, I encountered a police checkpoint. The Garda Síochána, or Guards, as the police in Ireland are called, are good people, dedicated to serving their community, but sadly underfunded and ill resourced. It is probably fair to say that the funding and training required to keep the Garda Síochána up to date, with the challenges they were facing from the year 2000 onwards, were out of step with the funding and training available to the drug dealers and gangs in Ireland. Sadly, during the "Celtic Tiger" years, so much money had become available to the young people of Ireland that they had run out of cars, gadgets and gismos to buy and had turned towards recreational drugs for their fun. The drug lords in the cities like Dublin, Limerick and Cork made obscene amounts of money , and being rather naughty people, didn't pay taxes, so the Government didn't have the money to fund the Guards adequately in the ensuing arms race. During the first ten years of this century, the poor Guards were obviously playing catch-up, after having started a long way behind this new band of criminals. Although not strictly correct, the media painted a sad image of a balding, slightly overweight village policeman, from the 1950s, furiously peddling his bicycle in a futile attempt to apprehend two "bling" encrusted drug dealers, in a bullet proofed Humvee. Fortunately the gangs seemed more inclined to turn their Ak47s and Uzi 9mms on each other, rather than on the whistle and notebook of the poor Guards. For a while it seemed that gangland killings were an almost daily feature on the news, and one did wonder how many of them could still be left alive, as they kept on shooting each other. Even after the crooks had been arrested, the blatant intimidation of the terrified witnesses made any justice seem difficult to achieve. In the end, the shocking and criminal mismanagement of Ireland's banks and economy achieved almost overnight what the Guards and Courts seemed unable to; the drug money stopped. Once the glut of excess money dried up, food and mortgage payments became more important than cocaine and ecstasy, and the drug gangs largely disappeared. In rural Ireland, I am pleased to report that the local Guards are still thin on the ground and wide in the hips, like the jolly policemen of old. Traffic checkpoints are a fairly common affair in Ireland, where the cars patiently line up to have their tax, insurance and car test window stickers inspected, and provided you are not obviously cross-eyed drunk, you are then waved on your way. I find the checkpoints to be a refreshing reminder of the relaxed way of life that we have here in rural Ireland. In England, a single broken down lorry could cause traffic chaos, urgent news reports and a visit from the traffic police helicopter, supported by an armed response unit; sometimes even fatal road accidents are insufficient grounds to justify a delay in the traffic. In my wildest dreams, I cannot imagine the pandemonium and recriminations that would follow if two English policemen were ordered to check tax discs, by standing in the middle of the M25! So I was naturally unperturbed when my hire car was stopped at the checkpoint, near Spancelhill cross. The young Guard checked my windshield stickers, and as all was in order, he started to wave me on. Suddenly he spotted that something was amiss and held up his hand. He approached my open window and asked,

"Excuse me, Sir," he said in a strong Clare accent. "Is this your ve-hackle?"

"Err – no, it's rented from Shannon Airport. Is something wrong?" I asked, wondering if I had obviously been driving too cautiously for the Irish roads.

"No, Sir, everything appears to be in order. Except I notice you were listening to the radio."

"Yes, I was," I replied cautiously.

"And singing, were you?"

"Not very well, but yes I was." I replied, trying to think where I could get a copy of the Irish Highway Code.

"Barry Manilow – wasn't it?" he asked with a devilish gleam in his eye.

Slightly embarrassed I replied, "Yes, I am afraid it was."

The Guard looked past me to the next car and with mock severity said, "Well, Sir, I believe it is a reportable offence, but I will let you off with a warning this time. Don't let it happen again," and then he walked away. You've got to love Ireland!

Chapter 7 – In which we move to Ireland

Back in England, Lesley had done a magnificent job with the packing, and our lives were now boxed in cardboard and ready to go into storage. It was March 12th, 2004 and, after a few nerve jangling delays and legal problems, the sale of our house in England was agreed and we were just waiting for the order to hand over the keys. Moving day had arrived. Once we had packed our respective cars with only the things we would need for the next few weeks, everything else was loaded into the removal vans and they departed – hopefully to be seen again in Ireland, very soon. After putting so much work and love into the house and garden, it was inevitably an emotionally painful day. Lesley and I took a few quiet moments to walk around the house and garden for the final time. After we fed the chickens, we walked slowly along the path that looped through the orchard and around to the vegetable garden. When we reached the point where we could see the entire property, we stopped and reminisced quietly about all that we had achieved together in the last few years, renovating a rundown cottage into a beautiful and desirable family home. Although this was supposed to be a happy and positive move, there was naturally considerable sadness and some apprehension as well; I gently pulled Lesley towards me and we hugged each other and shed a tear. Our moment of quiet reflection was rudely shattered by the ringing of my mobile phone. It was our solicitor calling to report that we were currently trespassing. He told me the house sale transaction was complete, the cash proceeds had been transferred to our bank account in Ennis, and that we should now hand over the keys to our neighbour. After exchanging pleasantries with Richard, we left him with our house and set off to our new life; Lesley, temporarily to her mother's house, and I towards Ireland.

My schedule took me past Birmingham and across North Wales to Holyhead port, where I would overnight at a hotel before taking the early ferry to Dublin and then on towards Corofin. Travelling from East to West, I would drive across the entire width of England, Wales and Ireland in around fourteen hours. One of the first steps towards living without debt was buying an affordable, reliable car that I could maintain myself. Ten days previously I had purchased a Ford Escort 1.8L that was decent value, as it had some slight accident damage. A local garage had replaced the front wing and one headlight and then given the engine a full service, changing the timing-belt, oil, filters and so on. Although I had already driven a few miles in the car, this was going to be a major test of reliability. Ultimately, the little car never let me down, but I never really grew to like it. Whatever I tried, I was unable to find a comfortable driving position, the steering was vague, the rear suspension sloppy, the boot space was unsatisfactory, and in Ireland the insurance was prohibitively expensive. After all its valiant efforts, I sold it after eighteen months and was happy to see it gone.

The journey to Holyhead on a busy Friday afternoon, driving an unfamiliar car, where I could barely see over the dashboard, left little time for contemplation or reminiscences. My stress levels were at manageable proportions, partly because I wasn't rushing to catch a ferry, which was fortunate because for the majority of the journey, the traffic was murderous. In some ways the torture of driving with a numb bum, in Birmingham's rush-hour traffic, whilst watching my wiper blades' lethargic efforts to rearrange the dead flies on the windshield, lifted my slightly apprehensive spirits somewhat. I had anticipated being giddy with excitement, but found myself feeling a little uneasy, perhaps because the house purchase was still up in the air, and perhaps because I was leaving Lesley behind. During that hellish drive, I gave much thought to those others we were moving away from – our ever supportive daughter, my two sisters and both of our elderly mothers and our friends – but was reassured that we would only be an hour's flying time away. Furthermore, it was conceivable that our new home would encourage friends and family to holiday in Ireland, or visit for long weekends; so I had high hopes of having more "quality time" with those people that we love, but miss so much.

I had visited the friendly folk in South Wales while on holiday in the past, and we had even considered the area, before Ireland came into focus. However, I had never before visited North Wales and, despite being forewarned, I was shocked by some of the venomous anti-British graffiti that decorated many of the bridges on the route into Holyhead. Given the recent history between England and Ireland, I started to worry unnecessarily that perhaps I had made an awful error of judgement and that we would soon be hounded from our new home by hordes of angry xenophobic villagers. After an uninspiring meal and an uncomfortable night in a lumpy motel bed, I drove through the morning mist to board the early ferry. As the fast ferry powered its way towards Ireland; with the rising sun on my back and the salt spray in my face, I held tightly to the railing of the observation deck and whooped like a ten-year old – to the obvious consternation of the other passengers.

As Dublin and the sun-kissed Wicklow Mountains came into view for the first time, I thought of my father and how he must have felt in 1943 when, after four years of struggling to survive in Russian prisoner of war camps, he had sailed into Liverpool harbour to begin a new life. Perhaps, like me, he may have had concerns about being an immigrant in a foreign land; like me, he may also have believed that the worst had now passed, and things were only going to get better. Although Dublin is the capital city of Ireland, it is only the size of a small English city like Colchester or Norwich – but much more difficult to navigate. All over there were jolly signs pointing the way to exciting places like Dundrum, Blackrock, Palmerstown and Coolock, none of which I had any desire to visit. Nowhere did I see any sign for the N4, which I did want to visit, or, more helpful still, a bloody big arrow pointing "West this way." Where there were street signs, they were helpfully placed just past the junction, as if to say, "Ah now see, you should have gone down that one!" Other signs seemed to lack any real confidence, only pointing vaguely towards where you might need to go, and one more confident sign actually pointed to a shop doorway. I wondered if it was even more lost than me and was suggesting that I ask in the shop for directions! Being a man, I am genetically unable to admit that I am lost, or ask for help; although I am delighted to offer copious and detailed directions to anyone else – even if I have no idea of where I am at the time. Mercifully, the streets were quiet for a Saturday morning, which was a good thing, as I constantly found myself in the incorrect lane. Unlike England, however, even when I indicated my intention to change lanes at the most inopportune moment, the other cars immediately made space and then sent me on my way with a jolly wave. On occasion I felt the need to justify my erratic navigation by shouting, "Sorry – I'm English" out of the window, but then I started to wonder if people thought I was just apologising for being English – which is not such a bad idea sometimes. In the end I decided that my obvious yellow GB licence plate was excuse enough, and I kept my mouth shut. In the end I navigated my way through the labyrinth of confusion that is Dublin and found the road west that would link with the N6 and cross Ireland to Loughrea, where I was to turn left towards Gort. As I travelled further west, the traffic thinned noticeably, making the drive ever more pleasurable by the minute. Once on the road west, I was able to relax and enjoy the drive towards a new life. Most of the larger roads in Ireland have the usual white lines in the centre, but unlike England they also have a yellow stripe on the left marking a second lane for tractors and slower traffic (we drive on the left in Ireland and the UK). I was unsure of the etiquette in the use of this lane. I wondered if it was reserved only for farm traffic, or were elderly farmers, who were driving a car, permitted to use the slow lane as well? I saw tractors, bicycles, some cars, a lorry, and a pony and trap using the lane, but on other occasions they stubbornly stayed on the main part of the road and held up the traffic. A couple of times, when being aggressively tailgated by a large speeding lorry, I crossed the yellow line to make room for them to pass, only to find myself bouncing around alarmingly on the unmade surface. During another attempt to politely allow some homicidal lunatic to pass, the yellow lane suddenly disappeared without warning, as the road crossed a small bridge, leaving me trapped between the uncaring lorry and a stone wall. For a moment I revisited my long discarded catholic schooling and sought divine guidance to slow my car on the loose gravel. God must have been with me that morning, or perhaps it was the ghost of Henry Ford; in any event I negotiated the bridge without any damage to my vehicle and took a moment to swear loudly, like a celebrity chef, at the back of the lorry as it disappeared into the distance. After that incident, I stubbornly stayed in my lane, forcing any traffic that was determined to break the speed limit by more than me, to overtake in the conventional way. However, the excitement wasn't entirely over because Ireland also has an impressive collection of some of the biggest and deepest potholes it has ever been my misfortune to drive into. For a while, many years ago, I lived in Lagos, Nigeria, during their period of extreme financial austerity. The Nigerian government had stopped all spending on road maintenance; consequently, one of the best forms of entertainment was watching the "new rich" wrecking their gleaming Bentleys and Rolls Royces in quarry like potholes. Ireland's potholes are more subtle. A more paranoid person would suspect that some shadow government department, in an effort to bolster the profits of the Irish motor industry, had deliberately placed potholes in positions most likely to surprise the unsuspecting motorist. Although I have now memorised and learned to navigate all of the potholes that have been allocated to my regular routes, I will still hit two or three on any new trip. They seem to appear in the most inconvenient and unlikely places, for example on the inside of a bend, at the top of a hill, or whenever you cannot swerve to avoid one because there is a bus travelling in the opposite direction. The most insidious of Irish inventions is the water filled potholes, which are disguised to look like all the other puddles that your car has been laboriously splashing through all day, but are actually massive pits, big enough to bury a dead politician, but filled to the brim with oily black water. So there you are, merrily driving along on a normal Irish road slick with rain and dotted with puddles. Your car is filled to the brim with the things that you will need to live in a rented cottage for a few weeks and, to relieve the boredom; you may be attempting to touch the end of your nose with your tongue. Then: splash, splosh, splosh, splat, splash, KERBANG!! Suddenly most of your belongings are on the front seat, the car has developed a pathological desire to turn left, you are choking on a boiled sweet and your glasses are jammed under the brake pedal, along with the end of your tongue. Occasionally the department of transport, in an effort to repair some of the most cavernous potholes, will send out teams of workmen in machines that look a little bit like giant anteaters. At the front end of each is a spout that hangs over the cab and periodically vomits streams of tar and gravel into water filled potholes. This magical mixture is spectacular in its ability to adhere to the tyres and bodywork of any passing car, whilst totally resisting any attempt to bond with the pothole.

I must have been somewhere near the village of Moate when I stopped at a garage for petrol, tea and a pee. Noticing that they had a deli counter, I asked the nice lady if she could make me a sandwich.

"Of course my dear and what would you like in it?" she asked.

I looked at a magnificent array of every conceivable sandwich filling, but being vegetarian and also not wanting to mess up the inside of my car any more than was necessary, I opted for simple and safe, "Oh, just a cheese salad please," I replied.

"Would you like a bit of nice ham with that?" she offered sweetly.

"No thanks very much, I'm a vegetarian," I explained.

"Oh you poor dear," she said as if I was afflicted with some incurable disorder, "Some chicken then, just to give it a little flavour?"

"Thanks for the offer, but cheese salad will do me fine."

"You're English, aren't you?" she asked, and I said I was.

"I suspected you were," she said with a smile as if my nationality explained my outrageous diet. "Are you on your holidays?"

"No I'm moving over here to live," I replied proudly.

"Are you?" She looked me up and down. "Well," she said, "you are most welcome," and she meant it.

While she prepared my sandwich, I looked around the shop for a few minutes and collected some items I fancied for evening snacks, along with the makings for breakfast for the following morning. When I came to pay, I discovered that my sandwich comprised an entire French stick, piled high with what must have been a pound of cheese, half a jar of pickle, a small lettuce and umpteen slices of tomato and cucumber. In shifts between meals, it took almost three days to eat – magnificent! Although my grocery purchases were a little costly, even compared to a village shop in England, the petrol was 30% cheaper, and my sandwich was an incredible bargain at just €2. Refreshed and refilled, I was soon back on the road again and making good progress towards Corofin. At Loughrea I turned left from the N6 towards the seemingly drab, concrete grey, village of Gort, where I needed to consult a map for the first time in 150 miles. Here I struck out across country on single track roads and into the setting sun, past the delightfully named Lough Bunny and several other loughs, along the southern edge of the Burren, finally arriving at Corofin, tired but elated.

After a few phone calls I managed to track down the holiday home manager, who gave me the key to the cottage and showed me around; this didn't take very long. The cottage was quite traditional, with a two-part front door opening directly into a sitting area with two rocking chairs, a slate floor and an open fire providing the only source of heat and entertainment. A galley kitchen had been squeezed into the corridor that led to two small bedrooms and an even smaller bathroom. Lukewarm water was dribbled out of the shower, thanks to an ancient and somewhat temperamental immersion heater which ate money faster than I could feed it into the electric meter. After I had unpacked my belongings and linen, made up the bed and called Lesley to let her know I had arrived safely, I decided it was time to eat. The cottage was rented through "Bofey Quinns," a delightful bar and restaurant in the centre of Corofin that Lesley and I had eaten at twice during our house hunting trips around Christmas. Not being inclined to visit pubs very often, except perhaps for the odd Sunday lunch, or when on holiday, we had very much enjoyed the friendly welcome and pleasant atmosphere at Bofey Quinns. They had an excellent menu, with several vegetarian options, and we found the food to be delicious and keenly priced, so it was no surprise to discover that it was rated in the top ten pubs in Ireland. Despite my enormous French stick lunch, I found that I was ravenous and in a celebratory mood, so I opted for my favourite – a veggie pizza and side salad. While my pizza was being prepared and cooked, I sat by the fire drinking a pint of Guinness and felt the stress of the last few years draining away. It seemed that, for the first time in almost thirty years, all of my bills were paid, I had ample money in my pocket, no debt to service, and I was no longer concerned about my career prospects. Although there might be some clouds approaching from just over the horizon, at the moment everything was looking pretty rosy. Perhaps it was the beer, perhaps it was the heat from the fire, or perhaps it was the years of stress draining out of my body, but I found that my eyelids were becoming unbearably heavy and my arms were so tired, that it seemed too much effort to reach for the remainder of my pint. I closed my eyes for a moment and took a slow, deep breath and allowed cotton wool to fill up my mind, trapping the few remaining wild thoughts and soaking up the last vestiges of fear. I fell into such a deep sleep, that it was all the waitress could do to wake me when she delivered my meal. She needed to wake me a second time twenty minutes later, when she discovered I had fallen asleep over my uneaten food, and a third time after it was re-heated. In the end with the help of some strong tea, I managed to remain awake long enough to do justice to the excellent pizza and even managed to eat a sweet. To compensate the bar staff, I forced myself to consume a second pint (it would have been rude not to) and, after leaving a generous tip, walked the hundred yards back to my cottage where I fell onto the bed, fully clothed, and slept like a dead man for twelve hours.

The next morning at ten o'clock, I was outside my solicitors' office, waiting for them to open. The purchase of Glenmadrie was still looking doubtful, partly because there were some genuine issues that we needed to resolve and partly because my solicitor considered any deviation from the norm to be an instant deal breaker. There were undoubtedly some problems with the property; I had spotted some considerable dampness and wood rot in the exposed southern end, and some aspects of the building were not consistent with the plans on file. I was confident that the structural problems could be fixed and had already renegotiated the price to take account of the cost, but the planning issue was a little more complicated. Ideally, plans would have been filed, approved and then followed religiously. In practice, there is a more relaxed approach to planning in the more rural areas. On further investigation, it transpired that the "filed plans" were actually just a grubby sheet of A3 tissue paper, showing a rough sketch and some outlandish ideas of how the house was expected to be developed, twenty years ago. Although the drawing was on file, and some aspects were consistent with what was actually there, much of the work had never been completed. This wasn't necessarily an issue because, in the first instance, the sketch was not a formal plan and second, the matter of "compliance" with any plans was a matter of opinion; as we were cash buyers, there was really no need to seek the opinion of the planning office. Both ours and the vendor's surveyors were agreed that property was broadly compliant, but our solicitor was still refusing to condone the purchase. He seemed to be acting like a father, refusing to marry his only daughter to some tattooed and pierced, pot smoking monkey, although I was starting to suspect he felt more allegiance to his liability insurance than he did to our best interests. In the end the saving grace was the "statute barred" rule that allowed any non-compliant structure to remain, provided it had been in place and uncontested, for more than eight years. My solicitor and I piled all of the documents on his desk and worked through each page, crossing off the completed issues as we went, until we were left with just the site clearance and payment to deal with. We arranged buildings insurance and agreed that the sale could proceed, as soon as I had confirmed that the pyramid and other rubbish had been removed. Then, to lodge the funds into the client account, ready for transfer, I wrote out the largest cheque of my life – clearing 70% of my bank account with a single signature. After a delicious celebratory lunch of leek and potato soup at a nearby sandwich bar, I set course for Glenmadrie. I had finally managed to navigate my way to the house without the repeated use of an ordinance survey map, so I was feeling quite chipper, until I saw a caravan boldly parked in the driveway. It was an old fashioned wooden caravan, horse drawn and brightly painted, like something a fortune telling gypsy might use at a circus or carnival. There was an equally old dappled grey horse eating grass on the front lawn, and inside the house I discovered a family of four, watching a portable television that had a bent wire coat hanger for an aerial. They were English "new age travellers," which seems to be a catchall description for "unwashed, unemployed and unemployable English tourists." Although they were pleasant enough in explaining that they were not squatting, only staying overnight with the permission of the owner (whose name they couldn't seem to recall), I realised that I needed them off the property and told them so, politely but firmly. They seemed disappointed to be losing a source of free electricity and heating, but they understood that I was not going to back down and after a while they grudgingly complied.

I spent an hour walking around the house and property, checking for any previously unnoticed problems and taking a few photographs – a pleasurable task since the pyramid had finally gone, as had the scrap cars and other items of rubbish. Once I was as convinced as I could be that everything was in order, I sat on a rock above the quarry and phoned my wife in England. As we chatted Lesley told me how her mother was moaning about our dog, Romany, getting under her feet, although she suspected that her mum was secretly happy for the company. She mentioned how her back was aching because of sleeping in an uncomfortable bed, and then she complained about how busy things were in Essex. Then I described the beautiful view before me across the moor towards the forest, where the mist was drifting silently through the tops of the mighty pine trees, like the ghosts of ancient smoke, and how the sun was setting in the west and turning the sky a glorious orange – as a harbinger of an approaching storm. I told her how much I loved her and was missing her and how I hoped to see her soon and then reported the good news that everything was now ready for us to complete the sale.

"Last chance to change your mind." I joked.

"No way," she replied firmly.

So I called our solicitor and give him the go ahead to complete the sale without further delay. However, it seems that the legal profession would require a further couple of weeks to complete its black magic. Then, barring any last minute disasters, Glenmadrie would be ours on April 4th, almost exactly six months since I had sat on the wall in Essex, looking at my doctor's car.

After such an intense period of activity, the next two weeks were like the calm after a storm, which was ironic, because the next day the weather started to deteriorate towards wind, rain and some spectacular thunder storms. I had very little to do, other than read, listen to the radio and make the occasional trip to the house, to check that nobody else had decided to take up unauthorised residence. In retrospect, perhaps I should have squatted there myself – it would have saved me a bundle of money in rent and petrol. Legally everything required to complete the sale was in place and like any house buyer, we just had to wait patiently for the process to end. I managed to fritter away a few hours trying to change over the billing of the electricity and telephone, as both companies seemed flummoxed by the challenge of a registering a foreigner who didn't already have three months of Irish utility bills as proof of identity. After a herculean effort to suppress my growing anger, I managed to convince both companies that it could be to their financial advantage, in the longer term, to exchange some electricity and telephone calls for some of my money, as was traditional in other countries. Apart from the prospect of seeing Lesley again and moving into the house, the only ray of sunshine in an otherwise dismal fortnight, was that I had already received several calls from new clients responding to the posters and advertisements I had placed. During the two weeks that I stayed in Corofin, I actually earned enough money to cover my rent and buy a pint of Guinness; it seemed that I was back in business.

On the first Sunday that I was in Corofin, we had yet another thunderstorm, an event which, although not entirely unusual for Ireland, was unexpected on such a frosty day in March. Sometimes, warm moist air flowing north-east from the mid-Atlantic hits the cold dry air sitting above the frosty ground in Ireland, and the warmer air rises rapidly, condensing its moisture to rain or snow. In some conditions the rapidly rising air creates a static charge that can lead to thunderstorms accompanied by torrential rain, hail, and even snow and the odd mini-tornado. The thunderstorms seem to worsen when the mass of warm damp air is forced to rise even faster as it encounters a line of hills. Although nowhere as spectacular as the thunderstorms seen in tropical countries, Irish thunderstorms seem to excel at causing flash flooding, and the accompanying lightning strikes are particularly adept at knocking bits from houses and trees. As there was no rain falling in Corofin, I stood outside the cottage watching as a series of purple thunder clouds passed a mere five miles to the north and politely lined up, before marching on legs of lightning across the hills towards Loughrea. The ground at the base of each cloud was darkly obscured by a solid wall of falling rain and repeatedly illuminated by vivid flashes of lightning. I found it strangely captivating to stand in the dry, whilst watching a deluge of water and hail of almost biblical proportions falling on the poor villagers a scant few miles away. In time honoured tradition, I measured the distance of each storm, by counting the seconds between the lightning flashes and the accompanying crash of thunder. Each wicked lightning flash was accompanied by an instant static crackle on my battery operated radio and the frequent flickering of the lights as the lightning connected with the ground. I counted eleven separate storms that day and I knew that many were passing close to the hills around Glenmadrie, which I could locate by spotting the distinctive radio mast that is nearby the house. At about three o'clock I saw the radio mast take a direct lightning hit, which instantly silenced all of the radio stations for the next three days; mercifully the electricity was spared on this occasion. Some years later, in bright sunshine on the drive back from Limerick, Lesley and I drove through the aftermath of one of these storms. Near Formoyle Beg, the road runs along the hillside which slopes very steeply, some six hundred feet, down to the river Glenomra. Here, the earlier deluge had created dozens of raging streams across the road as the water gave in to gravity in a desperate attempt to reach the river below. In retrospect, it was dangerous folly to attempt to ford any of these raging torrents and risk certain death had our car been washed from the road into the river, but others had passed ahead and I felt obliged to follow. Of course they were all in tractors and four wheeled drive SUVs, whereas we were in an overloaded and aging Skoda estate, with dodgy wiring. As luck would have it, we survived unscathed, but just like my climb up the quarry, I felt like a buffoon afterwards.

A few days after the thunderstorm, another quirk of Irish driving almost cost me dearly. I was driving from Ennis to Corofin, perhaps slightly faster than was entirely wise on a wet road and in the dark – but like all men, I live under the illusion that I am an expert driver. As I rounded a slight bend in the road, I was irritated to discover that I was facing a set of blindingly bright headlights, which were set on full beam. Now this is not unusual in Ireland, as many rural drivers seem to be rather reluctant to dip their headlights until the last possible moment, if at all. All one can normally do is flash your own lights repeatedly, while complaining loudly, then aim for a spot just to the left of the approaching car, in the hope that you will miss each other; remember that we (allegedly) drive on the left in Ireland. However, on this night, although I had been aware of the headlights for the few seconds before I rounded the corner, I was still totally blinded as they were not only on full beam, but accompanied by some slightly misaligned fog lights as well. With barely two seconds to manoeuvre, I was instinctively aiming to the left of the lights when I realised that the other car was actually parked on my side of the road and facing the oncoming traffic.

With a screech of tires and a squeal like a schoolgirl, I hauled my car to the right, missing the other car by mere millimetres and then swore like a big brother contestant, all the way home. The next day as I passed the same spot I could see that if I had turned left, then I would have driven directly into a very large tree, leaving everyone scratching their heads and speculate as to the cause of my unexplained fatal car crash.

Finally the day had arrived when we were to take ownership of Glenmadrie and officially become residents on the island of Ireland. To avoid unnecessarily paying another day's rent, I had to vacate the cottage at Corofin by ten o'clock that morning. Although I wouldn't have minded the additional expense, the truth was that I was as giddy as a child at Christmas and desperate to be in my new home. So I packed up my car and headed for Ennis; by eleven o'clock I was drinking my third cup of tea, in a café near to my solicitor's office, while still waiting for confirmation that the sale was finalised. At half past twelve, the call finally came, but there was a problem; the keys had disappeared and I wouldn't be able to get in to the house! For the next three hours I repeatedly called the vendor's solicitor, who was constantly unavailable and failing to return my calls. First I was told that she was in a meeting, then at lunch, then in court, and finally I was informed that she had just left the office to go on holiday for two weeks. I pleaded with my solicitor (who should really have made sure the keys were handed over), then the estate agent and finally with the poor secretary at the other solicitor's office; but no one seemed to understand that actually having the keys to the house that I had just bought might be nice. In the end I decided to take possession of my land, by parking my car in the driveway in the usual fashion, and to take possession of the house, by breaking in if necessary. After an extensive search, that lasted nearly fifteen seconds, I found the keys under a rock at the front door and, without any further ceremony, stepped across the threshold and into our new home.

Chapter 8 – In which we settle in

It was already getting dark and cold, and I had a lot to do to get settled in for my first night in Glenmadrie. After calling Lesley to relate the good news, I unpacked from the car only the few things I would need before the morning and then set about organising somewhere to sleep. The only furniture in the house was a large cream coloured couch in the sitting room, and although I had brought a collapsible camp bed and sleeping bag, I decided that the couch would make for a more comfortable night's sleep. The cooking and central heating were via an oil fired Rayburn cooking range in the kitchen. There were no instructions, but the operation seemed simple enough, so despite a disturbing smell of kerosene around the base and some loose wires sticking out at the side, I attempted to fire up the heating. Although I appeared to have all of the switches in the correct position, nothing seemed to be happening, so I tentatively wiggled the wires and was rewarded with a big blue flash. I hid in the corner for a couple of minutes, but nothing else happened and I was getting cold, so I daringly tried jiggling the wire again, and this time the boiler grudgingly came to life. Newly inflated with false confidence in my manly abilities, I decided to try lighting a fire, in the hope of keeping warm overnight. There was a pile of hand cut peat at the side of the house, which was loosely covered with an old blue builder's tarpaulin, but still reasonably dry, despite all of the recent rain. The small fireplace was set into a massive chimneybreast that came fully four feet into the room and was six feet wide. It was painted magnolia, the same as the rest of the room, but decorated with soot stains. I managed to start the fire without too much trouble, but the smoke seemed unwilling to take the arduous journey up the chimney, much preferring to stay in the room and keep me company. I sat on the couch in front of the roaring fire and examined my new surroundings, through the thin haze of smoke. The sitting room was thirty feet by about eighteen with a polished pine floor, and although the stone walls had a rough cement render that had been decorated with exterior masonry paint, any protuberances seemed to carry a highlight of dust, soot and cobwebs. On the end wall, beneath the staircase, someone, with a small amount of artistic talent and a large amount of mind-altering drugs, had painted a motif that looked like some Technicolor genetic experiment involving a dog, a sheep and a fire dragon. Although slightly higher than the seventy inches in the kitchen, the ceiling was very low and covered in strange wooden slats that provided easy access for spiders, and delivered a light sprinkling of dust whenever the wind blew. The wood was red cedar, probably recovered from old tobacco pallets and then nailed to the rafters to provide a makeshift ceiling. It was a thriving source of woodworm and also highly inflammable, which we discovered when we started the renovations. During the winter we would regularly pull down a few pieces and put them directly into the fire; they were all exactly the correct length and, disturbingly, burned like rocket fuel!

Once I had settled in I realised that I was ravenously hungry, so I had to risk life and limb again to cook a meal on the Rayburn. In the end I was delighted to discover that, apart from being caked in grease, the cooking side of this cast iron monster was in excellent order. Without a fridge I was temporarily relying on tinned vegetables and eggs, which took me back to my student days, but nevertheless provided a decent meal when washed down with some warm Guinness. Presumably in an effort to save some money on electricity, the previous owner had fitted low power incandescent light bulbs throughout the house; none of these bulbs were any stronger than a measly 40-watts, and a few were just 15-watts, which I had only ever seen in a fridge up to now. After I had washed up the dishes, I tried reading a book for a while, squinting in the gloom, but sensibly gave it up as a bad job before I ruined my eyesight. So with nothing else to entertain me I pulled the couch in front of the fire, climbed into my sleeping bag and curled up for the night. A few hours later, I was roused by my bursting bladder and took the shortest route to relief, by stepping into the courtyard. As I watered the shrubs three things struck me. First the total lack of light and dust pollution delivered a breath taking view of the stars in the night sky; above me I could easily identify Orion's belt, Venus, Mars, Saturn and Jupiter, as well as the smoky band of the Milky Way. It was awe-inspiring to look at stars that actually existed billions of years ago, but the light was only reaching my eyes today. I first saw such a clear night sky when a miscommunication over travel arrangements left me stranded in the bush overnight, in northern Nigeria. Fortunately a kind family let me share their mud hut for the night. This view was much the same as that in Nigeria (only with less lions and elephants), and whenever I see such a sky I always find myself saying the same thing – "Wow!" The second thing that I noticed was the absolute silence. The wind had dropped to a mere whisper, and all I could hear was a distant river and the whistle of my tinnitus, a legacy of too many loud discos during my long-lost youth. Finally I was struck by how lucky I was to be able to pee outside my own house – if I chose to, and then I remembered once before performing the same act outside that mud hut in Nigeria, when marooned in that far off land, and I found myself questioning if life hadn't just taken me full circle.

The next morning, I ate my breakfast in the conservatory while watching the wild birds squabble over some bread crusts that I had thrown down. Afterwards there was little else I could do but read, explore our new house and clean. Lesley and our lorry load of belongings were not due to arrive for a couple of days, so I drove into Ennis and purchased a few essential items of cleaning equipment and a box of 100 watt light bulbs. Then I kept myself busy clearing the dust and cobwebs, and mopping throughout, including the bare floorboards upstairs. Frustratingly, just by walking about upstairs I triggered a rain of woodworm dust and dead spiders, which fell onto the floors below, so I found that I had to clean the downstairs again, and again, and again. As we were planning to put most of our belongings into storage in the music studio, I spent some extra time preparing that space. The studio was the only room in the house that seemed to have been recently built. It was freshly plastered and painted, and fitted with a new carpet in a mildly offensive purple colour. The room was empty apart from a desk, made from a thick slab of pine on rough blocks of wood, a few shelves and some loose skirting boards. Two large wooden gates were fitted into the west wall, creating a doorway to the front of the property that would provide easy access when we were unloading our belongings. Given how recently the studio had been constructed, I was disturbed to note clear signs of water damage above the exposed south facing window, and I correctly suspected that this would link up with the dampness in the room above. At the time the studio appeared to be dry and I found myself incorrectly hoping that the dampness would not prove to be a major problem in the future.

After staying overnight in Wales, Lesley caught the early fast ferry to Dublin and made good time, arriving at the house shortly after lunch. Lesley resisted my half-hearted request to carry her across the threshold, but we took the time to share a kiss and hug as she stepped into our new home for the first time. The first and most urgent order of business, after such a long drive, was to let Romany out of the car to stretch her legs. As a "town dog," Romany was unused to having the freedom to roam that she was now facing, so we stayed nearby while she explored her new territory. Fortunately the garden and meadows are quite well defined, with fences and hedges providing a substantial enough barrier for a little lap dog, so we were confident enough that she wouldn't get lost; and there was so little passing traffic that the road wasn't an immediate concern.

After appropriately anointing the garden, she woofed at nothing in particular for a while and then decided to explore the house. We showed her where the water bowl was and then put her bed in the sitting room, which she proceeded to poke and prod, as if she was attempting to sculpture an origami dinosaur. Finally she circled the bed three times, let off a resounding fart and settled down to sleep for the rest of the day, evidently happy with her new home.

Our furniture had taken a slightly different route to the house, stopping overnight in Ireland, but conveniently arriving within an hour of Lesley. As would become normal practice for deliveries, until we were familiar enough with the local landmarks to provide useful directions, I drove out to meet with Big Dave and his unbelievably skinny assistant Wally, to help guide the lorry back to the house. The aging lorry was overloaded and clearly struggling to climb the hills of County Clare, so I took them on a more circular approach to the house, which at least avoided the steepest hills. Once parked in the driveway, they opened the back of the truck and we were presented with a nightmarish three-dimensional jigsaw puzzle, constructed from our most precious possessions which were jammed into the truck at all kinds of unbelievable angles.

"The big truck broke down, so we had to fit it all into this one," explained Dave, red faced and breathless from the exertion of climbing down from the cab.

There was nothing for it, it was going to be dark in less than five hours and the only way everything was going to be unloaded in time was if Lesley and I chipped in. We decided that I would work with Big Dave, moving the heavier items, while Lesley, with the help of wheezy Wally, would oversee operations to make sure that most things found their correct places within the house – when needed, everyone would run up and down the path to the studio with items for long term storage. We cautiously approached the gridlock of furniture in the back of the truck and like a giant game of "Ker-plunk," tried to identify which pieces we could remove without setting off an avalanche. With generous applications of care, swear and prayer, we managed to extract a few of the larger pieces without causing havoc, after that things progressed swimmingly. The bigger pieces like beds, wardrobes and dining tables were located to the rooms that they would be used in, along with various boxes of kitchen implements, clothing and tools. Amazingly we managed to unpack our entire lives in just four hours, collecting only two minor dinks in the freezer and an old chest of drawers; we even had time to stop for tea and sandwiches. We thanked Sweaty Dave and Lazy Wally for their assistance, settled our bill and sent them on their way with a bottle of whisky for their troubles.

Lesley was in the kitchen, unpacking boxes into the larder (called a press in Ireland) and I was in the room above, which I was going to use a temporary workshop and shed, for the next three and a half years. Thinking that it was starting to get dark, I foolishly turned on the light.

"Hey! The lights have just gone off down here," Lesley shouted up the rickety spiral staircase that bizarrely connected the kitchen with the two floors above.

"Try the switch, perhaps it's loose," I shouted back obligingly.

"Okay. That worked, the light is back on," she replied.

"Now the light has gone off up here!" I complained and flicked the switch again.

"Hey! Quit it will you, the light in the kitchen is off again."

I went up to the next floor and tried the light switch up there to see what happened – the light in the workshop went off and the light in the conservatory came on. In the end we figured out the sequence necessary to illuminate the rooms we were in and I wrote "fix the electrics" on my to-do list. Back in the middle bedroom, which was above the sitting room, I had finished assembling the wardrobes. I noticed that the floor sloped so severely that they leaned forward fully ten degrees and needed propping up to stop the doors swinging open. I sat on the bed to consider the options, only to hear a loud crack and the sound of falling debris below.

"Nick, did you know that the leg of a bed is sticking through the ceiling down here?" Lesley asked helpfully from the sitting room.

"Yes, thanks," I replied with a stiff smile, adding another job to my list.

Later that night, fed and watered, we sat together on the couch and enjoyed the peace and quiet of our first night "living the dream."

"You are going to have to get this chimney sorted out," Lesley said as smoke billowed into the sitting room for the third time in less than an hour.

"Yes, dear, I've already put it on the list," I replied sleepily.

The next few weeks revolved around settling in to our new home, cleaning almost constantly to keep ahead of the dust, unpacking only the things that we needed for daily use and getting out and about to discover the local area. We visited Galway, Ennis and Limerick to try and get a feel for the kind of shops we would have access to, not only for food shopping, but for our gardening and building needs as well. Living in England, we were used to having access to a wide range of shops, with local competition helping to drive down the prices. All of the towns and cities that we were familiar with followed a similar layout – major retailers in the high street, smaller shops in the side streets, and perhaps a major supermarket or two in a development out of town with major computer, electrical, DIY and garden centres in dedicated retail parks. The commonality and logic of this retail geography made finding places to shop quick and easy, even if you were a stranger to the area. Secondly, if you were to ask any two people at random, you would be assured of being correctly directed to the sort of shop you were looking for. Failing that, a five minute search on-line, or a flick through the local yellow pages would undoubtedly set you right. We found Ireland to be very different, as many of the retailers we were familiar with had yet to become established in the west. Also, because there is a very commendable tradition of shopping where previous generations of your family shopped, many stores did not feel the need to advertise their presence or whereabouts. Secondly, those retailers who were well established seemed to have shops seemingly scattered at random, in some of the most unlikely of places. Take Galway, for example. Being a university city, it has a centre a little like many old English towns, with narrow streets lined with varied and interesting shops, but the outskirts are scattered with shops, hotels, hospitals and factories, like a child's bedroom after a particularly violent game of monopoly. Limerick has a more modern feel, and has some retail parks that are very distant from each other, so comparing the price of a can of paint in three shops could require a twelve mile drive, in addition to the twenty mile drive to get to Limerick in the first place. Because of the overinflated wealth in the economy, up until 2009 when the recession really started to bite, most shoppers seemed prepared to shop at the nearest shops and pay whatever they were charged, and many shops seemed to have an almost contemptuous attitude towards their only source of revenue. In the "boom years" in Ireland, it would not be unusual for a farmer's wife to do the weekly food shop, for a family of six, in the local garage convenience store, paying thirty to forty per cent more than she would when shopping at Dunnes or Tesco. I was left almost speechless when told that I couldn't purchase several thousand euro's worth of building supplies, because the shop was "trade only," something I hadn't encountered in England since the mid-1980s. That same store would be happy to serve anybody today – if they hadn't already gone bust. Finally, one of the most frustrating quirks I have encountered in Ireland is the practice of not pricing big ticket items – in particular houses, cars and electrical items. Trying to buy a car for the first time was a hoot. We spent twenty minutes walking up and down the forecourt waiting for the salesman to finish his afternoon coffee and cigar, before we could finally ask the price of a particular car. He looked me up and down, presumably trying to judge the girth of my wallet.

"Well now, Sir, how much do you think it would cost?"

"What? Err, I don't know, why don't you just tell me?"

He smiled like a school teacher confronting a naughty but likeable child. "Ah now, go on with you – have a guess."

"Oh I don't know, perhaps €10,000?" I said, hopefully.

Our baggy little salesman staggered back in mock horror, "NOoo Sir, not even close!" and then like a slimy game show host, he said, "have another guess."

We quickly tired of these antics, amusing as they were, especially when it came to light that some retailers even applied an "English price" to unsuspecting foreigners. I am pleased to report that by 2011 things had improved considerably, jointly because of the recession, increased competition from large retailers and improved access to the internet and online retailers. However, not everything is rosy. Even allowing for the exchange rate and the additional cost of trading in Ireland, some large retailers still charge more for the same product in Ireland than they do in England. I may sound a little finicky about shopping and saving money, but we had a lot of work to do and only a little money to do it with. Without a formal budget for the renovation project, our savings account would soon resemble a leaky bucket, with me putting money in the top, rather slower than it was dripping out of the bottom. So it was vital, right from the beginning, that each and every purchase we made represented good value for our precious assets.

The first two jobs on my list took little of my time and money but saved thousands. First, on the list was the strong smell of kerosene in the kitchen, which I was able to trace to a leaking valve on the Rayburn that took just seconds with a spanner to rectify. As a precaution I also cleaned the filter on the oil tank outside and discovered a steady drip of oil from another loose valve, again easily tightened. Secondly, with just two telephone calls, I had been able to acquire ten gallons of commercial woodworm treatment and, using the same equipment I had saved from our previous house, spent two happy days crawling through hundred year old cobwebs in the loft, protecting our biggest asset. As the house had no television aerial, our first official visitor was the a satellite engineer who efficiently and quickly fitted the new dish, so poorly it turned out, that I had to replace the bolts the next day, for fear of losing the dish with the first light puff of wind. In 2004 the telephone reception at the house was appalling, frequently failing completely for days on end, and when it was working your conversation was muffled with a background of clicks and crackles. We had no less than eight visits from the engineers, but with no improvement; in the end I climbed onto the roof and fixed it myself. There was no worthwhile broadband access at that time in rural Ireland, and even with my upgrades to the telephone line, our internet connection speed was slower than a reluctant toddler going up to bed, and less reliable than a politician's expenses. Just keeping the internet security and windows patches up to date seemed like a full-time job, but it had to be done if we were to keep in touch with friends and family online. Trying to shop online was pointless at the time because, until about 2008, very few online retailers would ship to Ireland, so we used to get things sent to my wife's mother to be collected on the next visit over. Today things have improved substantially, thanks mostly to companies like Amazon who will now ship our beloved books to Ireland for free, and parcel2go.com who will pick up and collect anything, from anywhere to somewhere else, for less money than anyone else.

The countryside around the house is stunning, truly breath-taking, but oh so easy to take for granted if you see it every day. We thoroughly enjoyed discovering the new walks that we could take with Romany. Opposite the house, we could walk across the moor for several miles, with spectacular views towards Lough Graney, and at the time there was a rough hiking path, marked with a post every hundred yards or so, helping even the most hapless walker stay on course in the fog and snow. Immediately behind the house was a large forest with a logging trail that took a right hand loop around the hillside and back to the road where you started. Once on the far side of the hill you have an unobstructed view across the green valley, as far as Shannon and Lough Derg. Often in the early mornings the valley floor below will be shrouded in fog, stained light pink by the rising sun. Sometimes on a Sunday morning we would jump in the car and drive through Flagmount to the north end of Lough Graney, where a forest path leads down to a beautiful secluded beach, known locally as "Silver Sands," where we could walk for an hour without sight or sound of another person. The water is crystal clear and shallow for up to fifty yards out, so you can wade in knee-deep on a hot sunny day, and walk around Black Island at the head of the Lough, if the mood takes you. Alternatively there is a footpath that leads to the unfortunately named River Bleach, which flows down from Lough Atorick, high in the hills towards the Slieve Aughty Mountains. I am always amazed and grateful to discover that this idyllic beach is again completely deserted, when in most other countries, dogs would have to be kept on a leash, the beach would be covered in tourists and their discarded rubbish, and the water would be churned to foam by hundreds of speedboats and wake borders. God bless you, undiscovered County Clare!

Chapter 9 – In which we add to our family

Even before the purchase was finalised, we had started drawing up plans for how we would like to renovate the house. The options were to repair, rebuild or replace, and it was important to choose correctly at each stage, if we were to keep the feel of Glenmadrie as original as possible, while transforming it to a warm and pleasant home. On closer inspection it was clear that much of the existing structure had either been built poorly, in the wrong place or (more annoyingly) built quite well, but on top of something else that was about to fall down. For example, although there was a perfectly serviceable staircase from the lounge to the second floor, someone had seen fit to add a spiral staircase, but for some reason it was in the kitchen running up through two bedrooms and about as useful as a third nipple. In the event of a fire, the staircase would act as a chimney, fatally dragging smoke and flames up into the bedrooms above; it would have to go. Some nice rooms had been added on the second floor, but the floor they stood on could barely support its own weight – and so on and so forth, throughout the house. So we decided that we would save and repair the things that we liked, like the stone walls, windows, conservatory and roof – basically all of the external structure. Internally though, pretty much everything would have to go, mostly because it was rotten or in the wrong place. Secondly, it was very obvious to us that, although the house was generally watertight, it was in desperate need of insulation. The wind could blow, unimpeded from the loft into the bedrooms, and the stone walls, although over two feet thick, were constantly cold to the touch, sucking away any attempt to heat the house. The ceiling heights were less than six feet throughout the ground floor, and on the third floor, over the kitchen, the clearance was just over five feet. I decided that the second floor levels would have to be changed throughout the house with the walls dry-lined and insulated; this would obviously require moving or replacing all of the electrics and plumbing. Put simply, we were planning to gut our house and rebuild another, inside the stone shell of the existing building. You may be thinking that it would perhaps have been easier to demolish the house and build a nice new one, and you would probably be right – but if we had wanted a "new build" house, we would have bought one in the first place. At least the purchase price had left us enough cash reserves to pay a builder to do the bulk of the work, except for decorating which Lesley and I would tackle, as usual. We decided that the immediate priorities were heat and water. Our only source of water was pumped from a shallow well in the wood below the house. The well head was only the size of a kitchen sink and dangerously close to the septic tank, although the presence of frogs and water nymphs in the well suggested that it was currently unpolluted. However, apart from the risk of sewage seeping into our drinking water, such a shallow well would also be inclined to dry up without warning; we therefore decided that we would get a deep well drilled in a location that was at least one hundred feet above the septic tank. The huge stone fireplace intruded substantially into the lounge and was poorly constructed and inefficient. Our surveyor had recommended removing the external chimney, but we weren't sold on the idea as it would ruin the external appearance of the house. We opted instead for removing the internal fireplace, installing a wood burning stove, and calling in a chimney expert to help sort out the smoke problem.

Our other priority within the first couple of months was to get another dog. Since Brandy had died so unexpectedly, and we now had so much room, there never seemed any doubt that we would get a second dog once we had settled in, if only to keep Lesley and Romany company while I was at work. One day when Lesley was at the local village post office, she happened to notice some delightful puppies at a house just opposite. She was as giddy as a teenager on a first date when she came home and told me that she had already selected our new doggy. When she arrived three weeks later, "Amber," as we decided to call our new puppy, was just five inches long, dark beige in colour, with a pointy face, black button eyes, huge ears and a curly tail. She is a Pomeranian and wire haired Terrier cross, and being bred from a terrier she is playful, energetic, highly strung and totally fearless, charging at any perceived intruder like a kamikaze fur-ball. Her favourite games are tug, chase and rolling in any available poo, so as to smell like something larger than her fully grown size of eighteen inches. At the most inconvenient times, for example just after you have finished spring-cleaning, she will joyfully present herself, dripping foul smelling faeces at every step, after rolling in the runniest cow pat she could find (if you are lucky), or plastered in fox poo (if you are not.). Any available stick or rope will trigger a game of tug so ferocious that, if you relax for a moment, you are at risk of receiving a dislocated shoulder. Amber will refuse to let go during a game of tug, even if lifted clear of the ground, where she will hang by her teeth, growling and shaking in delight. She is very clear on the division of labour; her job is to sleep, play, guard the house and chase off all invaders, including the postman, passing walkers, cyclists and any passing aircraft. She is convinced that she is dominant in this last event as every jet, light aircraft and helicopter she has ever woofed at, has flown away without looking back. Our job is to feed her, stroke her or play, whenever she demands it. She doesn't care whether you are digging a trench, making jam, washing the dishes, taking a bath, balancing on a ladder, or trying to write a book. Whenever the mood takes her, Amber will march up, present her ball for you to throw, and then woof her "play with me bark," gr-rap, gr-rap, gr-rap, over and over again until you finally comply. You may think that she will get bored and give up if you continue to ignore her, but you would be wrong. If Amber feels she is being unnecessarily ignored, for example because you are washing the dishes, she will sneak up behind you and place a tennis ball directly behind your heels. Then she will sit silently waiting until you unknowingly step backwards, either kicking the ball with your heel or slipping over. At that point she will be guaranteed to get your undivided attention – even if it is only to angrily chase her away. For the residents of Glenmadrie, a friendly shout of "Amber alert" is sufficient warning that the determined terrier has positioned yet another man trap.

When moving a delivery of cement, garden peat, or some other unwieldy items to safe storage, we became quite adept at kicking her ball every eight paces, regardless of the weight we were carrying. However, when moving lengths of wood with Lesley, the generally accepted rule was that only the person facing forwards was required to kick the play ball. Like many terriers, Amber has quite short legs and a stiff, but muscular torso; she loves to be placed on her back and given a tummy tickly fight, and when she runs she goes "Hup-hup-hup-hup," like a Special Forces soldier abseiling down the side of a building. The first time I fell off a ladder at Glenmadrie was after the damn thing snapped in the middle, without any warning, just as I was half way up. I landed flat on my back in a flowerbed, with a clatter and yelp. My eyes watered with the force of the impact and I was temporarily winded. I expected my wife to come rushing to my rescue, with a first aid kit and a concerned look on her face, but no! The first sound I hear is "gr-rap, gr-rap, gr-rap," as Amber barks over and over again, demanding that I throw her ball and (as I couldn't quite reach to strangle her) I grudgingly obeyed, before trying to extract myself from the remains of the ladder.

Our house has three external doors, and although Amber is clearly an intelligent dog, she is firmly of the opinion that the planet outside each door is different to the planet outside the previous door; she believes this with illogical passion in the face of all evidence to the contrary. Presumably in an effort to be taken for a much bigger dog, Amber will launch herself out of the opening door, as fast as a greyhound, furiously barking and growling like a rabid hyena, until she has seen off all potential and imagined invaders. Ten seconds later, if you were to let her out of a different door she will repeat the process, ignoring my angry calls and convinced that she is facing new trespassers. Of course by staying on the same planet, she is entirely capable of going out of the front door and running around the house to the French windows at the back, where she will woof repeatedly until admitted. Conversely she will frequently make the journey from the conservatory door, around the house to the front door, where the "let me in" woofing will begin all over again. Her blind bravery took a literal knock, and almost cost us a dog, when Amber was about six months old.

I was taking some vegetable waste out to the compost bin when little Amber launched herself out of the front door with her usual gusto; unfortunately at exactly that moment, a car was approaching on the road below the house. Passing cars are rare at Glenmadrie, and it was unfortunate timing that it happened to be passing just as Amber exploded from the front door. She immediately caught sight of the speeding car and, ignoring all of my desperate shouts to stop, charged the eighty yards down the driveway to collide at right-angles with the front bumper. Time seemed to slow down, and I watched in helpless horror as Amber slipped past the front wheel and was then rolled along the underside of the car, like a rag doll in a tumble dryer. Miraculously she emerged from under the rear bumper and, still barking like a lunatic, ran back up the driveway, dodged my outstretched hands and disappeared into the house. After a short search I found the poor thing hiding under the couch, shivering in shock and matted with grease, but otherwise unhurt. Once Amber had been given a good wash and a long cuddle, she was feeling well enough to chase another car, albeit with slightly less enthusiasm than before – stupid mutt!

In the early summer of 2004, the Irish economy was booming, awash with pretend money from loans, overdrafts, mortgages and the proceeds of any service involved in building or buying houses. The majority of the tax revenue generated within the economy was coming from the profits of builders, property developers, stamp duty on house purchases and the registration tax on new cars. Although the country punched above its weight with exports from farming, agriculture and a healthy manufacturing sector, much of the domestic revenue was generated through loans against artificially inflated property values, and shares in companies that provided those loans. There was also a massive and expanding public sector, paid for from the tax revenues generated by the property and motor industries, and billions of euro in unsustainable State borrowing. To any outsider, particularly one who had just decided to start a new life without the burden of debt, the Irish economic model was as believable as the Emperor's new clothes – and as likely to be exposed as a deception. However, the "Celtic Tiger Economy" would continue to soar unchecked, like a runaway rocket, for another four years, when it would suddenly plummet into an economic disaster of almost biblical proportions. Our futile attempts to secure the services of even the most incompetent of builders, was testimony to how much work they had available. Those polite gents, that actually bothered to return my telephone messages, told me quite frankly that they were only interested in "new build" projects, which were quick easy money, and not prepared to entertain any renovation projects, regardless of how much money I was willing to throw their way. Most houses in

Ireland are constructed using nine by seventeen inch concrete blocks, and at the peak of the boom, block layers were getting paid as much as €2 for each block they laid, and other tradesmen were getting similar rates. If such inflated rewards were offered, for what was arguably the easiest work available, what hope did I have of getting a builder to take on a complicated renovation on a century old farmhouse? One builder suggested that, if I was to demolish the house and clear the site, he would make himself available to build me a new house in a couple of years. Another builder, who claimed to be a chimney expert even though he was suspiciously lacking any work, quoted more than the cost of a two week holiday in Hawaii just to repair my smoky chimney. We politely used the Irish "I'll call you," meaning no thanks, and sent him back to Limerick. In due course, we managed to secure the temporarily services of a nice burly builder to help remove the huge internal fireplace and chimney, but even he refused any further involvement in our renovation project.

"It doesn't matter how much money you have, nobody wants to do renovation work these days – it's too hard and too dirty," he said. "Why don't you just do it yourself? You English are supposed to be keen on DIY, aren't you?"

Following much discussion we decided that he was right. Our money was no good here, unless we were building a new house. We were going to have to do it ourselves. This was a huge decision because, although Lesley was a dab hand at gardening, sewing, baking and decorating, and I had done a bit of DIY like tiling a bathroom, moving sockets and radiators, neither of us had any real building experience. However, in the past I had done the majority of my own car maintenance, by simply following the step-by-step instructions in the relevant Hayes workshop manual. At the age of twelve, I had successfully stripped and rebuilt a lawnmower engine, and I am eternally grateful to my father for just letting me get on with it and the confidence that gave me. During the Second World War, he only survived his time in Siberia as a Polish POW, by claiming to be a carpenter and then learning the skills from another man. His eye for detail, confidence in his own ability and knack for figuring out how things work, helped him to escape prison camp three times and probably kept him alive during his twenty years as a pilot in the RAF. Although I was never consciously aware of it, I suppose I must have inherited some of his can-do attitude. I just accepted that I was going to have to do all of the carpentry, block laying, rewiring and plumbing myself. I figured that although the entire renovation project was truly daunting, provided I approached it methodically in small stages, and had a decent DIY book to guide me, I could do it. We had already heard some stories and seen examples of atrocious building work that some Irish builders thought was acceptable; so we felt that by doing the work ourselves, as well as saving a bucket load of money, we would know how well (or badly) things had been done. So we agreed that I would take on all of the renovations, leaving Lesley in charge of the decorating, vegetable garden and much of the housekeeping. With just one person doing the work, the project was obviously going to take a good while longer to complete than the original plan had allowed for. Furthermore, my business was taking off and I would need to go and see clients on most days, but at least the building work would be done to our satisfaction and at a much lower cost. If Lesley ever had second thoughts about what we had got ourselves into, or doubted my ability to complete the building work, she never showed it – full credit and love to her, for her unflinching support!

The first item on the home improvements list was getting a well drilled, so that we could have safe and reliable drinking water. We had a couple of quotes for the work, which involved drilling and lining a borehole down to around 350 feet, and then supplying and fitting the water pump and electrics. I was mildly amused when, during both site surveys, the drilling experts each used a "water divining" rod to "locate the best place to drill," which seemed to involve wandering around aimlessly until their broken twig magically pointed at the ground, indicating that water was only a few hundred foot below. Although they differed widely in their choice for the best location to drill, both of the sites selected provided suspiciously convenient vehicle access for the drilling rigs. Both companies quoted around the same price and seemed equally capable, so we made our choice based on a recommendation from someone local that had recently had a well drilled. As drilling the well would involve heavy vehicles traversing the front lawn, after which I would need to dig deep trenches across the garden for the power cables and pipes, it seemed prudent to do any landscaping we needed at the same time. This heavy digging was going to require something more substantial than a wheelbarrow and shovel, so we decided to hire a digger and dumper truck – it was time for some "Boys' Toys!"

It took a couple of days for the drill to reach down into the aquifer, where we would be assured of clean sweet water. Then it took almost another week for me to build a small concrete shed to act as a pump house. The completed shed is six by eight feet, with a corrugated steel roof and a concrete floor with conduits for where the pipes and cables come in from the well and go out to the house. As a first attempt at building anything, other than a doll's house for my daughter one Christmas, it was good practice for what was to come – the pump house was, in effect, just a small house with walls, roof and a door. It took a while to build, but as yet it hasn't fallen over and it remains dry, so I must have got something right. The well engineer fitted the pumping equipment on the wall in the pump house and connected up all of the electrics and pipes, and then we were in business. We now had an almost unlimited supply of sweet, clean, fresh water. I left the old pump in place and fitted an outside tap so that we could use the shallow well for watering the garden and suchlike. To dig the trenches and do the landscaping, I hired a three-ton digger with caterpillar tracks, along with a large dumper truck, so that I could move any excess rubble to the quarry. I had never driven either type of vehicle before, but I soon got the hang of things and then had tremendous fun roaring around like "Bob the Builder" and doing macho things for a week. Actually, the novelty wore off pretty quickly. The weather was miserable, it lashed down with freezing rain every day, turning the garden into a sea of sticky mud; and as we only rented the equipment for a week, I needed to work sixteen hour days just to get the earthworks completed in time. By the end of the week, all of the cables and pipes were down, the trenches had been dug and refilled, an eighty foot square area of land was levelled ready for our polytunnel and vegetable garden, and several tons of rock, concrete and rubble had been removed to the quarry. My "Boys' Toys" were due to be collected by the hire shop on Monday morning, and as all of the landscaping was finished, I had just enough time on Sunday to dig out a large pond at the north end of our meadow.

Both of our previous homes had garden ponds, which are excellent for attracting wildlife, like frogs and newts, so we were keen to have a pond at Glenmadrie as well. There was a perfect location in a distant corner of our land, where there seemed to be a natural spring just beneath the surface. I surmised that, if I dug a big enough hole, it would gradually fill with water and become a permanent pond. I roughly marked out an area of around forty by thirty feet to dig out, in a doughnut shape, to create a large pond with a little island in the centre which would give some predator protection to any visiting wildlife. I started the digger and scooped my first load of soil, only to meet with some unexpected resistance. As I was quite close to some large trees, I assumed that I had snagged a large tree root and decided to press on until the root broke. I was happily working the controls to manoeuvre the digging arm up and down when, from the corner of my eye, I noticed the telephone pole in the road above, rocking a full six feet with each tug of the digger; I was obviously pulling on an underground telephone cable. A quick inspection revealed that, to take the shortest route from the telephone pole at the roadside to the pole by the house, the engineer had simply buried the cable under four inches of soil as it ran directly across the top corner of my land, and I had unwittingly snagged it with the shovel on the digger. As the telephone reception seemed no worse than usual, despite the cable being stretched by three feet, I just buried it again and started my pond two feet further west. By bed time on Sunday night, I had created a pond with gently sloping shallow sides, deep areas down to five feet and an island to protect visiting wildlife from foxes and the like. As if by magic, the following morning my pond was full to the brim with crystal clear water and already home to some happy pond skaters and a couple of grateful frogs. After eight years, the pond is now well established and thriving with all manner of wildlife. It frequently attracts ducks, grey herons, snipe and curlews as well as hundreds of frogs. The frog population is maintained, despite the hungry herons, with the help of Lesley, who insists on rescuing any frogspawn that becomes stranded in puddles and ditches within a mile of the pond. In early spring, it is not unusual to find her merrily wandering along the country lanes, with the dog leads in one hand and a bucketful of frogspawn in the other. The neighbours may think we are slightly nuts, but at least the frogs and herons are happy.

When we first arrived, there were disappointingly few wild birds around, mostly because our house is remote and built at an altitude of around one thousand feet, so the growing season for their natural food of bugs, berries and seed is relatively short. Quite early on I decided to build a large bird table, using up some scrap wood and roofing felt. It stands on a stout post, protected from the worst of the wind, in the centre of the courtyard, close to the trees and overlooked by ten windows. Because the house is so remote, this single dependable food source has attracted a large variety of birds which nest in the area and return every year. During the winter we frequently get through twenty kilos of bird seed a week, and a dozen fat balls, trying to keep up with the ravenous hordes that sit in the trees and fall on the food before you can step away from the table. We now regularly attract at least eighteen different species of birds to the table, including finches, dunnocks, tits and thrushes. Recently we were delighted to see our first house sparrows that had obviously heard about the free food and decided to make the trip up the hill from the valley. Occasionally the local sparrowhawks will buzz the table in the hope that a tasty young bird will fly into a window in panic, and then fall to the ground stunned, where the lightning fast sparrowhawk will be on them in an instant. The trees in our wood and the nearby forest, and the beautiful but desolate moorland, also provide good nesting for kestrel, merlin, game birds, and several species of owls and ducks. If you are particularly lucky, you may catch a glimpse of the ever-elusive hen harrier, as it whips past your head and disappears over the hedge. Each spring is heralded by the return of dozens of cuckoos calling for a mate, in ever louder competition. Occasionally, if we are really lucky, we are treated to a visit from a night cuckoo. This dubious honour involves the bird sitting on our roof and delivering the loudest imaginable calls throughout the night, regardless of any amount of shouting and swearing by the occupants. The star-crossed bird will continue this insidious torture every night, for up to a week, pausing only long enough for you to drift into sleep for a few moments, before he delivers an extra loud "cuck-oow!" to startle you awake again. Oh, the joys of country living!

One mystery that took a while to solve was that of the elusive flying ghosts. Late one spring, as dusk fell, I was up in the meadow trying to spot the international space station flying over, when I heard a most peculiar sound. I imagined I was hearing half a dozen hang-gliding whales, doing ghost impressions whilst playing the low notes on pan pipes. This ghostly noise seemed to circle around my head and reverberate around the valley, without following any discernable path. It is such a deep, warm sound that, although it resonated down into my chest, I never felt in the least bit threatened. With the help of a local ornithologist we discovered that the monster behind this seasonal haunting was the little snipe – a ten inch short-tailed bird, with a face like Pinocchio lying about his expenses. This diminutive wader's mating display involves swooping dives at dusk, with its tail feathers extended laterally into the airflow, an action which creates the ghostly drumming noise that had so intrigued me.

Perhaps my favourite bird is the skylark, which can be spied each summer, high above the moor, hovering almost stationary for minutes on end, while delivering a most beautiful song, which even the most talented of violinists would fail to emulate. Whenever I hear a skylark today, I am instantly transported back to a Sunday morning during the hot summer of 1975, when I was still a lanky teenager, all knees, elbows, pimples and hormones. It was during a round of golf with my father near Cromer, in Norfolk, England, and we were taking a break from the heat to drink some tea and eat a sandwich. As we sat together on a grassy mound by the cliffs overlooking the sea, we watched a skylark performing its eloquent rhapsody, and my father told me exciting wartime tales of his time as a mosquito pilot. Seeing a skylark today refreshes my memory and makes me ponder if some small part of him is in that tiny bird, singing in delight as he swoops through the air.

Our growing community of swallows are endlessly entertaining, as they swoop and whirl, like spitfire pilots defending their airfield from the attacking hordes. However, the greatest flying displays are provided by the bat colonies that roost in the roof eaves of the north end of the house, and also in the quarry. These welcome little friends can eat millions of the devilish midges each night, by diving and twisting in delightfully energetic aerobatics. Just after dusk on warm summer evenings, I love to stand and watch the little pipistrelle and brown long-eared bats engaging in their adventurous displays, particularly when the air is so still that you can hear the clicks and whistles as they chase down their prey. One memorable hot summer night, I was rudely awoken after a young bat climbed in through an open window, and then flapped in panicked circles above the bed. It took half an hour before I managed to gently snag it with a tea towel and return it safely to the night air. Although I was unfazed by the invading bat, I must admit to a slightly less than manly reaction, when I first encountered the giant wood wasp. These delightful insects are almost identical to the common stinging wasp – except they are around five inches long, sound like a flapping umbrella and repeatedly try to fly up your nose. My initial reaction was to run around the garden in blind panic, screaming like a terrified schoolgirl, although further research eventually identified the species as a harmless member of the wasp family. That devilishly dangerous stinger is actually just a long probe used to lay eggs in the surrounding pine trees. Still – better to be safe than sorry!

With the well and pump house completed, the next thing on my "to do" list was the fireplace in the sitting room. Once the internal chimney had been removed with the help of the burly builders, and I had built and tiled a plinth, we were ready for our wood-burning stove to be delivered – or so we hoped. Constructed from cast iron to absorb the heat, it is the size of a rabbit hutch and as heavy as a car engine. The first time it was delivered, the driver and his assistant had successfully manoeuvred it all the way into the sitting room, via two sets of low stairs, through five doors, swearing and cussing all the way, before we discovered it was the wrong model. They then had to retrace their steps all the way back to the van, using even worse language and sucking on their skinned knuckles. The shop unapologetically told us that it would take six to eight weeks to get a replacement, which inevitably arrived on the wrong day, when I was out at work. The poor delivery driver was on his own this time; being a little old man, who probably weighed seven stones wringing wet, he had no chance fighting against the bulk of this cast-iron monstrosity and only managed a few yards, before he dropped it down the first staircase. The driver was uninjured, but a leg had been cleanly ripped from the stove and it had to be returned to the shop again. The shop manager was again unapologetic when he told us that it would take another six to eight weeks to get a replacement. The third stove was delivered undamaged, but when I opened the box I discovered that there was no chimney. Annoyed and frustrated, I telephoned the shop to report my missing chimney.

"I am very sorry, Sir, but I'm looking at the order here and the problem is, you didn't order a chimney," said the helpful manager.

"But I expected the chimney to be included with the stove," I explained, "We have been waiting for this stove for weeks."

"Yes," he laughed, "A lot of people make that mistake."

"Why don't you just ask people if they want a chimney?"

"Well, Sir, had you decided to use our stove fitting service, our engineer would have supplied a chimney at the time of fitting."

"But you wanted to charge me €400 to stand the stove on the plinth that it is already standing on!" I replied.

"And to fit the chimney," he pointed out helpfully.

"Oh, so now I understand. The chimney is included in the fitting?" I asked.

"No, Sir, the chimney and the fitting would have been extra," he told me happily.

"Well that's ridiculous. Where did you think the smoke was going to go, without a chimney?"

"It's not our job to think, Sir. If you wanted a chimney, you should have asked for one when you ordered the stove," he explained, as if he was talking to a child.

"Well I know that now, don't I? Can you please order one as soon as possible?" I pleaded.

"Yes, Sir, I will be delighted to. It should be here in six to eight weeks."

In the end I got our stove up and working, and after the first winter I added a back boiler and plumbed it into our central heating system. For several years we were able to feed it with free waste wood, cut from old rafters and floorboards, and strips of dusty cedar simply pulled down from the ceilings as we needed them. Like the beating heart of our home, the stove today sits proudly in our sitting room, providing enough heat to warm the entire house and heat our water as well.

Chapter 10 – In which Amber has a bad hare day

Once we were settled in, the days seemed to blur into each other, with cleaning, building, gardening and seeing clients. The cleaning became an almost hourly chore, or so it seemed, mostly because of dogs that refuse to wipe their feet, and the constant rain of dust and soot from the ceilings which was particularly noticeable on windy days. I had started work on renovating the old cow shed by taking down some of the old wood and demolishing the unstable walls. The walls were easy enough to remove, as they collapsed with just a gentle shove of my shoulder and were then broken up and set aside as rubble and infill for the new flooring. As we had decided to recycle all of the waste wood for use in the fire, replacing the roof in the wing and any other woodwork would take a little longer than one might expect. A "proper builder" would simply chuck it all in a skip, or on a big bonfire, but to us this old wood was a valuable source of free heat – so we had to carefully remove the majority of the nails and then cut each piece to a length that would fit in the stove. It was a lot of additional work and added considerably to how long each section of building work took, but we had plenty of time and probably saved thousands of euro on skips and firewood.

Outside, Lesley had made a start on clearing an area of land around thirty by fifty feet to be used as her vegetable garden. We knew that it had been a vegetable plot many years ago and should be fertile land, especially as it had also been used as a goat pen in the past. However, because of the extraordinary amount of buried rocks and rubble she encountered, Lesley quickly gave up trying to dig with a spade and fork, and instead attacked the land with a pick axe and crowbar. Although unacceptable, it is not entirely uncommon to find buried rubble in the garden of a newly built house, thanks mainly to the feckless builder and his lazy assistant; but finding rubble deliberately buried in the garden of an old house is surprising, particularly when there is a quarry just a stone's throw away. If we were going to grow any vegetables in that first year, Lesley needed to get her plants in the ground as soon as possible, but as I was already busy, and both of us are susceptible to back problems, we decided to hire some help with the heavy digging. We soon found a local English chap, who was happy to be paid by the day, and he did a reasonable enough job of removing the worst of the rubble, without bursting our budget. Although buried rocks and boulders would continue to be a problem, within a week, Lesley was able to start digging in compost and manure, to improve the soil, and soon after she began planting her first crop of vegetables.

Even at the relatively low altitude of one thousand feet, gardening can be a challenge, particularly after living for so many years in the warm and dry conditions of East Anglia where, during our last year in England, the south east corner had suffered yet another drought, a hosepipe ban and summer temperatures of over thirty-eight degrees Celsius. The west of Ireland is statistically only one degree cooler than Essex, but three times as wet, and the winters are generally a little milder. However, the real difference in temperatures at Glenmadrie is actually much larger, closer to five degrees. This is because every one thousand feet of altitude causes about a two degrees Celsius drop in temperature and secondly, living away from the "heat sink" (caused by the heat retaining qualities of the buildings and roads in towns) can reduce the temperature by another three degrees. During our first year, the weather at the house was unusually warm and the plants grew well, but the cold and rain in the subsequent years led us to build a large greenhouse and install a fifty foot polytunnel. During the long hot summer of 2007 we planted a small apple orchard, and Lesley added dozens of fruit bushes, so we would have enough fruit for jams, pies and her awesome sweet chutney. Over the next eight years we would buy or barter, to get tons of top soil, manure and compost, to help improve the quality of our thin and undernourished soil. Despite the difficulties that horticulture at Glenmadrie presents, Lesley has successfully grow apples, pears, peaches, grapes, berries, currants, squashes, potatoes, cabbage, sweet corn, tomatoes, beans and salad crops. She is an excellent and experienced gardener, who can work miracles in her battle to grow crops in the cool Irish climate, although as the great Irish potato famine proved – sometimes the weather wins.

Before leaving England I had purchased, second-hand, a solid American built petrol lawnmower, which has done sterling work keeping the grass on our acre of front garden under control. It was obviously designed for cutting large areas of dry grass in the heat of California or Texas, so I had to modify it for Ireland. When the fog and low cloud has been hanging around for a while, it would be almost impossible to cut the long wet grass we get at the house with a conventional lawnmower. To upgrade our mower, I removed the grass collection box and cut a twelve inch slot out of the back plate, to allow the wet grass to freely spray clear; otherwise it would get tangled in the blade and repeatedly stall the motor. This unique design worked splendidly, apart from coating the user from head to foot with a thick layer of wet grass cuttings, and breaching most European health and safety rules. I soon learned to cut the grass with my mouth shut, after I accidentally mowed over a hidden frog; but this minor tragedy paled into insignificance on the day that a large pebble shot out of the mower – and was only prevented from breaking a window by hitting me squarely in the groin. Cross-eyed and knock-kneed in agony, I let go of the lawnmower, grabbed my "crown jewels" and collapsed like a man shot; fortunately the mower stopped without hitting anything valuable and my fall was broken by some conveniently placed dog poo.

As Romany was getting on a bit, she was less inclined to play with other dogs, preferring to sleep all day, snoring like a drunken sailor, or sitting in her favourite spot on the hill above the garden, watching over her territory. Frequently she will woof at the world and then at her own voice, as it echoes from the cliffs on the other side of the valley. Lhasa Apsos seem to have a stubborn streak about a mile wide, and Romany was always eager to demonstrate hers whenever she could, most commonly when confronted with a closed door. On a nice sunny summer day, you could be reading a book, gardening, sitting in the bath or climbing around on the roof, when you would hear Romany begin barking. Without fail, and at the most inconvenient times, she will go out of the open back door and walk all the way around the house to the closed front door, where she will stand barking until someone lets her in. She will never walk back around the house to the open back door, but will remain rooted to the spot, stubbornly barking in defiance at this inconvenient obstruction. Try as you may, this persistent "ark, ark, ark" cannot be ignored as it will not stop, or even change in tone or frequency, so you find yourself climbing down from the roof to let her in, usually at exactly the same moment that your wife has just climbed out of her bath to do the same thing. Oblivious to our dagger like stares, Romany will trot past us and into the lounge where, after circling her bed three times, she will flop down with a satisfied grunt and fall instantly asleep. On one sunny autumn afternoon I was repairing fences in the meadow, when Romany started barking at the locked front door. As Lesley was away shopping in Limerick, and I thought I was far enough from the house to be unaffected by the persistent barking, I decided to ignore Romany, assuming that sooner or later she would give in and simply walk back around to the open door of the conservatory. After an hour of relentless woofing, I finally cracked; I could take it no longer – I was getting a headache. So I put down my tools, climbed the fence and trudged my way back down to the house and the prospect of blessed silence; sometimes it's good to know when you are beaten.

Whereas Romany will only play when the mood takes her, and then only for a few minutes, before she gets bored and needs to get back to the important business of sleeping, Amber, being part terrier, has no such problem. Once when some friends visited, Amber was delighted to discover that they had thoughtfully brought the gift of two young children for her to play with. The youngsters were happy to sit on the rug and take turns throwing a ball for little Amber to chase. Every few seconds the ball would roll across the polished wood floor of the sitting room and bounce down the stairs into the kitchen, hotly pursued by a scrabbling ball of beige fluff. Sometimes she would catch the ball, before she slid into the kitchen table, and sometimes she wouldn't. Regardless of any minor injuries, seconds later she would return with the ball, panting heavily and with her eyes twinkling with mischief, ready and willing to go again. The children laughed as Amber comically scrabbled for grip on the shiny wooden floor, and then teased her with a game of "piggy in the middle," delighting as she performed acrobatics of Olympic proportions, in an effort to steal the ball. Because of our conversation with our friends, we had become distracted from watching this game; so it was fortunate when one of the adults noticed that Amber was totally exhausted, barely able to walk, and called a halt to play, before her tiny heart exploded. Like many children of her age, Amber has had several toys, but only two that were her favourites. One is a fur covered pyramid that we call "Amber's sucky toy," because she will lie for hours sucking on one corner, even falling asleep in the process, just like a child sucking its thumb. On those occasions when the toy becomes so dirt incrusted and smelly that we have no choice but to put it in the wash, Amber becomes almost frantic with stress. Unable to sit still, she is like a furry drug addict in withdrawal, until her toy is returned to her. Her other cherished toy is a hard rubber ball on a stout piece of rope, which is excellent for throwing, chasing and playing tug. One trick she has developed (presumably from watching Olympic hammer throwers on television) is to grasp the rope in her teeth and then turn in ever faster circles, until she lets go and the rope and ball flies away, randomly bouncing off of walls, windows, crockery or visiting friends, only to be chased down with the usual gusto. Once Amber has grasped the rope again, the petite dog will growl and shake her head violently, so that the hard rubber ball repeatedly bashes her on each side of the head. Such a pounding must surely hurt considerably, but she remains remarkably unaffected, emerging with only a bad hairdo, slightly cross-eyed and with a momentary wobble in her step. As a hunter of rats and other vermin, Amber is generally useless, preferring to rely on barking ferociously and running around like a headless chicken, rather than using hunter-like stealth and tracking skills. Occasionally she will get lucky by trapping an unsuspecting field mouse under some weed control fabric in the garden, and then she will spend a happy hour, sniffing at the tiny lump and making little cat-like pounces. She seems blissfully ignorant of her failings as a hunter, preferring to trust that, if she makes enough noise, nobody will notice her shortcomings. In her dreams, as she twitches and growls on the couch, she is a respected and successful hunter, majestically bounding across the moor in pursuit of a magnificent stag. Sadly, even her most entrenched delusions were shattered on a sunny morning in May.

As it was such a beautiful day, I decided to take the dogs on a walk that was a little longer than usual. This picturesque track took us in a wide clockwise loop, up through the forest, across a field and then down to the lane that would take us back towards the house. Romany was trotting along at my side, occasionally stopping to sniff a stick, or pee on a tuft of grass. Earlier in the walk, like the perfect lady she was, Romany had found a suitably large bush to hide behind, where she had turned three tight circles before she did her business, all the while looking out for intruders. Little Amber had finally tired of chasing her ball, which was currently leaking doggy slob into the lining of my coat pocket. She was now leading the walk and making her little, "hup-hup-hup-hup" noises as she ran excitedly from bush to bush ahead of us. Towards the end of the walk, the forest path opens into a field with extraordinary views across the valley towards Bodyke and Tulla. At the bottom of the field our path joins with another running at right-angles. If you turn to the left the path leads through a meadow and on to the village of Feakle, and to the right, after another field, the path joins with a single track road that leads back towards the house. Bouncing along some fifty yards ahead, Amber suddenly spied something on the left and, oblivious to my calls, took off like a rocket and ran into the meadow. The knee high grass hid the action from my view, as the little terrier raced around the field barking wildly. Suddenly a large hare burst from the field, quickly followed by a ball of angry beige fluff. The hare was casually lolloping along the path, hotly pursued by Amber, clearly delighted to be chasing something that was almost twice her size. Directly ahead of me, the scene played out as the chase passed from left to right, seemingly in slow motion. First I saw the hare, calmly trotting along, with its ears up and white tail bobbing; I imagined I could hear it quietly singing "dum-de-dum-de-dum," as it enjoyed a gentle jog in the countryside. A few yards behind was Amber, head down and ears back, running flat out and slowly losing ground, but unwilling to admit defeat so early in the pursuit. Behind this chase, a second hare emerged from the field and trotted along behind Amber, presumably following its friend, as if they were out on their usual Sunday morning jog. As they passed my position, although Amber was clearly running out of energy, she still turned her smiling face to look at me, as if seeking my approval of her prestigious hunting skills. At that moment the hare at the back decided that it was about time it got on with the mornings exercise. So it lengthened its stride, easily overtaking the diminutive panting dog, and joined its companion hare running ahead. Poor little Amber was still looking at me and smiling, when the previously unnoticed hare crossed her field of vision and (dismissive of any potential danger) easily accelerated away. In that instant, I saw Amber visibly deflate, gradually slowing her stride as she came to terms with the hopelessness of the pursuit. As the two hares joined up together and effortlessly bounded away, Amber came to a halt, head down and panting like a heavy smoker. Somehow it all became my fault, and even after I had stopped laughing and dried my eyes, she snubbed all of my attempts to apologise by petting her, or throwing the ball. The two hares were presumably feeling a little guilty as well, because they repeatedly offered themselves to be chased again, but poor Amber was by this time inconsolable and stubbornly refused to have anything else to do with them. By the time we got back to our land she had perked up a little, taking a few moments to chase the ducks off the pond and woof at a passing jet liner, but it was only a half-hearted effort, lacking any real expectation of success.

Throughout that first year, we entertained a succession of welcome visitors. Friends and family from England came to stay, to see our new home and experience a little Irish "Craic" (pronounced Crack), which translates as "fun" from Irish to English. Typically we would collect our guests from Shannon Airport and bring them to stay at the house, from where we could take them on the usual selection of day-trips to see the attractions of the west coast. Although it is always a pleasure to welcome visitors, we noticed that, like professional tour guides, we were becoming bored with seeing the same attractions for the umpteenth time in just eight months. The usual week included trips to Limerick, to see King John's Castle, and on another day, Galway, for the side streets full of interesting little shops and some lunch by the harbour. During the midweek we would tour the farmers' market in Ennis, and then enjoy a delicious meal and an evening of tiddly merriment at Peppers bar in Feakle. A trip to Aillwee caves and the Burren would be incomplete without lunch at "Bofey Quinns," followed by a visit to the Cliffs of Moher and the nearby Rock Shop, which sadly had nothing to do with rock music. Finishing the week was usually a day out at Bunratty Castle and Folk Park, before taking our charges to the nearby Shannon Airport. Each and every attraction is excellent entertainment and well worth the visit, but by the end of the first year, Lesley and I were drawing lots to see whose turn it was to take our latest guests to "bloody Bunratty Castle again!"

Actually there are probably umpteen attractions in Clare that we have yet to visit, partly because, until recently, we have been too busy renovating the house to take the time off, but also because they are so poorly promoted. Ireland in general and County Clare in particular, are way behind the curve in how they promote the marvellous visitor attractions. There are close to three hundred and fifty castles in Ireland, but only a few are advertised and maintained as attractions. Many castles are just partly preserved piles of stones that are marked on maps, but are only visible from the roadside and remain inaccessible without climbing fences and ditches. Others can be visited without cost and may even display a sign saying "Please bang on the door of number 23 behind you, if you would like to purchase a visitor's guide." Similarly, with a few exceptions, the natural beauty of the Irish countryside remains largely inaccessible to tourists. For example, there are several substantial waterfalls near our house, all clearly marked on maps, but Lesley and I have failed repeatedly to reach them, even after climbing through brambles and over fences. In England, it seems like every possible monument has been exploited to the full, with car parks, concession stands and children's play areas; in Wales many of the waterfalls have footpaths for easy access and specially prepared areas for taking photographs. Although I am happy that the countryside of Clare remains largely unspoilt, I believe that there is a good case for exploiting more tourist dollars than we currently do, provided it can be achieved without damaging the countryside.

When one of my sisters visited, after the usual round of attractions, we happened to take a trip to Ennis during the annual street festival. This was a lucky coincidence as we had seen no advertising of the event whatsoever. We spent a delightful day watching demonstrations of Irish dancing, music, listening to storytelling and visiting the open air market, where we feasted on succulent olives, laced with enough garlic to ensure safety from even the most determined of vampires. Apart from a splendid pub lunch at the Old Ground hotel, the highlight of the day was an elderly gent giving an animated and hilariously funny demonstration of Irish folk music, using only his voice, hands and feet.

A few weeks later, our daughter Joanne came on holiday to Ireland for the first time since we had moved. She had always been totally supportive of what we were doing and had nothing but good things to say about the house, Ireland, and just how well we both looked. We had a lovely time showing her around Clare, discussing our plans for the house, taking long walks in the forest and across the moor with the dogs. One sunny afternoon we drove down to Lough Graney and walked the dogs on "Silver Sands" beach. This was the first time that Amber had experienced such a large expanse of sand and water, so she made the most of the opportunity, madly charging around on the beach, kicking up the sand and digging dozens of holes with frantic energy. Eventually she worked up enough courage to venture into the water, partly encouraged by a game of fetch that gradually extended further and further into the shallow lake. She learned to paddle a little, which is an essential skill for any dog in Ireland that only stands four inches tall, but it took her several attempts to get the hang of not breathing when her face was under the water. During the middle of the week, we took a trip to Mountshannon, which is a pretty village on the banks of Lough Derg. Near the centre of the village there is a public park and garden with a maze that overlooks the lake, and nearby there is a very posh sailing club. Being not so posh, we rented a rowboat with an outboard motor for the ridiculously low price of €20 for half a day. We donned our lifejackets, piled into the boat and set off for an afternoon cruise around the lake and across to Holy Island, where there was an old monastery. It seems that every lake in Ireland has a monastery and island in the centre called Holy Island. The one in Lough Derg is such a beautiful location that I can understand why someone would want to live there, irrespective of religion or a desire for solitude. The weather that day was so glorious that we could easily have been in the south of France as we cruised along the shore front, passing dozens of yachts gleaming white in the blinding sunlight. Their rigging lines played a soft symphony as they slapped against the masts, in harmony with the gentle rocking of the waves, intermittently punctuated with the chime of a ship's bell and the sharp call of the moor hens. On the last full day before Joanne flew home, we went to Bunratty Castle (again) and made a day of the trip, by giving our full attention to every detail of the castle and Folk Park. The castle is actually more of a tower house, with a long history of being repaired and renovated, not unlike Glenmadrie! The name "Bunratty" means castle at the mouth, or bottom, of the river Ratty and from the top of the castle one can see the River Ratty, the Shannon estuary, the motorway and the airport – perhaps not the best view in Ireland. Despite the abundance of wildlife and the salty tang in the air, I have always found the mudflats associated with such tidal estuaries to be rather dull and depressing places. In common with most castles in Ireland, Bunratty has an interesting history, as well as enjoyable architecture, with many narrow corridors, passages and winding stairways providing various ways to access or defend each floor. Some of the stairways are deliberately constructed with risers of various heights and sizes. These "stumble steps" will force a sword wielding attacker to look down to ensure better footing, or risk a trip and fall, at a time when any distraction could make you bleed all over your opponent's sword. The steps have much the same effect on visiting tourists, making them stagger and giggle like drunken teenagers. The easy going nature of the Irish was again demonstrated, when we noticed a "bag lady," sleeping full length on one of the benches in the Folk Park. She was roundly ignored by the park staff, whereas in another country she would have been unceremoniously woken and told to move on. However, the two massively rotund American tourists, who became stuck in the dungeon passageway of the castle, received a less than sympathetic response, when they suggested that the ancient stonework should be widened to make more room for portly visitors. The Folk Park is an appealing and accurate reconstruction of nineteenth century Irish village life, with a main street, a post office, shops, a school and a bakery. Many of the buildings have been moved from other locations and faithfully reconstructed, to add to the authentic feel of the park; perhaps this would explain why some tourists have asked what possessed the Irish to build the castle so close to the motorway! There is also a working pub that is guaranteed to deliver a hearty welcome and plenty of "craic" every night, or, if you prefer, the castle is now famous for its medieval banquets and the associated entertainment that is provided by the local artists. Although there were many tears at the airport as we waved goodbye to our beloved daughter, our sadness was brief, for we knew she

126

would become a regular visitor, as she and her friends discovered the magical beauty and solitude of rural Ireland. On the other hand, we didn't move to Ireland to become tour guides; there was work to do back at the house.

We knew from the engineer's report, that there was water getting into the south end of the house. Some of the floorboards in the master bedroom were wet and rotten, and there was water dripping from above one of the windows in the studio below. It was clear that, on the south facing wall, there was a small amount of water running down the concrete behind the plaster board; the engineer suspected condensation, but I suspected there was a more substantial leak. Not wanting to start ripping down walls unnecessarily and on the basis that water runs downhill, I started my investigations in the loft. Immediately above the wet area I discovered several old bird nests and a considerable amount of damage to the roof felting, which could easily allow wind-blown rain to enter the house. Although it was a bit of a squeeze, I managed to extract the empty nests, block up the hole that the birds were using and fit some new felting, without needing to remove the roof. On the assumption that the problem was probably fixed, I replaced the water damaged floorboards and skirting in the rooms below and then waited for the rain to fall – which inevitably it didn't. I should explain at this point, that there are 236 different types of rain in Ireland, ranging from light drizzle, to lashing fire hoses and everything imaginable in between. Here you can experience the soft humid mists which gently caress you on a warm day, or the big fat rain drops that instantly soak through your shirt when you have forgotten your umbrella, as well as the vicious cold-steel rain, which only falls when you are wearing your best suit and trying to change a flat tyre. Because Glenmadrie is at altitude, we are privileged to receive a very special version of the rain that, when wind assisted, can travel sideways and occasionally upwards. On the days when the house is enveloped in cloud or hill fog, the wind can push the water around, and even under, the best fitting doors – leaving large puddles in the porch, which we incorrectly used to blame on the poor dogs. This kind of soft mist can last for days, particularly when you need a dry day to cut the grass or paint the outside of the house, and over time this unrelenting moisture will cause any exposed or untreated wood to swell and warp. On "wild days" the rain will unremittingly pound the south end of the house, as if it were an ancient sailing ship rounding Cape Horn during a winter storm. This kind of weather will find even the smallest crack or cranny and force water into the house, and because water can easily follow unseen gaps in the stonework, leaks can be very hard to repair. The plan was to start my repairs in the attic and to work my way downwards until the problem was fixed. But to prove that the repair was successful, I needed lots of rain, and 2004 turned out to be a very dry year. So all I could do was to repair the obvious leaks and then wait until there was some really serious rain, before declaring that the problem was finally solved. Inevitably, about three months after I claimed my first success, the rain returned with a vengeance and water started to drip through into the studio again. Repair plan "B," which involved removing the plasterboard on the internal south wall to try and find the problem, would have to wait until the following spring, because by then I was busy converting the old cow shed into an office, shower room and utility room in an area we would call "the wing."

Mr Rain finally reappeared at Glenmadrie, towards the end of 2004, and quickly seemed determined to make up for his long summer holiday. Within days he had invited his two superhero friends, Gale and Storm to help him make up for lost time. They soon set about flooding the meadow, battering the house, knocking over trees and randomly disconnecting our telephone and electricity, at the most inconvenient of times. Gale is cold at heart and insisted on pointing out all of the places where she could get into the house, by howling through every gap in the walls and blowing dust down through the ceilings. I used up several cans of expanding foam, just trying to keep her out of the older parts of the house, and in the end I had to temporarily box off the spiral staircase, to try and keep the drafts below hurricane force. Storm, the other visiting superhero, is a moody cow, inclined to violent tantrums, moaning and wailing all night long and stealing anything that isn't well secured. In late October, when Lesley was back in England visiting her mother, I was rebuilding a wall in the wing when the weather took a turn for the worse, demonstrating the full force of an Atlantic storm. So that I could remain reasonably dry while I was building the new walls, I had left the original corrugated steel roof in place and added some tarpaulin, to protect the sides where the old walls had been removed. Late one evening I was working under floodlights, laying a few more blocks to use up the last of the mortar I had mixed, when both Gale and Storm decided to pay a visit. The trees around the house started to thrash alarmingly and there was a ghostly moaning from the hill opposite. Then the wind and rain increased to a startling ferocity, as the unseen squall approached. Just at that moment, the winds peaked and the entire roof of the wing (comprising five hundred square feet of corrugated steel, with a frame of timber and tree trunks) reared up, like the lid on a giant toilet seat, and balanced precariously on one edge. I stood transfixed; watching what was probably a couple of tons of rusty steel and rotting wood, hanging motionless above me, apparently unsure of which way it should fall. Suddenly the wind subsided into an eerie silence, and then, to my horror, the roof slowly dropped towards me. With a yelp far less manly than I would have liked, I covered my head with my arms and threw myself onto the ground; with a mighty crash, complimented by a shower of rust and dead spiders, the roof landed perfectly back into place, on top of the wall. Fortunately, the ropes that I had used to attach the tarpaulin to one end of the roof had acted as a hinge, ensuring that the whole thing fell back into its original position, balanced on top of the remaining walls, rather than squashing me like a bug as it would surely otherwise have done.

In time the winter storms gave way to unseasonably mild, but unpleasantly wet, weather throughout December. Fortunately the lack of frost allowed me to make good progress with the new exterior walls for the wing, and by Christmas week I had moved on to digging up the floors, ready to lay the sewage pipes for the bathroom. Lesley and I are not particularly inclined to celebrate Christmas just because some retailers say we should, although we would make a special day of it, if we had guests. However, as nobody was expected to visit until the spring, we had no special plans for the day, other than a roast dinner and perhaps a glass of wine to compliment the inevitable television re-runs of classic Christmas movies. When Joanne was still young, we would always make a big effort for Christmas. Lesley would carefully manage our money, so that she could buy little gifts and treats all year to be hidden away, ready for Christmas; I am sure there are still some toys hidden somewhere in the old house. Then on the night of

Christmas Eve, after Joanne was safely asleep, I would construct an elaborate treasure trail, with cryptic clues and little treats hidden around the house, before helping Lesley to decorate the tree and lounge, so that on Christmas morning Joanne would be completely surprised. It was delightful to see the astonishment on her face when she discovered the tree surrounded with gifts and tasty treats, combined with the smell of turkey, slowly roasting in the oven. Joanne still maintains that her favourite gift by far was the large doll's house that I had secretly built during the weeks before Christmas, at a time when we had very little money. Conversely, at the end of 2004, there seemed very little point in taking time out to add a tree and decorations to the cobwebs and dust, particularly when there was so much else to do.

So we had no special plans for our first Christmas at Glenmadrie, other than eating rather too much and having an afternoon walk with the dogs. But on the morning of December 25th, I opened the curtains to discover that the altitude and weather had combined to deliver a special Christmas treat – six inches of thick snow! The snow suppressed the noise and made the branches on the trees hang low and, with visibility reduced to less than one hundred yards by the hill fog; it felt like we had been wrapped in cotton wool, or Santa's beard. I lit the fire and after telephoning our friends and family, I cooked our traditional Christmas breakfast, of thick slices of French toast with lashings of maple syrup. Personally I prefer my French toast smothered with strawberry jam, but it seems that this dietary quirk is unacceptable in polite company – unless you happen to be pregnant. Once we were washed and dressed, we set out like two polar explorers with mismatched dogs for a walk in the forest, before dinner. Amber ran, rolled and jumped in the snow with a childlike delight, chasing after every puff of snow that was disturbed by our boots. Occasionally she would dive headfirst into a drift, in pursuit of some particularly devious snowflake, only to emerge moments later, eyes dancing and grinning widely, with her face covered in snow and looking as if someone had just thrown a custard pie. Romany, on the other hand, had seen it all before and trudged along with grudging indifference, collecting ever larger snowballs on her feet and underside – until finally she could walk no further. Then she would sit down and refuse to move until one of us held her upside-down like a turtle, and the other risked frostbite while breaking off the lumps of ice with our fingers. Back home and exhausted by carrying ten pounds of ice, Romany lay by the fire, steaming gently and slowly leaking water across the floor as the ice melted. As it was too cold to work outside, we took the rest of the day off, watched some television, did some reading, ate too many mince pies and then dozed on the couch until it was time for bed. The snow lingered for two weeks and because the rural roads are seldom gritted or ploughed, we were pretty much confined to the house throughout, but that caused us little inconvenience. We have two large chest freezers that are kept well stocked with frozen milk and bread (for those days when we don't bake our own) along with Quorn, vegetables and other essentials, so that we don't have to make the forty mile round trip to the shops every day.

Glenmadrie quietly slipped into 2005, without ceremony or the usual barrage of fireworks which seems to punctuate every party in England from mid-October through to the end of January. Just after midnight, I let the dogs out, to do what they must, before bed time. While I waited for their return, I stood in the deep crisp snow, revelling in the silence, and breathed deeply of the deliciously pure air. As I stared in awe at the star filled vista of a crystal clear sky above me, I took a moment to remember my father, as it would have been his birthday, to think of our friends and family abroad and to give quiet thanks for our new life in Ireland.

Chapter 11 – In which our family grows, again

By 2005, with the economy of the "Celtic Tiger" booming, it appeared that most people paid little regard to the prices they paid for big ticket items like cars, white goods and electrical. They seemed happy to pay outrageously inflated prices for the illusion of getting the best products. Although I recognise there is a correlation between price and quality, it seemed that in Ireland at that time there was a limited market for "value" with, as an example, even the lowliest of new properties opting for custom built kitchens. Very few of the well-known DIY retailers had shops in the west, and the builders merchants were operating without any real competition, willing and able to charge substantially more than the UK prices. With our limited budget for the renovation, we had to get the best possible deal on every purchase and keep our spending under control. Had we lived closer to the UK, either via Dublin to Wales, or to the North, I would probably have been making regular trips across the border to pay in sterling, but the time and travel costs from Clare would have made the benefit questionable. Although, whenever one of us visited family by taking a car on the ferry, rather than the much cheaper Ryanair option, we would return with the car so laden with bargains as to be practically dragging the exhaust along the road. On one trip, Lesley found a pet shop selling twenty kilogram bags of wild bird seed, for just £7.00; at that time in Ennis, we were paying £19.50 for the same product. In her desire to capitalise on the bargain, Lesley so insanely overloaded her little Skoda Estate that she was stopped by customs officials at Dublin Port. The poor guy refused to believe that anyone would willingly buy so much seed, just for wild birds, and unloaded more than half of the bags, before coming to the conclusion that Lesley wasn't a drug mule, just an eccentric English lady. When we renovated our previous house in England, we had saved a good bit of money by making many of our larger purchases in the January sales, and our plan now was to do the same thing, but on a much larger scale. I had decided that there was enough space in the studio to store most of the big purchases, in particular the kitchen units, the bathroom furniture and the floor and wall tiles. As buying these items was unavoidable and represented a large proportion of our eventual spend, I wanted to save as much money as I could and complete the purchase before we ran out of money. One particular store, which we knew from England, had a shop in Limerick that stocked a reasonable range of kitchens, bathrooms, building materials and garden products. Incredibly, along with the 50% reduction in their January sale, they were also adding a further reduction of 20% on this particular weekend and then giving 10% back in vouchers on all purchases. Consequently we saved some €3,000 on buying the kitchen and bathroom, and I even managed to negotiate free delivery into the deal. Later that week we found a tile warehouse in Ennis that was having a clear-out sale and saved another €1,500 on wall and floor tiles, cement and grout. Once the deliveries were completed and the studio was stacked to the roof, with barely enough room for a mouse to slip between the boxes, we could relax, secure in the knowledge that everything was paid for, safely stored and ready to be fitted when I had completed the construction.

Because we had run out of storage space, the lumber, blocks, insulation and other building materials had to be bought locally, and delivered when I was ready to start each new phase of the renovation. For most of these deliveries, we stuck with a couple of local builders merchants that gave us decent prices and free delivery on the thousands of euro's worth of supplies that we bought over the next seven years. It felt good to put some money back into the local area, although in those heady days of the booming "Tiger economy," it was sometimes surprisingly difficult to get people to take your money. When the first lorry load of building materials arrived, we were surprised to find that we were unable to pay the driver because he had not been given an invoice. Even though the load was worth a couple of thousand euro, it seems that the girl in the hardware store who took the telephone order had automatically opened an account and extended us a substantial line of credit.

They actually seemed quite put out when we insisted on paying for all of our purchases with cash on delivery. A couple of weeks later, Lesley arrived home from a shopping trip to Ennis and came over to where I was working in the wing. She leaned against the wall and watched me cutting some wood for a while, before she spoke.

"I've been thinking," she said brightly.

A cold shiver went down my spine, ran across the floor and hid in the corner quivering.

"Now we talked about this dear," I joked, dodging her swinging foot. "We agreed that you would stop thinking for a while."

"I said I've have been thinking," she repeated, teasingly.

I sensed that she wanted to tell me something and I could see no obvious means of escape. "Go on then, what have you been thinking?"

"Rugs!!!" She said triumphantly.

"Oh jolly well done!" I teased. "What are we having for dinner?"

She ignored my caustic wit. "I think that we need rugs, for the sitting room floor."

"We do?" I asked, picturing the constant snow of woodworm dust and dead spiders that coated the floor daily. "Won't they just get dirty?"

She rolled her eyes and sighed dramatically, "Not for now! For afterwards – when the work is finished."

Sensing at least a temporary reprieve, I relaxed. "Oh. You mean for later. Well that's alright then."

Then she spoke quietly, whilst carefully inspecting a fingernail. "Only we need them now – because they were on sale."

I eyed her suspiciously. "Were on sale? What did you buy?"

"I didn't buy anything – yet. I was at a shop in Ennis and they had these Persian rugs; they are really beautiful and they were practically giving them away."

"Okay, fine," I conceded, "The next time we are in Ennis, we can go and have a look."

"No need!" She said jubilantly, "They are in the car. All six of them!"

"But you said you didn't buy them," I whined.

"I didn't," She said proudly.

"What, and I suppose they just gave them to you?" I asked mockingly, "Without asking you for a deposit or anything?"

"Actually they did," she said with a big smile.

Incredibly Lesley had arrived home with several thousand euro's worth of rugs in the back of her car. The staff in the shop were so keen for her to buy that they had insisted she take home half a dozen Persian rugs – just to try them for size. Amazingly, they didn't ask for any deposit, credit card details or identification; in fact, they didn't even bother to take a note of her name! Again we found this level of trust to be evidence of how delightfully innocent and crime free County Clare was at that time. Although things may have changed a little now, mostly because of the recession, in general it is still an admirably safe and pleasant place to live – particularly when it isn't lashing with rain. One day in early May, Ireland's weather made a bad first impression on some guests.

I was at Shannon Airport to collect two gents, Tony and Stan, who I had invited over to address a meeting in Ennis. It was a lovely day, warm with a beautiful blue sky, although there were a few very tall and angry looking clouds around. I had arranged the meeting at a local hotel with twenty colleagues or so from around the island of Ireland. My plan was to get everyone together, to share best practice, arrange training sessions and to benefit from some group purchasing power for supplies, insurance and suchlike. This was our third such meeting, and they were proving to be popular, as we had recently formed ourselves into an official association of members who could happily work together, because we were not geographic competitors. Previously, we had to travel to England or Spain for any meetings and additional training, at a considerable cost in time and money. Also, all administration, insurance and supplier negotiations were being handled by an office in Kent, who did not appreciate the challenges of doing business in Ireland. Recently I had secured an excellent deal on public liability insurance for the group, arranged some local training sessions and agreed preferential rates with our equipment suppliers. At the previous meeting, my good friend Richard had been chosen to be the official representative for contact with our European headquarters, and I was honoured to be elected as chairperson, or chief dogsbody. The two gentlemen that I was meeting at the airport were from a company hoping to become new suppliers of equipment and stock to our members. Tony was the slightly self-important sales director and was smartly dressed for his presentation, wearing a beautifully cut, and obviously expensive, Italian woollen suit; whereas since Stan was at the meeting as the equipment specialist, he got to carry the samples and wear more casual clothes. This was a first visit to Ireland for both men. After the usual handshakes and welcoming comments, I proudly led the way as we set off across the ten acre car park towards my car. I was just pointing out the distant Slieve Bearnagh Mountains, which they had so recently flown over as their flight came in to land, when far to our right I heard a car alarm begin to bleat, followed by a second and then a third. Tony stopped dead and looked across the car park as a forth car alarm added to the commotion.

"What the hell is going on over there?" he asked, squinting into the distance, where yet another car was now flashing and honking.

"Perhaps it's vandals – you know, kids or something," Stan said as we walked on past.

"No it isn't. There's something odd going on," he replied tersely.

I had finally spotted my car in the distance and took a moment to look across towards where another two alarms had just started honking, with a sound like geese preparing to migrate. Finally I noticed the boiling blue clouds above us and what appeared to be hundreds of bouncing golf balls, marching across the car park in our direction, battering the cars and setting off the alarms along the way. Suddenly the penny dropped.

"That's hail – big hail," I shouted, "Quick, run to the car!"

We made the sixty-yard dash in record time and, after a mad scramble for keys and stock samples, threw ourselves, damp and laughing, into the safety of the car. Just then, the full force of the storm hit with an explosion of lightning, water and ice. I started the car, turned the fan to "full" to try and clear the misted windows, and then I looked around to check on my guests. Immediately I noticed that we were one short.

"Stan, where's Tony?" I asked.

"I don't know. He was running along beside me and then he dropped his suitcase. Last I saw he was picking up his clothes," Stan replied, trying to keep the smirk on his face under control.

"Christ, he's going to get soaked," I said.

"Yes, and him in that lovely new suit as well," Stan chipped in brightly. "I suppose we'd better go and look for him."

"I can't see him anywhere," I said, peering over the roofs of a thousand rain lashed cars, "Perhaps if I drove around a bit, we might spot him."

We unsuccessfully circled the car park for a couple of minutes, but it seemed like hours, as the rain and hail intensified with each mighty crash of thunder.

"Maybe he went back into the terminal building," I proffered.

"If the weather is always like this, maybe he just went home." Stan joked, and then pointing, "Ah! There he is – oh dear, that doesn't look good!"

"Oh dear indeed," I agreed as I spotted a bedraggled Tony, who seemed to be soaked through to the skin. He was standing pathetically alongside his broken suitcase and clutching an armful of muddy clothes.

As we did our best to maintain our poker faces, poor Tony told us that after his suitcase had burst he had become lost and, not knowing which car we were in, had no alternative but to chase his clothes around the car park as the full force of the storm hit.

I tried to make light of the situation by pointing to the large "Welcome to Ireland" sign at the exit of the airport. Tony refused to see the humour of the situation, particularly when it emerged that all of his clothes were soaked through, and because of his slightly rotund shape we were unable to borrow any replacements. With only an hour to go before the meeting, and to avoid the prospect of the poor guy doing his sales presentation in a hotel bathrobe, I asked the hotel manager to arrange for Tony's suit and clothes to be dried as quickly as possible. However, to add another memorable moment to the trip, when his clothes were returned half an hour later, he discovered that the laundry had tumble dried his beautiful woollen suit on maximum heat, leaving it looking a bit like an undersized potato sack. In the end the meeting was a roaring success, and Tony cheered up considerably after securing several sales, despite his suit looking like it had been found in a skip outside a charity shop.

Sometimes in rural Ireland, it's the little things that make you laugh, like the relaxed approach to medical care.

A few weeks later, Richard and Karen, some friends of ours from England, arrived at the house unexpectedly. This was their second visit to Ireland, but as they had brought David and Andrew along, their rambunctious young boys, this time they were staying in a holiday cottage in Corofin, close to the one I had rented. We were delighted with the surprise visit and had a cracking day chewing over old memories and discussing our plans for the house. Meanwhile, the boys kept out of any significant trouble, by playing with the dogs on the land and climbing around in the quarry, like two hyperactive kittens. At the end of the day, we were sad to see our friends go, but they had places to see and we had plenty of work to keep us occupied. Richard and Karen spent the week touring around the west coast, sightseeing and trying to keep the boys entertained; towards the end of the week, they came to the house again for a farewell dinner. I noticed that Andrew, the older of the two boys, had a big bandage on his thumb. Knowing of his susceptibility for attracting accidents, I asked what had happened. Richard casually explained that, despite numerous warnings to take care with the knife, Andrew had managed to slice a bit off the end of his thumb whilst doing some crafts. The injury was not a particular problem and would soon have clotted over, except that the young boy continued to lift the bandage to inspect the wound. Being just a flat spot missing from the tip of his thumb, the cut was less than a centimetre square and unlikely to require stiches; all it needed was time to clot and heal, but Andrew insisted on fiddling with it, until the bleeding started over again. In the end Richard, who is a calm and practical guy, went to the local pharmacy to ask if they had something that would help clot the wound. He was delighted with the results of his purchase, a potion painted on the wound which quickly stopped the bleeding and manfully resisted Andrew's further repeated inspections. Karen and Richard are lovely people, good parents, excellent company and trusted friends, with a great sense of humour. We all laughed ourselves to tears when Richard showed us that the magic potion bore the words, "If symptoms persist, please consult your vet."

Andrew seems none the worse for his visit to Ireland and the unusual medical care he received – apart from a tendency to chase passing cars and bark at the moon.

Rural Ireland has two types of dog, known as "indoors" and "outdoors" dogs. The majority of dogs in towns and cities are "indoors" dogs, permitted access to some part of the house and walked on a lead daily. Most farms and rural houses have outdoors dogs that never ever come into the house, living outside all year, perhaps sleeping under a tractor or in a shed, even during the worst of the weather. Outdoors dogs are never taken for a walk, but are free to roam as they please, feeding on a daily handful of dry food thrown on the ground and perhaps some juicy kitchen scraps. By law, all Irish dogs are required to chase cars, tractors and passing bicycles; or so you would imagine, given the number of canine terrorist incidents one must endure on each road journey. The desire to chase passing traffic is now so inbred, that it is almost impossible to stop any Irish born dog from taking off in pursuit of a passing vehicle, regardless of any threats and scolding. Some dogs are happy to get their exercise by running along behind a car for a few seconds, then waiting patiently until another car passes in the opposite direction, so that they can run back to where they started. Usually these harmless chases will go completely unnoticed, unless the driver happened to look in their mirrors. However, the unexpected sideways assaults are much more disturbing, particularly for passing tourists. In this form of pursuit, the dog, or sometimes several dogs, will make a fast lateral approach, creating the impression that they are suicidally depressed and about to throw themselves under your front wheels. Frequently the initial phases of these kamikaze attacks are concealed by hedges, farm tracks or buildings, so that the dogs only become visible at the very last second. Even drivers experienced in driving in rural Ireland and familiar with the tactics of certain dogs, find it difficult to resist swerving and breaking in panic.

One of our neighbours has a mongrel dog of uncertain parentage. Large in size, but small in brain, it has a coat of short black wiry hair and on his flanks there are two white patches, as if he had recently brushed against some wet paint. He is imaginatively named "Patch" and may well be the champion car chaser of all Ireland. Tom is a short but surprisingly energetic pensioner, with snow white hair, a ready smile and a wicked quick wit; he drives a large black car which is permanently shadowed by his dog. To be fair, Tom tried his best to discourage Patch from his passion for chasing, but to no avail. When he was a puppy, we would see Patch running along behind passing cars, trailing a rope or chain and some part of whatever it had originally been attached to. Sometimes it would be a stake, or a small tree, and on one occasion we even saw a large concrete block, gradually becoming smaller as it bounced along the road behind this energetic dog. In a desperate attempt to discourage Patch from chasing cars, Tom even constructed an ingenious and elaborate arrangement of straps and trusses, to secure a heavy pipe with a line of little bells, just below his chest. The idea behind this fiendish contraption was that, if he attempted to chase a car, his knees would bang repeatedly against the bar, causing discomfort and ringing the bells. Not to be outdone, Patch quickly taught himself to run sideways. In the end Tom accepted the inevitable, and Patch now covers dozens of miles each day, proudly running along the road, twenty yards behind Tom's car. Nowadays, if I see Tom's car parked while he is tending to his cattle and horses, I know Patch will be hiding in a nearby ditch, ready to spring out like a ninja greyhound and chase my little car for up to half a mile. He is an incredibly fit and determined opponent; once, in my rush to get away before he seized my bumper, I missed a gear change and he almost caught up with me. I could see his eager face in my wing mirror, tongue lolling and eyes sparkling as he revelled in the chase. He equalled my pace and ran for several hundred yards, at thirty-five miles per hour, until I finally got onto a downslope and managed to open up a gap. Just then another car passed, travelling in the opposite direction, and I was horrified to see Patch perform an athletic back-flip into the ditch, as if he had been struck by a bolt of lightning. I stared in shock for an instant, until I saw Patch chasing after the second car; then I realised that the aerial acrobatics were only the lovable pooch's pea size brain trying to change direction, without consulting his body.

Lesley had a birthday approaching, and as we had often discussed the possibility of getting another dog, I decided to make a visit to the Ennis dog pound to see if I could spot a likely candidate. Many of these homeless dogs find themselves in the Ennis dog pound, along with a regular supply of "outdoors dogs" that have been mistaken for strays and brought in by well-meaning tourists. Unfortunately the dog pound in Ennis has the dubious record of euthanizing more dogs each year than almost any other place in Europe. I know the dog pound staff are kindly and well-meaning people who care well for their charges, but there is only so much they can do with limited resources. At that time the pound was unstaffed over the weekend, and consequently most of the unclaimed dogs were being put to sleep by close of play on a Friday, leaving the pound empty and ready for the next batch on Monday morning. Unless you have a particularly hard heart and a strong will, you should never visit the dog pound on a Friday afternoon, just before "Putting to sleep time." We are both dog lovers, a soft touch and occasionally impulsive, so it should not have been a surprise that we left the pound that Friday afternoon, having saved not one, but three puppies, from certain execution – they were all about three months old and we named them Lady, Kia and Scruffy.

Lady is an older style English Foxhound. With sharp intelligent eyes and floppy ears framing a proud and noble face, she is slender but strong, a natural long distance runner that also loves to howl at the moon. Although equipped with slightly shorter legs than the modern hounds, she is a real hunter nonetheless – away into the woods, with her nose down and tail up, at the slightest hint of a scent. With a short coat of smooth soft fur in the brown, tan and white colouring of a beagle, she is an elegant dog; but pushy to the point of rudeness, to ensure her rightful place as the centre of attention. Kia is a Collie Spaniel cross, with beautiful dark brown eyes that make her look worldly and wise. She has a jet black coat which is as soft as the finest silk, but sticks relentlessly to carpets, furniture and visiting friends. Her distinctive fur magically appears, in cricket ball size dust bunnies, as soon as you have finished vacuuming and liberally coats any item of dropped food. She has a little white fur on her muzzle and chest, as if she had dipped her snout in some cream, and recently she grew some light grey eyebrows, just to be fashionable. Although she is an extremely affectionate dog, we suspect that she may have had some early bad experiences. She is very wary of people, particularly men, and dislikes any sign of admonishment – so much so that she will typically wet herself on the spot if someone tells her off or attempts to pick her up. Scruffy is a Wire-Haired Terrier, crossed with something unidentified, but probably large and aggressive. She has rough honey coloured hair with golden eyes, big ears and a light-brown nose. She is an odd sort of dog to look at. I imagined that she was hurriedly assembled by God, five minutes before going home time on the Friday night of a long bank holiday weekend, in an attempt to use up some of the left over dog parts before they went off. Rather like a badly constructed Mr Potato Head doll, her features seemed to be in constant conflict with each other, and there was a sinister undertone in those eyes, presenting all of the compassion you would expect from a drug addict mugger. In any event, our family of five dogs quickly became friends, although Romany remained slightly aloof, treating the others with mild disdain, as if they were guests that had overstayed their welcome. Amber, on the other hand, was delighted to have three new friends to play with, despite the fact that each puppy was already three times her size.

Shortly after our new dogs had arrived, we noticed that Kia had an upset stomach and had lost interest in eating; she seemed to have gone rather quiet, spending the day just lying alone in the conservatory. This was not particularly concerning, as the stress of being in the kennels and then moving to a new home, along with the change of food, can cause a short period of mild illness. We spoke with the vet and decided that, as long as she was drinking plenty of fluids, a short period without eating would not cause any harm; as anyone who has had food poisoning while on holiday will know, the best treatment until things settle down, is to keep warm, drink loads and sleep near a toilet. However, within two days it was clear that Kia was going downhill fast, lethargic and unable to drink or eat anything, so we took her to Cathy our vet, who sadly diagnosed "parvo." The canine parvovirus is the most infectious disease among dogs and the most deadly, particularly in puppies. The commonest form is enteritis, where the intestines are infected, causing fever, vomiting, diarrhoea, general lethargy and a loss of appetite. After invading and inflaming the small intestine, which stops the absorption of nutrients, the virus assaults the dog's weakened immune system, opening the road to secondary infections. The most effective treatment is to keep the dog warm, hydrated and clear of secondary infections, with the use of IV fluids and high dose antibiotics; the mortality rate for dogs left untreated can be as high as 80%. Cathy sympathetically told us that Kia would be lucky to survive. Perhaps it was because she was such a gentle puppy, who looked so desperately helpless and frightened as the virus raged through her body, or perhaps it was because some vets have a kind heart and love dogs, but Cathy refused to allow Kia to die. She cared for her around the clock for a week, administering fluids, heat blankets and gallons of antibiotics, until the worst was over and Kia finally started to eat and drink without incident. Once we had her home, Kia's appetite improved and she started to put on a little weight, demonstrating remarkable resilience as she quickly returned to full health. It was delightful to see her joyously running along with the other dogs, joining in all of the games and adding her distinctive woof to the others in the pack. We will be forever grateful to Cathy and the other vets in Tulla for another life saved.

Because we live in a remote area, the dogs are free to explore our land, the adjacent forest and the moor, although they usually stay within sight of the house and return when called. There are a few exceptions; here are the rules as they were explained to me by the dogs:

1.   Passing hikers and walkers must be woofed at and followed for several hundred yards, to ensure that they have been seen off.

2.   Walkers who demonstrate any signs of friendliness, or show little obvious fear of dogs, can be followed further, but with less woofing.

3.   Should any walkers stop to converse with the servants and feeders of the dogs, all woofing will cease while stroking and playing takes place. Once the conversation is over, rule two applies again, even if the walkers came into the house for the afternoon and had tea and scones.

4.   Amber is exempt from the first five minutes of any stroking, as she is required to continue running around wildly and woofing jealously at the heels of any walkers who attempt to pay attention to any dog, other than her.

5.   Romany, if woken from her afternoon nap by the racket of barking dogs and shouting owners, shall walk a few yards in the opposite direction and then woof myopically at a tree.

6.   Cyclists must always be chased, but only until they fall off. Once they pick up their bikes again, they are classified as walkers and can be dealt with under rule one.

7.   On warm days, all dogs shall be required to sleep in the sun in the courtyard area, remaining motionless until passing hikers (exhausted from the muddy eight hundred foot climb from the river below) are level with the stone wall at the back of the house. At that point the hikers will pause and draw enough breath to say loudly, "What a lovely house," whereupon Lady will launch herself over the wall barking like a rabid hyena, and the other dogs will run into the lane via the greenhouse, in a flanking manoeuvre designed to confuse and trap the terrified enemy.

8.   On quiet days, when no walker, hiker or passing traffic is available, the dogs will (on a previously agreed rota system) take turns running outside and woofing wildly at nothing in particular, thereby causing the dogs' servant and feeder to again stop whatever it was they were trying to get done and go outside to investigate the non-existent intrusion.

9.   At the most inconvenient of times, Lady will be required to identify the scent of some imaginary prey and disappear in chase, for no less than thirty minutes. She should ignore all shouted demands to return, by howling defiantly from nearby hills. On every third such chase, Kia will be required to join in by running along several hundred yards behind, breathing heavily and promising to go on a diet. She will return twenty minutes after Lady, but only after collecting in her coat several sticks, two large pieces of bramble and some smelly mud from a ditch.

10.   On any night when there is a full moon, Lady shall stand on the hill tops, at each of the four points of the compass, and howl at her own echo. This activity will be treated with disdain by everyone else.

While we have never had a break-in, one would suspect that any visiting burglar would be roundly ignored by our ferocious guard dogs, as they lie like furry starfish by the fire. Although to be fair, when two white vans full of ne'er-do-wells pulled into our driveway at two o'clock one August night, the pack of snarling, barking dogs that charged menacingly across the lawn soon encouraged them to head towards Galway and presumably easier pickings. Extra dog treats all around that night!

With five dogs to care for, we became regular visitors to the vets, first for Kia's illness, then for puppy inoculations and of course for Romany's frequently infected eyes and dickey tummy; in general, however, the dogs were all in pretty good health, apart from the occasional mishaps. When in full hunting mode, Lady is inclined to run into barbed wire fences, or cut a paw on a sharp rock, but these wounds usually heal themselves without needing medical attention – except for one rainy night in September. After hunting excitedly for almost an hour, she trotted back into the house, soaking wet, muddy and steadily dripping blood from a large cut, where she had obviously caught her ear on a bit of barbed wire. Before we could react, she enthusiastically shook herself off in the lounge, leaving the cream coloured walls splattered with dirty water, mud and suspicious looking splashes of blood. The cut would only require a couple of sutures to stop the bleeding, but the walls required a lot of cleaning before visitors stopped calling the Guards to report a murder. After surviving her early brush with death, Kia is now blest with a robust constitution – apart from occasional sinus infections, which cause bouts of violent sneezing along with magnificent snot bubbles, worthy of a toddler with a heavy cold. Amber is almost indestructible, delighted to join in the rough and tumble of doggy life, able to endure more punishment than your average superhero and as willing as a heavyweight boxer with gambling debts.

It took Kia many months to learn how to play nicely. We had to be sure to protect Amber's "gaming rights," and on our walks during that time, a clandestine version of the little dog's favourite game "Stones" operated, whereby we would attempt to kick a small pebble for Amber to pounce on like an excited kitten, while escaping detection by Kia who would, of course, have wanted to join in had it dawned on her that a game was in progress. After much work we have finally trained Kia and Amber to play in a way that avoids any possessive fighting. This new game basically involves throwing a tennis ball to Kia, who, at the command "Give," will drop it so that Amber can bring it back – it's complicated and tedious for the ball thrower, but good team building for the dogs! Lady considers such games to be beneath her lofty skills and prefers to augment her walks by sniffing out squirrels and foxes. Her attitude is unsurprising, given that Kia, in her determination to get to the ball first, has been known to body-check like a line-backer on steroids. Although excessive body-checking is not actually a breach of the "Queen's rules of doggy ball games" (second edition), it is certainly contrary to the spirit of fair play, which requires the chase for a ball to be won by "a fair pursuit, demonstrating fitness and enthusiasm." After one particularly violent body-check left Lady upside-down in a gorse bush, I imagined I could hear her mumbling, "bloody Kia...taking it a bit seriously...only a game after all," as she limped away. Lady is a legendary biscuit catcher, who has never been known to miss, but when she has a realistic opportunity to catch a ball, the delicious anticipation will usually overpower her skill. Like an eight-year old child, challenged to make the winning catch in a little league game, Lady will invariably panic and lunge too early, causing the ball to bounce off the end of her nose and arc perfectly into Kia's waiting jaws. In some ways it is a good thing because, if Lady ever manages to get the ball, she does her "happy dance" from side to side along the road, with legs and ears flopping like a rag doll, before disappearing into the wood, where she will bury her prize so that it can safely remain hers forever. Incidentally, the game of "stones" has been banned since an operation proved that Amber (with a tummy like a bag of marbles) was jealously guarding her prizes by swallowing them – GAME OVER!!

Lesley mentioned one day that there had been an incident between the dogs; she was walking them along the forest path when, as she described it, "suddenly – all hell broke loose." She hadn't been paying much attention to the dogs at that moment, but presumed that something had happened, because suddenly Scruffy had hold of Amber, while Kia was running around barking wildly and diving in with the occasional nip. Poor little Amber is less than half the size of the other dogs and she was squealing and struggling like a baby piglet as Scruffy attacked her. Luckily, during a brief pause in the melee, Lesley was able to snatch Amber out of harm's way. Within seconds calm was restored, but Lesley was wary of a second assault, so she carried the terrified Amber all the way home and then drove her directly to the vet, where she had her wounds dressed. Lesley discussed the incident with the vet, but as no one had seen the precursor to what had happened, they decided that Amber had probably overstepped her status, and Scruffy was just delivering some discipline, when things got out of hand. Nevertheless, we committed to watching the dynamic between the dogs very closely, just to be on the safe side. This proved to be a good thing.

Lesley and I have kept dogs for many years, and through our experience we have developed a good eye for how they are getting along together. Over the next two weeks there was absolutely no indication of any problems approaching; in fact, Amber and Scruffy seemed to have become very friendly together – making what happened next even more shocking.

We were all up on the meadow, where I was throwing a ball for the dogs, and Lesley was walking alongside with Romany, who was getting a little too old for running around. I had probably thrown the ball about twenty times, without any hint of an impending incident. The dogs were all having a grand time running around and playing energetically, but without becoming overexcited. I was at the top of the small hill that sits in the centre of the meadow, when I threw the ball down the slope again and watched the dogs chase after it. Then, right in front of me, I saw Scruffy suddenly change direction and, without any warning attack Amber from the side. In the few seconds it took me to run down the hill, Scruffy had already flipped Amber over and, with teeth digging deeply into her belly, was shaking her like a rag doll. I grabbed hold of Scruffy, gave her a sharp whack on the rump and told her to let go, but her attack only intensified; the screaming and growling was terrible to hear. By using all my strength, I managed to prise her jaws apart with my fingers so that Lesley could rescue Amber, limp and bleeding heavily. As suddenly as the ferocious assault had started, it was over. As if someone had flicked a switch in her head, Scruffy seemed completely calm and normal, except for the blood smeared on her face. Poor Amber had several large rips on her belly, she was bleeding heavily and clearly in shock; fortunately there was a vet on duty at the surgery, who was able to treat her within the hour. She was lucky that nothing was fatally damaged, but she needed several stitches to close her wounds, along with antibiotics to fight any infection from the bites and a big dose of something for the pain and shock. Scruffy was less lucky. She had twice assaulted a smaller dog without any warning, and without my intervention she would surely have killed Amber. We were convinced that Scruffy could no longer be trusted, and it was likely she would attack another dog at some point, or, even worse, a child. Dogs that have a history of violence cannot be offered for rehoming, so, after a long discussion with the vet the decision was clear; she had to be put to sleep. It broke our hearts to do it, but the situation was evidently untenable. Even so, we all cried like babies when the deed was done, particularly as Scruffy licked my hand as she slipped away. It seemed like she was saying, "I'm sorry for what I did, but I just couldn't help myself."

I buried Scruffy on the hill behind the house, taking some comfort from the vet's earlier comments. "Don't feel too bad. If you hadn't rescued her, Scruffy would have been dead six months ago and would never have known the loving home you guys gave her."

True words, but little comfort, even today.

Chapter 12 – In which Nick has a smashing time

Like the wife who only realised that her husband was a drunk, when he came home sober one day, after Scruffy was gone, we noticed a different atmosphere in the house, a sense of calm. Only then did we realise that when Scruffy had been in the room, the other dogs were constantly changing their positions, unable to settle for any length of time. Now that she was gone, they all quickly settled onto their beds and relaxed, perhaps for the first time in months. I was annoyed that I hadn't picked up the warning signs earlier, but it was too late for recriminations; at least now our dogs were all well balanced and happy.

The work on the wing was progressing well, the roof and walls were completed, new windows had been fitted, and I had mixed tons of concrete for the floors in my new cement mixer. Once the building was sealed to the elements, I got busy dividing the large internal space into a granny annex, with a shower room, and added a utility room for the washing machine and tumble dryer. I was thoroughly enjoying myself, building the wooden framework for the plasterboard or "slabs" (as they are called in Ireland) and laying in the wiring and plumbing. There was a real sense of satisfaction to be had from adding quality and value to our home. Also, because I tend to over-engineer things, we could be fairly confident that it was well insulated, and it wouldn't fall over – even if it happened to be hit by a falling asteroid. Although Lesley was keeping busy, creating and tending to the new garden and vegetable plot, and making delicious jams and pickles, she helped with the building work whenever I asked – and sometimes when I didn't. I arrived home from a four day trip to England, to discover that she had taken it upon herself to put a cement render on the new wall of the wing. Neither she nor I had any previous experience of rendering, but she had somehow managed to do a magnificent job; her efforts blended perfectly with the existing lumpy render. I asked how she had done it.

"Well, I am quite good at icing cakes, so I figured that the technique would be much the same, only on a bigger scale!"

I was delighted; not only had she saved me several days of work if I had done the job myself, but more likely had saved the thick end of a thousand euro in wages for a plasterer to do the job. The time saved was not to be wasted; water had started to leak into the studio again, so I took a break from building the wing to re-investigate.

Clearly, the only way to find the source of the problem was to remove the internal plasterboard wall at the south end of the house and trace the leak. The result was a little shocking and became an early example of some of the shoddy building work we would uncover as the renovations continued. There were two large windows in the south wall of the upstairs bedroom, separated by an eighteen inch concrete pillar. Normally windows are securely screwed to the external walls of a house and then sealed with mastic to prevent any water intrusion, but the walls above the studio were constructed from reinforced concrete, which can be difficult to drill into. Rather than buying a decent drill bit to attach the windows securely against the winter rain and gales that routinely lash the south end of the house, the builder had simply attached the windows to the wooden frame of the internal wall, then filled the remaining two inch gap with some old newspaper and a bit of render. The repair had lasted for just eighteen months before the water slowly penetrated; then it began pouring through, almost unabated, soaking the floorboards and the walls in the room below. Adding to the problem, the cement render on the external wall was "blown," meaning that it had detached from the brickwork, allowing water to seep in and making the internal wall damp. That weekend I had hired some aluminium scaffolding, so that I could knock off the blown render and allow Lesley (my "builder's apprentice") access to set about doing the repairs. My first plan with the windows was to refit them correctly onto the external wall, but that was going to be a bit tricky as they were slightly too large for the opening, probably because they had been purchased second-hand. Also, they were old leaded windows with thick chunky frames that didn't let much light through. Then I had the inspirational idea of simply removing the centre pillar and fitting one large window, which would have modern double glazing, provide better insulation and let in more light. I discussed my idea with Lesley and after checking out the price we placed the order, and I set to work preparing the hole.

Although it was going to be a couple of weeks before the new window would be ready to be fitted, I decided to get everything ready anyway and then temporarily refit the old windows while we waited. To ensure that the new window fitted correctly, without causing further leaks, the old render had to be knocked off, the centre pillar removed and a new concrete window sill fitted. Mostly things went along swimmingly, except for that blasted centre pillar. This turned out to be made of solid concrete, reinforced with steel rebar – a slight case of builders' overkill, as there was nothing for the pillar to support, except for a lintel and the guttering above. If I hadn't already paid for the new window, I would have just refitted the old ones and shut the door on the damn thing – that pillar seemed to be impervious to damage, the pick axe just bounced off and my drill bits bent as if made of plastic. After several hours using an electric chisel and a disc cutter, which sprayed everything for fifty yards with dust and sparks, I managed to cut through the top of the pillar. Luckily, before moving to Ireland, I had bought two sets of purple motor racing overalls in a sale for the princely sum of £10. Not only were they an excellent value purchase, but the bright colour would make me easy to spot in the rubble should I ever cock up the construction. More importantly, they are fireproof, which is a good thing, as I seem to set myself on fire – a lot. After almost a full day of hacking away, I had managed to cut a three inch slot through the cement at the bottom of the pillar, exposing the four pieces of rebar that were still holding the pillar stubbornly upright and in place. My plan was to cut through the two rebars on the inside of the pillar and then, by bending the two outer bars, lay the pillar onto the scaffolding, prior to cutting the remaining rebar. I would then use a couple of stout planks to safely slide the pillar down onto the ground below for removal to the quarry.

At first everything went swimmingly; I used my diamond edged disc to cut the first two rebars and then I laid the pillar down onto the top platform of the scaffolding. But as I finally cut through the second set of rebars, there was a sudden sound like a freight train driving through a lorry, as the scaffolding folded like a cheap lawn chair and disappeared in a cloud of dust and bent aluminium. Our dogs would often sit and attentively watch me working, but luckily they were at the other end of the house, sitting and attentively watching Lesley putting food into their dog bowls, so no lives were lost. I ran outside, swearing like a Glaswegian squaddie on a stag do, to survey the damage. It wasn't a pretty sight. The scaffolding was comprehensively wrecked – looking like a Chinese knockoff of a Transformer toy with rickets, which had been dropped from a passing spaceship. On the positive side, the window pillar was out and sitting, undamaged, in the dent it had carved in the vegetable garden. I did my best to unbend and reconstruct the scaffolding, but in the end I had to admit defeat and phone the hire company to report the damage. I must have caught the manager on a good day, because he commended my honesty and gracefully accepted my grovelling apology, without charging me for the damage.

Although we had agreed to allow a local farmer to graze his cattle on our land, we delayed letting them in for as long as was practical, so that the wild flowers could bloom and seed. During the spring and summer of 2005 our meadow became a sea of fragrant colour, alive with bees and butterflies. There are daisies, clover, poppies, tansy and hundreds of other flowers, including beautiful wild orchids. Each summer, with the moor on one side, the forest at the back and the grass on all of the other fields already cut for winter silage by the local farmers, our little meadow becomes an oasis for insects and wildlife. The grass and flowers can get up to waist height and are delightful to walk through, even when the dew makes your jeans as wet as if you had been standing in the pond. I love to take long walks on the moor with my dogs, particularly on those early mornings when the sky is a pale blue, the air is fresh and the valley below is still shrouded in thick mist. Even though the moorland seems barren and lifeless, there is actually a good deal of wildlife to see if you keep your eyes open. Because of the generally harsh conditions on the moor, every sheltered nook and cranny will become a little "micro climate," like an island of colour on a beige ocean, as these sheltered hollows are exploited by nature. Even the seemingly consistent colour of the moorland is misleading; watch it throughout the seasons and you may notice how it subtly changes. As the winter snows gradually clear, the moor appears brown with the dormant grasses and flecked with areas of black, where the peat has been exposed by the goats, cattle and (sadly) motorbikes. In spring the grasses start to sprout, along with the heather; then the fragrant gorse begins to bud, adding light greens and bright yellows to the palette. By the summer the bracken, ferns and bramble have made much of the moor a rich green, interspaced with violet and white heather. In the autumn the fruits and berries have added red and purple, and the wild cotton heads have created a sea of waving white along the sheltered slopes. Without any doubt, the moor is a strangely attractive place, seemingly desolate, isolated and unchanging, but at the same time alive with change and colour – rural Ireland at its most beautiful.

After Lesley's car crash, as a result of being run off the road by some idiot in a speeding 4x4, the doctor gave her some strong medication for the resulting back and neck pain. A few days later she became unwell.

At first we thought that she had just gone down with a bad dose of flu, but she soon developed a severe rash and a fever. Whenever Lesley is sick, she will go to bed and sleep deeply for several hours and then awake refreshed and magically healed; on this occasion, however, her symptoms gradually worsened. After she had spent two days in bed, sleeping almost constantly, I decided that action was required. When I brought Lesley a bowl of soup and attempted to get her to drink some much needed fluids, I realised that she was confused and worryingly unresponsive, even after I opened the curtains and got her to sit up in bed. In the harsh light of day, it was obvious that her skin and eyes were shockingly yellow and, ignoring her slurred objections, I swiftly packed her into the car and drove straight to the doctor's surgery. We were allowed to jump the queue and, minutes later, we were back in the car and on the way to Limerick General Hospital. Lesley was diagnosed with severe liver failure, probably caused by a reaction to medication, and immediately admitted for tests and observation.

Over the next eight days she became desperately weak and unwell, as the toxins washed out of her system and her liver gradually started to heal. Every day, I made the two hour round-trip to the hospital; sometimes I made the journey twice, just to sit and hold her hand while she slept, or chat quietly when she was awake. For several days she made no discernable progress towards getting better, and I feared that my wife might be slipping away from me. On many of those journeys, I cried all of the way home, broken hearted that I had been unable to protect her. However, the human body is a phenomenal machine and able to heal itself, given enough time, fuel and space. In time, Lesley turned the corner, and after several weeks she was discharged into my care. She was still rather yellow, very weak and immensely tired, but at least she was getting better. Once at home she could eat properly, rest as much as she needed and, most importantly, sleep without being disturbed. Although it had been a close run thing and she remained unwell for a while, everything worked out fine in the end – except for her little car, may it rust in peace. My lovely wife continued feeling very run-down and unhappy for a long time and clearly needed some expert help to cheer her up, so I asked our daughter to come over for a surprise visit. We conspired together to keep the arrangements secret and I went alone to collect Joanne from the airport, under the pretext of meeting with a client. Two hours later, when Lesley saw Joanne walk into the house, they both instantly burst into floods of tears; it was an exquisite moment and cheered everyone up immensely. Joanne could only stay for the weekend as she was busy at work, but we all had lots of fun and a lovely time, just lounging around the house, playing board games and enjoying each other's company. At one point as I sat quietly, watching my wife and daughter chatting happily together, my chest constricted painfully as I imagined how dreadfully different things could have been.

Early on Sunday morning, Joanne and I decided to drive down to "Silver Sands," the beautiful beach at the head of Lough Graney, so that we could take the dogs for a long walk. It was Joanne's first visit to the lough, and she was amazed by how beautiful and unspoilt it was. We thoroughly enjoyed this quiet time walking together, despite the biting cold wind. Lady and Kia were having a fantastic time looping about in the shallow water, unsuccessfully chasing after the waterfowl and running like wild children through the woods, but still keeping us within sight. As usual Romany plodded along behind and Amber ran frantically back and forth, chasing sticks and woofing crossly if we didn't throw quickly enough. Sometimes Lady and Kia would decide to join in the stick chasing, causing things to get a little too boisterous, so I took to throwing the sticks out into the water, in an effort to calm them down a bit. It worked perfectly; Lady and Kia happily crashed into the water with a mighty splash and paddled out to recover the stick, while Amber was left behind, able to chase a second stick without risking any further unpleasantness. We repeated the stick throwing exercise several times, until the dogs were looking tired and we were getting cold and hungry. As we walked back towards the car, I threw one final stick for the always energetic Amber. But this time she paddled in the wrong direction, towards a small branch that was sticking out of the water about fifteen metres out. The branch was bobbing up and down with the waves, rather like a fishing float, and was an irresistible challenge to the tiny dog. Joanne and I laughed as Amber paddled determinedly against the waves, pausing occasionally to check her bearings, before paddling on reinvigorated as she neared her target. After nearly a minute of tenacious swimming, Amber grasped the stick in her tiny mouth and turned for home, cheered on by our shouts of encouragement from the shore. Unfortunately, despite her best efforts, Amber could only swim in little circles; the stick she had captured was attached to a submerged tree, washed downstream by the swollen river above. Initially we giggled helplessly as she gamely paddled in circles, clearly confused by her inability to progress towards the shore. But terriers are tenacious, and Amber was unable to admit defeat, so she continued paddling relentlessly, ignoring our shouts to "leave" the stick. Soon it became clear that the cold and exertion were taking a toll on the little dog. I could see that Amber was in danger of sinking, and the stick she had initially refused to let go of, had become the only thing keeping her afloat. Joanne had just joked that I was going to have to rescue my little dog, when some water lapped into Amber's face and she started to choke; moments later she started to sink. There was nothing else I could do – so I threw off my coat and waded in to rescue her. The icy water came to chest height and was so devastatingly cold that it took my breath away and shrivelled my man bits in an instant. I reached Amber just as she went under for the third time; she literally threw herself into my arms, coughing and shivering uncontrollably. Back on shore Joanne took charge of the pathetic bundle, wrapping Amber inside her coat for warmth, and then she laughed at my predicament, while I poured water out of my wellies and debated whether to undress, or just drive home in my wet clothes.

As we trudged along the forest path back towards the car, with Amber keeping warm inside Joanne's coat and Romany refusing any invitation to walk faster as she plodded along behind, I looked forward to a roaring fire, a hot cup of tea and getting myself dry and warm. The other two dogs were paralleling our path somewhere in the trees and, with timing worthy of an evil genius, Lady decided that this would be a good moment to go hunting for the first time – hotly pursued by Kia. I had never before heard our foxhound go into full "hunting mode," but I can assure you that the sound is devastatingly awful – particularly if it comes from deep in the woods and you have no idea what has happened. Suddenly the air was filled with horrifically desperate yelping and squealing, supplemented at odd intervals by Kia's frantic barking. The sound was so awful and unexpected that I could only imagine our terrified dog, caught in a deer trap, while being set on fire and repeatedly startled by evil monsters in ghost costumes. We know now that once Lady gets scent of some prey, regardless of whether it is real or imagined, she will set off with her nose down and tail up; yelping loudly, she will embark on an illogical serpentine chase, oblivious to any obstructions, dangers or attempts to call her back. She will always return, occasionally within an hour, muddy, bloody and panting, with a bedraggled Kia in tow, who is usually decorated with samples of twigs and bramble from each hedge and bush that they have visited along the way. Sometimes I have seen Lady running up and down the same field for several minutes and circling like a runaway lawnmower, although there was clearly nothing to chase – and never had been. She once set off along the forest path, like a policeman chasing an escaping jewel thief, only to reappear some minutes later being chased by a herd of red deer and a large stag, with the most magnificent antlers. As she ran past me she showed no sign of embarrassment or apology, even though I had to throw myself into a ditch to avoid being trampled by her wild-eyed pursuers. On another occasion I watched Lady running excitedly back-and-forth between fields, repeatedly crossing the path I was on and yelping ever more frantically, while the fox she was chasing sat a few feet away from me, watching the entertainment – before walking away, shaking its head in obvious disgust.

After seventy minutes of pointless calling, encouraged only by the distant prospect of getting warm and dry, and occasional glimpses of Lady and Kia as they splashed through the shallows in pursuit of a bird, we gave up all hope of recovering the dogs and headed back to the car – only to find our delinquent duo waiting patiently for us, with tails wagging as if to say, "Ah – there you are!" Seething, shivering and swearing, I drove home sitting on an old shopping bag that I had found in the boot. Lesley was unimpressed with the tale of my bravery in valiantly rescuing the little dog from the raging river, but she laughed enthusiastically as Joanne described how I had waded into the freezing lake to recover our stupid mutt. So I received neither a medal nor any sympathy for my heroics. On the other hand, Amber is a short dog with an equally short memory; she was none the worse for her adventure, but delighted in the additional attention of a rubdown with a fluffy towel and a bowl of warm milk. I was pleased to remove my cold wet clothes and stand in a hot shower until some feeling returned to my frozen feet, and some bit of the river smell had gone. After the weekend, Joanne had to return to England, and there was again much hugging and crying as we left her at the airport.

Back at the house, Lesley went full steam ahead on the gardening, only taking breaks to help me with the building work and to pick fruit for jam making. I had finally finished building the wing, which is really a granny annex, comprising a small bedroom and sitting room or office, a bathroom with a shower, and a utility room that could double as a small kitchen. The original plan was for us to live temporarily in the wing, while I completed the renovations in the main part of the house, and afterwards to keep it as a den or self-contained flat for visitors, tourists, or elderly relatives. In the end we made occasional use of the kitchen area and the bathroom, but only when there was no other alternative, and so, for the most part, even during the worst of the construction work, we carried on living in the main part of the house. I think that this was so that we remained constantly aware of the need to keep chipping away at the job, even if it meant living with dust and dirt and constantly needing to climb over or under obstructions. Had we moved into the comfort of the wing, it is possible that the renovation could have become a much longer job, being "out of sight and out of mind." One acquaintance of ours admitted that he and his wife had lived without a bathroom for seven years, because they had moved into a mobile home during the renovation of their house. By the beginning of 2006 I had started work on the kitchen, which, like most things, was turning out to be a much bigger job than I had expected. To turn three stories into two, thereby creating useable rooms with decent ceiling heights, I needed to remove the upper two floors and the spiral staircase. This posed some problems, as all of the heating and plumbing was located in this section of the house. Also the metal staircase was thirty feet high. It was connected to each floor, as well as the roof, and could conceivably have been the only thing stopping it all from falling down. After much head scratching, I propped the floor up with a few bits of wood and, starting at the top, bravely set about reducing the staircase into moveable sections with my disc cutter. Within a few hours I had set myself on fire three times, but had reduced the staircase to a pile of steel bits, piled in the garden, ready for the scrap metal dealer to collect.

The next stage was a little more complicated. After I had installed temporary lighting and sockets and then stripped out hundreds of feet of old electrical wiring, I started to remove the old floors, rafters and ceilings. The hot and cold water tanks were situated on two floors, both of which were to be replaced with a single floor, and although the tanks would ultimately return to the same locations, only several feet higher, they needed to be relocated temporarily. So that we would still have access to water and heating, I first constructed half of the new first floor three feet above the existing first floor and then add a temporary "H" frame, to hold the hot water cylinder, with a cold water tank above it. Only then could I remove the old floors, where the tanks previously were, and continue construction on the new floor level. It sounds simple, but it was a lot of extra work, plumbing and re-plumbing the system as the new floors went in; for many weeks parts of the house looked like a cross between a power station and a William Heath Robinson drawing. However, it all worked out, after a fashion, and once the upper floor was complete and I could start removing the kitchen ceiling. There was an expensive polished wooden floor in the kitchen, which we had hoped to keep, but the "spur marks" left by the previous cowboy builders would again ruin my plans – although on this occasion it proved to be fortuitous. Almost a quarter of the original kitchen space was taken up by a walk-in larder, made up from rough bits of wood and some planking. The larder was a shaky looking affair, ready to fall down at the first shove and painted bright purple into the bargain; it needed to be removed. But on closer inspection, I was horrified to discover that the lovely wooden flooring had been laid around the larder, rather than under it. It only took twenty minutes to carefully remove the purple monstrosity, but its absence revealed a gaping hole in the wooden floor which could not be patched. So, with no alternative left, I had to rip the floor up as well. Predictably, the wood had been nailed and glued so comprehensively that I could only save a few pieces, which I later used to patch some damage to the sitting room floor; the rest of the kitchen flooring ended its life as firewood. The fortuitous part of this frustrating episode was that, as soon as the protective plastic sheeting under the wooden floor was removed, the kitchen started to smell like an old oil tank. With a little detective work it soon became eye-wateringly obvious that the culprit was the small, but easily fixed, oil leak underneath the Rayburn, which I had rectified on my first night in the house. Although my repair was sound, over the preceding years, many gallons of kerosene must have escaped and run underneath the plastic, soaking unnoticed into the concrete floor below. The smell was never going to dissipate and I knew that the kerosene would gradually degrade the concrete, so it had to come out as well. It took several days of hard digging to remove the concrete floor by hand. During that time, the smell and fumes were so appalling that we had to keep all of the doors and windows open. Even then, I flinched each time there was a spark from my pick axe, imagining the misunderstanding should the fumes combust like a bomb, scattering bits of Glenmadrie and Nick all across this once Republican part of County Clare. Once the concrete floor was replaced and tiled, I was able to remove the old roof joists, with the enthusiastic application of my chainsaw – which was a quicker method, but unfortunately filled the house with exhaust fumes. After just an hour of cutting, pulling and swearing, the old joists were out, and we had a lovely high ceiling in our kitchen, almost three feet higher than before.

One of the nice things about doing renovations yourself, apart from the cost saving, is the ability to modify your plans as your wife changes her mind about things like: the number and location of electrical sockets, the placement of kitchen units and what size of fridge we need. Although the stone walls throughout the house looked delightfully rustic, they were cold to the touch, giving easy passage to mice and drafts and were so lumpy as to be completely impractical for hanging kitchen units. So I had decided I needed to insulate and dry-line the kitchen walls. To create a kitchen that was exactly the right size to house the kitchen units that we had bought and stored the previous winter, I had to build the walls perfectly square, vertical and exactly the right distance apart, as well as correctly positioning additional supports to hold the heavy wall mounted units. I had just completed the wooden framework, run through the wiring for sockets and lights and was well into attaching the plasterboard slabs when I heard an innocent little voice beside me.

"Nick? I've been thinking," Lesley said, sweetly.

A cold chill ran down my back. "Oh dear! – Err, I mean, oh good! What were you thinking?" I asked with trepidation.

"Well, here's the thing. The Rayburn is nice to have, it looks lovely, but it's not very practical for cooking on – particularly if you just need to boil an egg or something."

"Okay... so what did you have in mind?" I asked with further trepidation, whilst trying to remember the last time we had eaten boiled eggs.

She gave me a bright smile, "I think we need to buy a gas cooker."

I gave a silent sigh of relief. "I agree, it would be an excellent idea; unfortunately we are twenty miles from the nearest gas main."

"That's not a problem!" she told me triumphantly. "I've checked, and the cooker I like is available with bottled gas."

"Oh good," I said with a stiff smile. And then I set about redesigning the kitchen.

Actually it turned out to be one of her better ideas – I think that makes three now! After a trip to a well-known Australian retailer in Limerick and a goodly amount of measuring and head-scratching, I was able to rearrange the kitchen design. Now our new gas cooker is fitted against an external wall, providing easy access for the gas pipe and in a position that works well for cooking. The only compromise in the kitchen layout was the loss of sixty centimetres of worktop space and a three drawer unit, which would find a good home in my new workshop some years later. The bottled gas cooker has since saved us a small fortune, as it is quicker and more efficient than the Rayburn for most of our cooking needs and along with electricity, oil and the wood stove, provides a fourth method of boiling a kettle – which is a good thing to have, in such a remote location.

Once the walls were completed and the room was decorated in a light pastel colour and then thoroughly cleaned, it was time to start fitting the new kitchen units. On any renovation project, although the knocking down and rebuilding phase can be fun, or at least satisfying, I have always felt a great sense of excitement when the final installation begins; rather like reaching familiar territory at the conclusion of a long journey, you sense that at last the end is in sight. Given our limited budget, the kitchen was inevitably a self-assembly type, but of a surprisingly decent quality. Provided you follow the directions and apply a little common sense, fitting a flat-pack kitchen yourself is not an especially difficult job; and in this case, I would be working with square and true walls – which makes life a lot easier. Because it was still in the flat-packs, I planned to move all of the boxes into our spacious conservatory where I could figure out what everything was, before I started to put the units together. Once the shells were assembled, I could move them into the kitchen and secure them all in place, before adding the doors, worktops and trim.

By this time, the kitchen units had been in storage in the studio for almost two years, and I got a nasty shock when I went to move the boxes for the first time since they were delivered. Although they were well wrapped in plastic and carefully stacked, in a part of the studio that seemed to be dry, many of the boxes were clearly very damp and mouldy. I feared that our kitchen was ruined before it had ever been fitted. Luckily the damage was confined to the packaging and apart from needing a good wash with some cleaning solution to remove the mildew, the units were unmarked. As always seems to be the case, the assembly instructions bore little resemblance to the process required to successfully assemble the units and were about as helpful as a telephone help line. I suspected that the person who lovingly crafted the exotic work of fiction, which masqueraded as the assembly instructions, had actually translated them correctly from the original Klingon, but had accidently used the wrong pictures. To add to the entertainment, a partially illiterate and completely innumerate drunk had obviously been recruited to count and bag the small accessories required for each unit. He, or perhaps she, had obviously panicked under the strain of the new job and had resorted to randomly stuffing great handfuls of irrelevant screws and hinges into plastic bags, which had somehow ended up with my kitchen. After I had successfully completed assembly, even adding some extra screws for good measure, I still had almost a kilo of nails, hinges and screws left over. There were also dozens of obscure little metal thingamajigs that had a screw at one end, a lump of plastic at the other and a strange bump in the middle; they refused to fit anywhere in the kitchen, and may have originally been intended for the Large Hadron Collider. Not to be outdone, the "kitchen design expert" in the DIY shop had somehow managed to calculate that my kitchen would require twice as much base board as I had kitchen units – but only half as much pelmet. After such a long time there was no chance of getting the shop to correct the error, so I had to buy the additional pelmet, which was fortunately still available, as a gut wrenchingly expensive special order. Perhaps one day I can sell my collection of surplus screws and unidentifiable widgets to pay for the missing parts.

By mid-year the kitchen was finally finished and we could take a few moments out of our relentless schedule to admire a job well-done. The old kitchen was cramped, dark, cold and rather too well ventilated, with a low ceiling that rained dust and dead spiders onto the food below. Now, with an eight-foot high ceiling, well insulated walls, unpretentious white units, black marble worktops and cream floor tiles, the kitchen had become warm, bright and simplistically functional. With the addition of a large pine table and four chairs, it was now the welcoming heart of our home. Lesley was delighted with her new kitchen and I was quietly proud of my work.

Chapter 13 – In which we have visitors

Now that the kitchen was completed, it was time to begin work on the room above. This was actually still two rooms, on separate floors, and was being used as my workshop and a place to store tools. My plan was to make the space into one large bedroom, with a high ceiling, fitted wardrobes and lots of natural light, courtesy of three large windows. Because of the layout of the plumbing, the room would also need to house the hot water tank, in a traditional airing cupboard (called a "hot press" in Ireland) as well as the cold water tank, which I planned to hide in a false loft. The house is similar in layout to a Dutch barn ¬– a long narrow building, a single room deep, with windows on both sides. In the original upstairs layout, the rooms above the kitchen and sitting room were connected with doors in the centre of the house, exactly the same as the rooms below. We were quite happy with the design of the downstairs rooms, where you had to go through one room to get to the next, but we wanted to modify the upstairs to add a connecting corridor, to provide privacy for each bedroom and to act as an escape route in the event of a fire. The corridor upstairs would run along the entire length of the northwest side of the house, connecting the two master bedrooms at either end, with a new centre guest room, the bathroom and the staircase. It was a nice idea, but to connect the new corridor with the bedroom above the kitchen, the original centre door into that room needed to be blocked up and a new doorway would have to be created in the corner. That sounds easy enough, but the connecting wall where the door had to go was stone built and over four feet thick; I am not a builder and I was starting to think I was getting out of my depth. Luckily my ignorance and pig-headedness is sometimes more dominant than my caution and common-sense, so in the end I pressed on, regardless of my construction inadequacies. By climbing into the tiny loft above the middle of the house and squirming, snake like, through the ancient cobwebs and mouse droppings, I managed to examine the offending wall from above. I was pleased to discover that it was no longer a supporting wall – the task of cutting the new doorway was going to be easier than I first thought. Although the wall between the new kitchen and the sitting room was once the external north wall, after the house was extended it became an internal wall and, since the roofline was raised by several feet many years ago, the top of the wall was no longer being used to support the roof. So rather than having to tunnel my way through four feet of possibly unstable stone, propping, shoring and adding supports as I went, all I needed to do now was to remove the stone from the top down until I had created a new doorway.

This good news made the job something that I could take on with reasonable confidence, but the bad news was that, by starting twelve feet further up and working down through the four foot thick wall, I was about to remove a lot of stone, a hell of a lot of stone – all by hand. Lesley informed me that carting so much stone and associated dust through the entire length of the house upstairs, then back in the opposite direction downstairs, through her new kitchen, the porch and out through the front door was not an acceptable option. I had seen long chutes used on building sites as a method of channelling waste into rubbish skips, so I decided to try and do something similar. At the north end of the house there was a tall narrow window with a conveniently placed opening at the bottom, about a metre square, and by nailing together some old joists and a bit of left over chipboard, I managed to construct a fairly decent slide. The window was only fifteen feet from the wall I was demolishing, so now all I had to do was to remove each stone, carry or slide it across to the window and let gravity help it down the chute to the driveway below. One strange quirk I have noticed about the construction of these old stone built houses in Ireland is the tendency to put the very largest stones at the top of the walls. I am sure there is some sound building related reason for this, but I have yet to figure it out. It seems like a lot of trouble to put such massive blocks of granite or sandstone, at the highest point of the wall, and (I can assure you) it's an absolute bugger trying to get them down again! The overall construction method used in these old houses is much the same as that used by the Romans, thousands of years ago. The wall is actually two parallel walls of stone, close together, the gaps filled with sand, mortar, small stones and the occasional dead mouse. The filling acts as a binding agent, spreading the load and keeping the entire wall stable. Taking the wall down was a dirty and somewhat dangerous process because, as each stone was pried out, it was accompanied by a shower of dust and sand or, just when you didn't expect it, a small avalanche of larger rocks. I had escaped most of the landslides with nothing worse than a face full of dirt, and a few dents in the waste wood I had laid to protect the new flooring; however, when a huge block fell unseen from the top of the wall, it trapped my right hand, slicing through the skin of my little finger like a guillotine The stone was far too heavy to lift with one hand, the pry bar was inevitably just out of reach and Lesley was away in Limerick doing some shopping. I was stuck. With great care I managed to wiggle my way free, but it took almost fifteen minutes and by then my finger was completely numb, which made washing the wound less painful than it would otherwise have been. It seems that every cloud has a silver lining!

As a DIY builder I have developed extensive experience of what can go wrong when you are doing any building work; usually what can go wrong, will go wrong. In Ireland this is sometimes known as "Murphy's law". In the same spirit, "Nick's rules" for building cock-ups state the following:

1.   You almost only ever bang your head when not wearing a hard hat.

2.   If you are wearing head protection, then your hard hat will inevitably collide with a low beam, jarring your neck so that, in your surprise, you will drop the rock that you were carrying.

3.   A dropped rock will only land on your foot when you are wearing an old pair of trainers.

4.   If you have remembered to wear your steel toed boots, a dropped rock will always miss your foot, preferring to hit you on the knee, or shin, or both.

5.   If you miss a nail when swinging hard with a hammer, you will always hit your thumb.

6. If you swing softly with a hammer, the nail will always shoot sideways and hit you in the eye.

7. Your last nail will always bend as you attempt to hammer it in.

8. A hammer, when accidentally dropped, will strike the least protected part of your body, usually your knee, shin or big toe and sometimes all three.

9. A dropped hammer will only miss striking an unprotected part of your body if, as an alternative, it can hit your new ceramic toilet.

10. Plumbing joints will only ever leak after they are concealed in a wall and the decorating is completed.

11. You only ever run out of something that you desperately need, just after the shops have shut.

12. An electrical wire will only ever be "live" if it is touched accidentally.

13. If you need thirty feet of something to complete a job, there is no need to measure – you will only have twenty-nine!

14. When you have crawled to the deepest part of the loft and noticed a huge, hairy spider, which is just inches from your nose, your torch will instantly cease to work.

15. You will never need something that is just out of reach when someone nearby is available to pass it to you.

16. The telephone will only ring when you have reached the top of the ladder.

17. Your ladder will only ever slip when your wife is no longer holding it.

18. The most important information in the DIY manual is always on the page you didn't read.

19. The clearest and most helpful instructions are always provided with things that any idiot could figure out unassisted.

20. The most expensive and fragile things always come without any instructions at all, or with directions so misleading that you will accidentally cut two feet from the wrong end and then have to wait

six weeks for another one to be delivered from China – rather than returning to the shop and admitting to the smug shop assistant that you really don't know what you are doing.

The gap in the wall gradually became large enough to be called a doorway and the pile of stone in the driveway had started to resemble a mountain – but not for long. I returned from a weekend visit to England, to discover that Lesley had shifted the lot – about fifty wheelbarrow loads; not bad for a petite fifty year old housewife with a bad back! She had kept the larger stones for edging the flowerbeds and repairing garden walls and then used the rest to fill in the potholes in the farm track at the back of the house. It was an almost super-human feat as some of the potholes were more than fifty yards away and the ground was rough and steeply sloping. I am happy to admit that I was suitably impressed and very grateful for the help.

Although the English and the Irish share a common language, sometimes there are differences in pronunciation which can be quaint and humorous – but there are also variations in definition and application that can cause problems. In County Clare some people pronounce a double "t" as "th" so butter becomes "buther" and batter, "bather." I have noticed that, somewhat like many of the Poles we have met since Poland joined the EU in 2004, many outwardly well-educated Irish men casually use "fuck" as a precursor to both verbs and adjectives, but reserve the official Irish swear word "feck" for polite profanity.

I once nonchalantly described someone's unsuccessful attempt at a repairing some equipment as "shoddy," which in England means "not well built, or not using the best materials" – only to be informed that in Ireland it is a dreadful insult, meaning "work that is worse than excrement." Similarly in England, you may get away with saying, "Don't be a git" (a puerile person), but in Ireland it has the potential to earn you a split lip. One day, Lesley was chatting in a local shop, when she lovingly described our dog Amber, as being "a little toe-rag" (an endearingly silly dog), only to discover that the other customers were staring at her open mouthed. It seems that in Ireland it means something considerably less endearing; this was ironic, given what happened the next day...

Lesley was strolling along the farm track at the back of the house, returning from walking our dogs, when she encountered an extremely large black bull – five feet high and six feet wide, with ominous looking horns and testicles like two basketballs in a sack. This two thousand-pound behemoth was ambling its way up the hill, clearly on the scent of some fertile and willing cows in the fields behind the house. For a moment Lesley considered standing her ground, in the mistaken belief that the bull, wanting to avoid confrontation, would return meekly to the field from whence it had escaped. It quickly became frighteningly obvious that the bull was not to be deterred, either by the wildly yapping dogs or the mad English lady – who proved to be surprisingly spritely for her age, as she dived over a nearby fence. A short while later, our friendly but geographically distant neighbour Jim walked along the lane with three of his children in tow, looking for his lost bull. Spying us in our garden, he stopped by the gate and waved politely.

"Hello, Sir. How are you and missus, Sir, today?"

"Fine Jim, we're both just fine – how are you?"

"Ah we're grand. Fecked off though, me bull's escaped again. Have ye seen it?" he asked.

"What colour was it?" I teased.

"It's a big black one, it is. Went right through the fence again. After the cows it is."

Lesley chipped in. "Yes Jim, it came up here an hour ago. I tried to stop it, but it didn't want to know." She smiled, "I had to jump over the fence to get away."

"Oh ye don't want to get in his way," Jim confided, "He's a big black ….." and then Jim used an impolite word reserved for a woman's reproductive organs, but delivered with virulence more appropriate to a Glaswegian football hooligan, renaming the judge who has unjustly sentenced him to twenty years hard labour for an unpaid parking ticket.

I heard Lesley take a sharp intake of breath, "Really?" she enquired with a fixed smile.

"Oh yes," Jim replied, and then he proceeded to describe his bull's Houdini like escapology, coloured with generous applications of the same expletive.

As each profanity landed, I watched Lesley's eyes become ever wider and her smile more fixed, until she looked like a waxworks model about to topple over backwards. Slowly she raised her arm, pointed a shaking finger towards a distant field and mumbled, "he went that way!"

"Ah that's grand," Jim said, giving us another friendly wave. "See ye soon!" And with that he set off in pursuit of his bovine escapologist, with his children following along behind.

Lesley went indoors for a lie down.

Over the years we have made many friends here in Ireland, but strangely, very few seem to be Irish. Although we have many Irish acquaintances, most of our new friends are, like us, foreign nationals, sometimes called "blow-ins" by the locals; though "blow-in" is an accepted label for anyone, from anywhere, who has been living in the same location for less than thirty years. We believe that there are two reasons why Lesley and I have so few Irish friends. First, although we have always found the Irish to be hugely friendly, they are less inclined to actually be your "friend" – unless you happen to be related by marriage or birth. This may seem to be a little strange, particularly given the reputation for affability that the Irish have throughout the world, but in Ireland they appear to form close-knit circles of friendship that are difficult to break into, particularly for outsiders. Incidentally, I have detected little, if any, real xenophobia here, but for a Clare man, someone from Cork or Galway is as much an "outsider" as an Englishman, a German, or a Martian, and the reverse probably applies to the Cork or Galway man. Secondly, particularly in such a remote area, the communities revolve around farming, the pub, the church and the schools; if you don't attend the livestock mart, have children of school age, regularly visit the pub or the church, then you are unlikely to have a large circle of Irish friends. Apart from my good friends from work, who are all Irish and the very nicest people you could wish to know, we have met most of our friends when walking our dogs, or by rescuing passing walkers who were corralled by our pack of unruly dogs. Reflecting the international nature of the local residents, our friends come from as far afield as America, Germany, England and Australia.

Of course not every passing walker appreciates the attention they may receive from our dogs. Although our little band of canine ninjas are fundamentally friendly and not at all aggressive, they see their job in life as protectors of the territory – a task that they undertake with joyful enthusiasm. In an effort to encourage some "couch potatoes" to get out and see the countryside, a local rambling group arranged a bank holiday weekend walk in the area around Glenmadrie. To add to the fun, someone decided that it would be interesting to take in the sights, by marching fifty or so unsuspecting individuals along the path at the front of my land. In an effort to keep them on track, somebody had helpfully put up a cardboard arrow with "walk this way" written on it. Knowing the enthusiasm with which our dogs would greet a group of fifty tired and bedraggled strangers, I had half a mind to add a second sign just opposite the house that said "and now run!" The dogs stayed in the house for most of that weekend.

I wouldn't want to give the impression that the house is anything other than remote and quiet; we have very few visitors other than our friends and family. In the last eight years the only uninvited callers have been the postman, the nice old fellow who reads the electric meter, a census taker, one politician, two Jehovah's witnesses, a policeman who was lost and two separate people who had previously lived at the house when they were children and wanted to see how things have changed. The most frequent callers would be members of the local wildlife, some welcome, some not so much.

We know that some years ago, one of the previous owners used to farm goats at the house, selling milk and cheese to the locals. The remains of the milking parlour was still visible in one of the old out-houses and the dogs frequently find goat bones buried around the place – at least we hope they are goat bones. Feral goats are quite a common sight in the woods and on the cliffs overlooking the moor, but they are shy creatures, particularly if you are with a group of boisterous dogs. So we seldom get to see the goats up close – except for the day when I discovered a large Billy goat, just sitting in the middle of our driveway. Judging from his calm and inquisitive demeanour, we presumed that he had previously been head of the original herd that once lived on our land and had simply decided to pay us a visit. I have never found goats and sheep to be particularly appealing creatures, perhaps it is the odd shaped pupils that give them a slightly alien expression, but this fellow was truly magnificent. Physically very large, with a long grey coat, he wore on his head the biggest set of goat "antlers" I have ever seen; almost like an old style television aerial, each of his horns came out horizontally fully three feet, before branching upwards for another foot and a half. Including his head, the span of his horns was easily seven feet; if we could have tamed him, we would have had a unique and interesting way of drying our laundry. Despite our best efforts to make friends, he seemed to view us with some disappointment, and after a little while he gave a disillusioned "huff" and casually walked away. Occasionally when walking across the moor, we will spy him in the far distance, marshalling his harem toward safer ground, but the visit to our land still remains a solitary affair.

Some of the local farmers have a somewhat relaxed attitude to fences, boundaries and road safety when it comes to grazing their cattle. Sometimes it seems like they just open the gates and with a merry wave and a shout of "off you go," they send their cows out to forage for their own food. Certainly it is a good idea when driving to anticipate a herd of unsupervised cattle just around the next corner. Certain cows seem particularly adept at getting into my meadow, especially when they have eaten all of the spring grass in their own fields; at that point the sight of so much lush grass, just out of reach, can inspire them into climbing over, under and even through the most robust fences. Often the mother will have got in and will be happily munching away, but the calves will still be in the road, mooing pathetically. Fortunately we have become quite adept at rounding them up so they can be reunited with mummy – and we can have some peace and quiet. It can be frustrating when a herd of cattle break into your meadow, devouring the sweet spring grass before the wild flowers have blossomed and seeded; worse still are the times when cattle get into the vegetable garden. If they are not spotted quickly enough, even a comparatively small herd of cows will wreck several weeks of Lesley's careful gardening in a few short hours. Inevitably, an opportunistic herd of cattle will find their way into the garden when one or other of us is "home alone". It then requires some careful planning and quick action to get them out through the gate without causing even worse damage.

The first such social call occurred during our initial summer at Glenmadrie, while Lesley was visiting her mother in England. I had just finished my list of gardening chores and had sat down to eat my dinner, when I was startled by the sight of a large cream coloured cow looking at me through the front window. After coughing up a lungful of beer and bits of partly masticated French fries, still wearing my bedroom slippers and armed only with my fork and half an uneaten chip, I bravely ran outside to confront a dozen large cows happily grazing on my front lawn. In my blissful ignorance, I assumed that our dogs would dredge up their natural herding instincts and calmly and quietly help me to guide the cattle back towards the open gate and freedom. What actually happened bore an alarming similarity to the stampede scene from one of those old cowboy movies. First the dogs chased all of the cattle clockwise around the lawn for a while… and then anti-clockwise for a while longer. Next they split the cows into two smaller groups and encouraged them to comprehensively trample the seedlings in the vegetable garden – all the while barking hysterically and ignoring my frantic calls to stop. Not to be outdone, the cows then chased the dogs until exhaustion set in and they were content to watch impassively as I used a series of threats and bribes to persuade all of the pooches to return to the safety of the house. Once I was on my own and armed with a couple of bamboo rods from the remains of the vegetable garden, it was a fairly simple matter to guide the cattle out through the gate. Sadly, by then my slippers were ruined, the garden was a wreck, I needed another shower and the dogs had eaten my dinner – living the dream!

Pine martens are sweet looking creatures, rather like a large black cat, but they are vicious killers of small rodents, birds and (given the chance) chickens. More annoyingly, those that live in the woods around our house are all rather short-sighted, or perhaps merely stupid, because they will occasionally just wander out of the bushes, perhaps ten yards ahead of me, when I am walking the dogs. The first time this happened, I had all five dogs on their leads and in the resulting melee, as they enthusiastically tried to give chase, my left shoulder was almost dislocated. The next time, Lady was already off the lead, but in her excitement she "dropped the ball" by yelping frantically and loudly enough to forewarn the pine marten, who managed to slip away in the confusion. Once, Lesley was interrupted from her ironing by the sight of a particularly large pine marten, staring myopically through the French windows into the sitting room; perhaps it was hoping that the dogs would come out to play. Late one Sunday afternoon, during a distressingly long and cold winter, we watched for over an hour while a splendidly large black specimen dug industriously through the snow around the bird table, in search of the seed and peanuts that were scattered on the ground. The dogs were all warming themselves in front of the fire, arranged in various poses, like accident victims in a daytime hospital soap opera and fortunately oblivious to our hungry visitor.

I know that there are badgers living in the woods near the house, because I have seen their distinctive footprints in the soft silt left when puddles dry out and occasionally, late in the day, I will spot one of these shy creatures ambling along the nearby road. Although I have never seen them in the meadow, it is obvious when they have been digging for worms because the land looks like someone has been throwing hand grenades. Badgers use their strong front paws and snouts to scrape away the grass so they can get at the sweet roots and juicy worms, leaving such random damage as can seem, to the untrained eye, like an act of mindless vandalism. At present, there is a lot of talk about culling badgers to prevent the spread of bovine tuberculosis, but the jury is still out on the evidence. It is very hard to prove that badgers do not spread tuberculosis without first exterminating them all – which seems a little extreme. Perhaps they should try exterminating all of the cattle, to see if that helps; or is that just vegetarian logic? Anyway, badgers are always welcome on my land, even if they occasionally make a bit of a mess. While I am on the theme of visitors making a bit of a mess, five or six times a year, a wild bird will find its way into the house, typically via an open door and then on through the conservatory. The resulting scramble to rescue the poor creature, before it is devoured by one of the dogs, generally only requires the righting of some disturbed furniture, sweeping up a few feathers and then mopping up any spilled beverages. However, only days after we had completed decorating our new kitchen, a blue tit managed to slide down the chimney of the Rayburn, announcing its presence by making scrabbling and tweeting sounds from behind the hot plate. Clearly there was no way that the hapless bird was going to fly back up the chimney. I was under strict instructions from Lesley not to make a mess in her freshly painted kitchen so, after some head scratching; I decided to attempt a rescue by carefully removing the inspection cover. The instant I lifted the cover plate from the cooking range, the soot covered bird burst into the light and made a desperate break for freedom. With a shriek, Lesley dashed forward with a tea towel, endeavouring to snare the wretched feathered chimney sweep before it could be killed by Amber – who had been roused from her afternoon nap by the commotion and was now running in circles around the kitchen going "Hup-hup-hup." Fortunately the bird soon became tired of this game and settled on a window sill, allowing itself to be caught and thoroughly cleaned before being released back into the wild, but not before it had left several bird shaped motifs in oily soot on our new walls and kitchen units.

The more common, but much less welcome, visitors to our humble abode come from the local population of rats and mice. By feeding the local birds so generously, composting all of our food waste and keeping some chickens, we also involuntarily support a few families of rats and mice. These periodically increase in numbers and will then invade the house – given half a chance. Along with the assistance of Kia and Amber, the local population of owls, kestrels, sparrow hawks and pine martens do a decent job of keeping the vermin under control for most of the time, but occasionally there is an explosion in numbers that requires the application of traps and poison. I despise using such methods, because it is difficult to control which animals can gain access. Sadly, I have found innocent sparrows, finches, frogs and one particularly big spider that were killed in the mouse traps; worse still, a mink and some voles have managed to get into the rat poison, with deadly results. Nevertheless, when faced with a plague of vermin, there is sometimes little choice. When we first moved into the house and the internal walls were still exposed stonework, the rats and mice could find their way through quite easily. I had to get busy with a bucket of mortar, filling in any obvious gaps, after Lesley was surprised by a large rat that was calmly sitting on a shelf in the pantry. Actually, "surprised" rather understates her reaction at the time, although she has become rather more laid back these days. After that we kept a few traps around the house and in the loft, until it was evident that the rats and mice could no longer get in. It takes a while to clear the infestation and just when you think you have succeeded, a trap will go off in the dead of night, proving there is still more work to do. On one particularly memorable night during the summer of 2006, I lay awake in bed and listened as three rat traps, which were in the loft space above my head, went off in quick succession; then an hour later I was rudely awoken as the trap behind the wardrobe went off. Unfortunately in this instance, the creature was not killed instantly, and it spent the next ten minutes running around the room, making an awful noise by squealing and crashing into things, before gradually succumbing. I bravely hid under the covers, as my mind pictured something much larger and more ferocious than the medium sized brown rat that had found its way into the bedroom that night. When faced with a prolonged period of heavy rain and flooding, vermin will naturally move to higher ground and before I realised where they were getting in, higher ground became our loft and roof. All of our downpipes and gutters are now well protected with wire, but not before we killed twenty-two rats, during a ten-day period one wet summer. As a vegetarian and an animal lover, I sometimes find such slaughter difficult to live with, but when the population of vermin gets so far ahead of the population of predators, something has to be done.

More recently I purchased some eco-friendly electronic gismos that are designed to keep rats and mice away. When plugged into the sockets in various locations throughout the house, they set up an electromagnetic pulse that will discourage vermin from setting up home. I was a little sceptical at first, but combined with my efforts to block access to the drainpipes and fill in the gaps in the stonework, we have been free from unwelcome guests for a couple of years now. You may be pondering why we don't own a cat, or rely on the hunting skills of our dogs to deal with rats and mice. Although we both love cats and would have no trouble introducing one to our household, in our experience it would be almost impossible to stop a cat from going after the birds which we have put so much effort into attracting to our home; so the idea of having a cat has been introduced, discussed and discarded several times. Sadly, the dogs are embarrassingly bad at "ratting," as we like to describe the activity of failing to catch rats and mice. Our foxhound, Lady, clearly considers hunting vermin to be something that only "common" dogs would do; she prefers to save herself for the more regal duties of chasing deer, foxes and hares. Even though she once killed a hare, which was a surprise for everyone, it was a lucky kill – so she cannot claim to be a successful hunter. Whilst excitedly running around on the moor one day, she accidentally tripped over a sleeping hare, partially stunning it in the process and leaving it vulnerable to the assault that followed. Of the other dogs, only Amber (the terrier) and Kia (the black collie) have ever shown any interest in being useful by hunting close to home. Amber is awash with noise and enthusiasm and totally fearless as she launches herself into the attack. However, blindly running about and yapping loudly only serves to forewarn any vermin of the need to sit still and wait patiently until the storm has passed. Kia just likes to run around and bark at Amber, although I am confident she has no idea why she is doing it, other than that it seems to be fun. Once, when Kia disappeared for several hours, we feared that she had met with some sort of accident, until we discovered her just yards away, hidden by a bush and sitting by one of the dry stone walls; she had her nose pressed up against a crevice, which was presumably hiding a tiny vole or field mouse. Waiting patiently for prey to emerge, she will sit for hours, still as a statue and unmoved by our calls and offers of food. I have never seen any evidence that she has been successful, probably because, once alerted to her presence by the hot doggy breath blowing through the stones, the mice simply decamp to safety from the opposite side of the wall. Kia is a kind and gentle dog, without pretension or ambition; she does not keep score and is confident that a successful outcome is inevitable and so her patient waiting continues.

Chapter 14 – In which Nick gets a shock

By the summer of 2007, I had completed work on the new bedroom above the kitchen. Although the work may have been progressing slowly, it was progressing and we were both pleased with the results. The block that had housed the original dark, low-ceilinged kitchen, with a spiral staircase connecting to two useless rooms above, now had two large, airy rooms filled with light. The new bedroom above the kitchen has three large windows, a vaulted ceiling that reaches almost twelve feet in height, fitted wardrobes and an airing cupboard (or hot press, to bow to Irish terminology). To improve the efficiency of the heating, I had added a back boiler to our stove and modified the plumbing. Now the fire could provide us with free hot water and, on colder days, top up the central heating. The parts only cost around three hundred euro and although my modifications to the plumbing may appear a little complicated, with hand operated gate valves, "T" connections and alternate flow diagrams, it works – and it saves us around 20% on our oil bills. The next stage in my plan was to remove all of the woodwork, floors and rafters from the middle of the house before constructing a new, higher, upper floor level with a staircase, bathroom, guest bedroom and connecting corridor. Before starting on what was clearly going to be a long and difficult build, we decided that there were a few projects outside that needed some attention. I had already constructed a large makeshift greenhouse by reroofing the goat shed with clear corrugated plastic, but to have any chance of growing a practical quantity of vegetables in the cool, wet climate, Lesley needed a polytunnel. Secondly, I was going to need a large dry space, where I could both store the old wood from the house, before it was cut up for firewood, and store and prepare the new wood prior to fitting. By making half the area around the courtyard into a cover-way, I would create over eight hundred square feet of dry storage and working space, which would prove invaluable in Ireland's inclement weather – even after the building work was finished. Ideally, when doing any building work, one wants to avoid moving things twice, by having the bulk items delivered and stored adjacent to where they will be fitted. Unfortunately, because of the layout of the house and the limited accessibility, almost everything that was delivered ended up being moved several times – and some of those moves were tortuous. While constructing the bedroom above the kitchen, each plasterboard slab had to be carried from the conservatory, where they were being stored, twenty paces north into the kitchen, then thirty paces south through the sitting room, up two flights of stairs and another thirty paces to the north again, to reach the bedroom. It sometimes seemed a little like we were following a treasure map. I almost expected to see a sign that said "Dig here!" Apart from providing some much needed shelter, the new cover-way would also ensure that my storage and working area was adjacent to where I would be working for the remainder of the project.

The previous winter I had rented a digger and tipper truck to prepare the ground before the contractor came in to drill our well. While I had the equipment on site, I had also cleared the uneven concrete from the area that would one day become the cover-way, as well as levelling a large piece of ground at the south end of the house, where we were going to site the polytunnel. After much shopping around and internet research, we selected a fifty foot, heavy-duty polytunnel from a firm in Cork. It was surprisingly decent value for Ireland, given that we needed something robust enough to cope with the high winds and violent rain that can frequent the area. A few days later we were the proud owners of a very large pile of steel tubes, some with curves and others with joints, a massive sheet of thick polythene, folded into something the size of a double bed, and a grubby sheet of A5 paper bearing words of wisdom to guide me through the construction process. The instructions seemed to have been written onto the back of an envelope, along with a few hand drawn sketches and then photocopied onto some yellowed paper just prior to delivery. I imagined that the research and development department had met with the only person in Ireland to successfully build a polytunnel and, during a pub conversation over a few pints on a wet Sunday afternoon, had copied down verbatim his description of how the mighty deed was achieved.

I stared in amused disbelief at instructions like: "Around now you might be looking at a big pile of bits and be thinking 'Feck me! How am I going to manage', but don't fret, it will all come right in the end."

And, "stick the stakes into the ground and bend them in a bit like."

And finally, "and fer Christ sake, don't try and put the polythene over the frame on a breezy day. If the wind catches it you won't see it again before it reaches Birmingham."

At some point I stopped laughing sufficiently to telephone the supplier, who was kind enough to explain the construction process in idiot-proof steps. It took a day to assemble and erect the frame, which was constructed from two-inch galvanized steel pipes that fitted together to create a series of interconnected loops, ten feet high in the centre and firmly anchored to the ground at each end. The tricky bit was getting the base pipes hammered into the ground at the correct angle (about ten degrees) and in an exact square. For the first time since I was at school, I was able to make use of the hypotenuse in calculating the sides of a right-angled triangle; this brought me half way towards making my squares... well... square. Everything went swimmingly and I soon had the framework acceptably in place. I then had to secure it together with special bolts that drilled their own holes into the steel pipes. Unfortunately, my old Black & Decker electric drill did not have a torque release (to stop the drill head turning in the event of the bolt jamming), so several times when the bolt suddenly stopped turning, the drill continued going around, taking me with it. Usually this only resulted in some swearing as I was flicked off my ladder, as if by an invisible judo instructor. But when I was fitting the very last bolt, it inevitably jammed and for some reason the drill refused to stop, and I watched in horror as my right wrist and forearm were rotated through some four hundred degrees, before the drill was finally wrenched from my hand. Nothing was broken, but my wrist swelled up like a pregnant rat and continued to give me problems for the next three years. We had to wait for over a week before the weather was calm enough to fit the polythene, but at last we were able to drape it over the frame where, by burying all the edges in a three foot trench, it is now secured against even the highest winds. With the polytunnel completed, Lesley was finally able to launch into some serious planting, confident that the weather would not wreck her plans by being too wet, dry, hot, cold or Irish. Although the polytunnel is pretty large, around one thousand square feet, it seemed to be bursting with plants no more than a few weeks after I had finished the construction. Apart from the usual range of beans, carrots, potatoes, squashes and cabbages, Lesley also planted peach trees, grapes and a range of companion plants to discourage unwanted bugs. I am a vegetarian, I love good food and I enjoy eating; Lesley loves gardening, she is an excellent cook and enjoys making jams, pickles and cakes – it seems we are well-matched to each other.

The next thing on my list of construction chores was the new roof and concrete floor for the cover-way. The existing roof had rotted away and collapsed many years before, so there was plenty of clearing and preparation to do before construction could begin. Although to many people, such preparatory work may seem like a bit of a chore, I find the process rather enjoyable, primarily because with an old house, even knocking things down can make it seem better and cleaner. It also lets the dog see the rabbit, so to speak. Once all the old wood, roofing materials and weeds were removed, I was able to work out how to build the new roof and then set about ordering the parts from the local builders merchant. I decided to construct the framework with standard four by two inch sawn pine, which I find is easy to work with, readily available and strong enough for walls and some other projects; leftovers are never wasted in Glenmadrie! Lesley wanted the part of the cover-way that would attach to the conservatory to be fitted with a clear plastic roof to make the area as light as possible; on the other half I was able to reuse some of the old corrugated steel sheeting, which helped considerably to keep the costs under control. On and off it took about two weeks for me to finish building the roof, a task which I thoroughly enjoyed. It then took me about another month to lay the new concrete floors, which is a job I dislike intensely.

With a new build property, you would prepare the area and then a nice man would drive up in his shiny lorry and pump your self-levelling concrete precisely into place, leaving you with a perfect, flat floor. At that time in Ireland, with so much new construction underway, it was almost impossible to get a delivery of ready-mixed at a reasonable price, but to make matters worse, the cover-way was eighty metres from the nearest road access and most of the suppliers "don't do complicated pumping." Secondly, I had recently heard a cautionary tale that encouraged me to put more "do it yourself" into my D.I.Y. project. Freddy, a friend of ours, was similarly engaged in renovating his house and had decided to move things along by getting a delivery of concrete to finish the kitchen floor. All of the preparation work was finished, he had laid the damp-proof membrane, the insulation and all of the pipework for the under floor heating, and was ready for his concrete. The delivery was promised and delayed more frequently than a visit from the gas board and inevitably arrived on the wrong day, when Freddy was away from the house. His diminutive wife did her best in the circumstances, faced with a foul-mouthed and belligerent driver who was threatening to dump the load on the front lawn. She managed to contact Freddy on his mobile phone and then, carefully following his instructions, directed the driver to pour the self-levelling compound through the window and into the kitchen. Once the lorry had gone, it quickly became evident that there had been a horrible mix-up with the delivery, which was actually quick-setting concrete that refused any attempts to be levelled. Sadly, by the time Freddy had arrived back, the fully-set concrete covered half of the kitchen, from the centre of the floor to the bottom of the window sill; the guilty company refused to accept any responsibility, and it took poor Freddy several weeks to dig out the unwanted "brick" by hand. So in some ways I was reasonably happy to spend several weeks mixing endless loads in my little mixer, spreading and levelling the concrete by hand and then doing it all again whenever the dogs decided to take a shortcut to chase the postman. In due course the cover-way was completed. With the new roof in place and all of the exposed woodwork treated with preservative, I thought it looked rather smart. Even the new concrete floors were finished, fashionably lumpy, but adequate for storing and cutting wood.

Before I could begin work on replacing the sagging floors in the centre of the house, I needed to add some lead flashing to the cover-way to prevent rainwater from running down the walls and onto the walkway below. This fairly simple, but somewhat dusty, task involves using a disc cutter to cut a horizontal groove along the wall, a few inches above the cover-way roof. A long strip of lead sheet is then fitted into the groove and bent downwards, overlapping a second sheet of lead that is bent into an "L" shape on the joint between the cover-way roof and the wall. The two sheets of lead act as an effective barrier, deflecting any rain away from the wall and onto the cover-way roof, where it will run into the guttering. So, armed with gloves, goggles, ear defenders and my disc cutter, I climbed onto the roof and began cutting the required groove, along the cement render that covers the wall. My disc cutter has a powerful electric motor that spins the heavy diamond tipped steel blade at an incredible speed; because of the gyroscopic effect that makes the motor want to turn around the blade, one tends to use it rather carefully. Also, I did not want to accidentally step in the wrong place and put my foot through the new roof, or inadvertently cut through the cable, or my leg. Since I was working so cautiously, I was somewhat surprised to see a sudden burst of yellow sparks, followed by a large blue flash and a loud bang, which blew me backwards fully six feet. I found myself sitting precariously on the edge of the roof and clinging desperately to the disc cutter, which was jumping around like a wild stallion, as the unpowered blade gradually slowed down. When it had finally stopped, the cause of the violent gyrations was immediately obvious; almost one third of the blade was missing, having been melted into an ugly lump, and there was a large soot mark on the yellow paint, where I had been cutting the wall. Further investigation revealed that the house was now completely without power and, with the help of the local linesman from the power company, I was horrified to discover the reason why – I had unwittingly cut through the mains electric cable. In normal circumstances the mains cable runs from the utility pole along the roofline, or along some other clearly visible route, until it enters the house behind the mains fuse board. However, at some time in the past, a builder had seen fit to run the mains electric cable diagonally along the side of the house for around fifty feet, before painstakingly hiding it under a thick coat of cement render. I had been merrily chunking my way through the render, some twenty feet away from the fuse box, when I had cut right through the cable with some spectacular pyrotechnics. The linesman explained how lucky I was to still be alive and then he suggested that I should go out and purchase a lottery ticket. As we are the last house on the line, there is a transformer on the last but one utility pole and from there, the power runs uninterrupted directly to our house. Because I cut through the cable between the utility pole and my fuse box, there was nothing to stop the flow of electricity; in fact, the business end of the cable was still "live" right up until the linesman climbed the pole and pulled the breaker. A stout new cable now safely, and obviously, brings electricity to the house and the only expense for the entire incident was the cost of replacing the blade on my disc cutter and the two euro I wasted on a lottery ticket.

While I had been working on the renovations indoors, warm and dry, Lesley had been doing great things with the garden, working outside in the rain, mist, wind, sun and whatever other weather this fine country chooses to throw at us. We now had a fully functioning polytunnel and a well-stocked greenhouse. Several beautiful embankments featuring various sturdy bushes were providing pretty, but practical, windbreaks as protection for the flowers. Because we divide our labour in relation to our relative skills, except for when a second pair of hands are required, I do the majority of the building work and Lesley does all of the gardening. She is a skilled and knowledgeable gardener, or so she tells me. Gardening is very much her preserve and I am careful to know my place as the heavy lifter, digger, and idiot husband who is happy to compliment her hard work and then eat the beautiful vegetables that she grows. Her knowledge of flora and fauna seems encyclopaedic. I am always impressed when I point out some random plant at the garden centre and she can immediately summon the name and its history, although I sometimes suspect that she has just made up the names to humour me.

"Lesley – that's a pretty flower," I say, pointing. "What is it called?"

"Oh that? It's a 'Syllyarsehusband' or 'Hubsbanda-pratticus' in Latin. It's rather a gentle little flower. It thrives best when kept well-shaded and fed a little manure from time to time."

"Well, it looks nice. Do you want me to buy one?"

"No need dear, I already have one at home and that's plenty."

She is quite sensible to keep the garden as her domain, firstly because it provides her with her own space within the marriage, a place of quiet sanctuary and secondly because I am a clumsy and ignorant horticulturist. I seem to have an almost dyslexic inability to recognise the difference between plants and weeds – unless I am standing in a flower bed, where I will unerringly trample every plant with my size ten wellington boots, but miss all of the weeds. I have tried to help in the past, but since an unfortunate incident with a strimmer and some weed killer, I am now restricted to cutting the lawn, fetching and carrying and obliging with some carefully supervised digging. Lesley waited until the hottest day, in the glorious summer of 2007, to task me with digging dozens of deep holes to plant fruit trees. I had watched a few episodes of "Gardeners World" on television and recollected how to do this digging stuff; whenever the presenter plants a young apple tree, he gently pushes his spade into the soft loamy earth and tips it to one side a few times, before carefully easing the plant into its warm safe new home. At Glenmadrie, digging a hole requires a spade, a pick axe, a crow bar and a whole lot of hard work. In many places the top soil is barely a few inches deep, cunningly hiding a sub layer of shale and large rocks, sometimes larger than a car. The best technique is to use a crow bar, a five-foot long steel bar, an implement the thickness of a broomstick, with a sharp point at one end, to probe the ground for a relatively rock free spot. Then, using the combined weight and leverage advantages of the pick axe and crow bar, loosen the rock and shale sufficiently to be lifted out by hand. Once the hole is large enough, the tree can be added along with fresh soil, water and some well-rotted manure. To create an orchard, we had twenty fruit trees to plant, mostly just south of the polytunnel, with the remainder to be dotted around for cosmetic effect. In practice, each tree took around half-an-hour to rehome; in the end we both put in a good day's work, on what turned out to be the hottest day of the year.

It was a glorious summer, with seemingly endless days of warm sunshine and barely a sign of rain. The lane at the back of the house, which doubles as a stream during wet weather, was so dry that I was able to walk out with the dogs while still wearing my slippers. Ireland is without doubt a glorious place to be when the weather consents to be pleasant for a while – and it consented a lot that year. At the same time, the economy was superficially as bright and sunny as the weather, although I sensed that storm clouds were brewing on the far side of the horizon. As we had lived through previous recessions in England, I think that to some degree we had an eye for the warning signs, or at least a profound feeling that the outrageous spending, by Government and many individuals, could not continue. Much has been written about the reasons for Ireland's spectacular financial demise, by people far better qualified to comment than I am, so there is little narrative value in attempting my own analysis of the crash. However it may add some colour to my story to relate a few of the things we saw that made us both say, "this can't continue!"

Much of the money being generated in Ireland at the time was coming from outrageously inflated property values. It seemed that any plot of land with road access was considered "prime" building land and valued accordingly. The banks were lending wildly, for fear of missing out on their share of the profits and many property developers were neither building the proposed houses and flats nor even repaying the mortgages, preferring to simply borrow more money against the inflating value of future house prices. The ready availability of cash encouraged the overpricing of basic household commodities and, because it was so easy to make a large profit, many retailers casually increased their margins and allowed standards of customer care to fall. This left many shops with high debts, unwieldy business models and a vulnerability to outside competition. As the pretend money from the property boom flooded through the system, the Government found it had an ostensibly endless supply of taxes to back up the States borrowing requirements. But most of the taxes were coming from just three sources, the service sector, property and new car sales – the Irish badge of wealth. With so much money in the coffers, the Government was unwilling to deny the strong trade and public sector unions – so wages and benefits increased to unsustainable levels. Not to be outdone, the Government awarded itself huge pay increases, as well as outrageous benefits like free parking for life and generous compensation should a minister have to resign – even if it was because of misconduct. They were also guaranteed a gold-plated pension and allowed extraordinary expenses, generally paid without the need for receipts, along with a daily allowance of so called "walking around money," which was more than many people were earning – including me.

There was a trend towards ever more excessive demonstrations of wealth at social events like birthdays, weddings and religious holidays. The prices of many gift items in Ireland had risen to such heights that thousands of shoppers were flying to New York to do their Christmas shopping, and then proudly displaying their purchases to the waiting television cameras on the return journey. When I was a child, we were delighted to receive a badge and perhaps a certificate after our church confirmation and first communions. Here, in the new, glitzy Ireland, most children were dressed in new expensive clothes for these ceremonies, with some arriving at the church in a stretched limo, or even flown in by helicopter. These religious events were usually followed with a lavish party, where the child received several thousand euro in cash gifts from friends and relatives. Extravagant weddings became another badge of wealth and success. Even a relatively basic wedding would cost in excess of €50,000 and several notable celebrities and "new rich" publicly spent more than a million. For some people, the money seemed to have become more important than the event, with many children beginning to expect such lavish spending as a right: "If every other child has dozens of presents, a hundred guests and two bouncy castles at their eighth birthday party, then why shouldn't I?"

On the other hand, we were growing much of our own food, doing our own renovations on a strict budget, driving a ten-year old car and living without debt. In retrospect it may look as if we had a premonition of the events to follow, but in all truth we had barely survived the English recessions during the 1980s – and so late in life, I was terrified of repeating the nightmare. Consequently we managed our money carefully and watched the madness with disbelief, in the sure knowledge that it would inevitably end badly, although I would never have predicted just how badly.

The up-side of living alongside such a glut of wealth was that my business was doing extremely well; in fact, I was so busy that I had little time to work on the house and my diary was full for a month in advance. My income was so high that I was almost keeping pace with the money we were spending on the house renovations – but not quite. After one very long hot and busy Friday at work, with little fluid to drink, I was disturbed to discover that I was peeing blood. As it was late in the evening and I didn't want to waste the weekend unnecessarily waiting around at A& E, there was little to do but drink as much water as I could and see if things settled down. Although the bleeding stopped over the weekend, to be on the safe side, first thing on Monday morning, I presented myself at the local doctor's surgery. After a short discussion we both agreed that the bleeding was probably due to dehydration, which dislodged a small kidney stone. There was no pain, infection, or sign of further bleeding, but as I was entering the age range where prostate cancer was a statistical possibility, the doctor decided he should examine my prostate. This delightful procedure involves having a gloved finger thrust up your bum, while the doctor asks you about your holiday plans and feels around for suspicious lumps. For some reason doctors who perform this kind of examination all seem to have hands like a bunch of bananas and a desire to economise on the lubrication. Fortunately nothing of any interest was discovered by the doctor's exploring digit; nevertheless, he decided that I should pop over to A&E for some precautionary tests. Even at the height of the financial boom in Ireland, hospital waiting lists were ridiculously long. The quickest way to circumvent the logjam was to present yourself at A&E with a doctor's referral letter. Although the entire health service may be systemically flawed and shot through with well-intentioned but disastrous anomalies, the medical staff are all excellent people and they do an outstanding job, despite the conditions they have to work under. So, an hour later, I was lying on a trolley and discussing my symptoms with an Nigerian doctor, who appeared to be far too young to be out of secondary school and far too large to be a lumberjack. As he joyfully snapped a powdered glove onto a hand that was slightly larger than a coal shovel, he explained in broken English that he needed to examine my prostate. My eyes bulged as I watched him apply a pea-sized blob of KY jelly to his cucumber like middle finger.

"Is this strictly necessary?" I croaked, "My doctor has already examined me, he said my prostate was okay – it was all in the letter I brought."

His broad smile revealed perfect teeth, gleaming white against his jet black skin. "Yes, is good in letter, but I am the dokt-oor now and I must feel also. Is good?"

I pulled a face and assumed the position, resigned to my fate. "Yes, is good," I said with a sigh.

He fiddled around behind me, as if he was hunting for a favourite watch that had accidentally fallen into the toilet; his tuneless humming only occasionally drowned out by my squeaks and grunts of pain. After what seemed like an eternity, he proudly announced that everything was "Goo-wed," but that I should wait to see what the senior A&E doctor thought. So I continued reading my book and tried to relax while I waited.

About two hours later, a tall but slightly hunched Asian doctor peered around the curtain and enquired as to my wellbeing. Disappointingly he was not the senior doctor I was hoping to see, just the regular A&E doctor for the afternoon shift. I gave him a concise medical history while he flicked through my notes, squinting occasionally as he tried to decipher the squiggles that the Nigerian doctor had evidently made in response to my earlier answers. He added a few of his own unintelligible squiggles and then announced that he needed to examine my prostate. I was starting to feel like the new boy in prison and defensively explained that I had already been examined twice, my prostate was found to be absolutely fine, and it was recorded in the notes – twice. Nevertheless, he explained in thick but perfect English that he needed to feel for himself. "To check – you see," he said with a stiff, formal smile and a slight bow.

Resigned once again to the inevitable examination, I lay on my side with my knees drawn up to my chest and tried to relax and ignore the mop-wielding cleaner who was squinting into my cubicle as if he was trying to read a distant road sign. The doctor, obviously ignorant of the hospital's policy of cost saving, liberally slapped a litre of lubricant around my buttocks before expeditiously inserting a curry hot finger, and possibly half his arm, to facilitate his investigation. The examination ended abruptly, with an audible "pop," as he removed his hand with a speed worthy of someone avoiding a snapping dog. As my diligent doctor peeled off his glove, he reported proudly that all was well – but that I should still wait to see the senior A&E doctor. He gave me a couple of sheets of stiff blue tissue paper, and left me to the impossible task of attempting to wipe the gelatinous lubricant from my derriere, before I accidentally slid off the trolley like a wet fish.

Some forty-five minutes later, a flurry of activity from the nurses and junior doctors suggested that either the US President had suddenly been taken ill while on a secret visit to County Clare, or the elusive A&E senior doctor had finally arrived. Given the prospect of an even longer wait and the real possibility of the Secret Service conducting a cavity search, I correctly hoped for the latter. Moments later he arrived at my bedside, accompanied by an entourage of nervous student doctors. The softly spoken senior doctor had kind eyes, a pleasant smile and looked rather like my old maths teacher would have – had I actually gone to school in India. He was a short, portly sort of man, in a dusty tweed suit with a pocket full of pens, wearing a stethoscope and a brightly coloured tie that proudly displayed samples from his last twenty meals. He took my hand and shook it formally, but then refused to let go, addressing me as "Sir" and enquiring empathetically about my health, as if he was an employee who had heard whispered rumours of some malady. All the while I squirmed uncomfortably as his large but disturbingly soft hands continued their embrace after our initial handshake and I almost panicked when he started to softly stroke the back of my hand with his fingers. In the end I faked an itchy nose in an attempt to break his hold without further embarrassment, although I noticed several of the attending student doctors sharing a wry smile on my behalf. Undeterred by my well-used, but futile objections, he insisted on examining my prostate as well. Once he had his gloved finger inserted where the sun does not shine, in a surprisingly loud voice, he explained every detail of the procedure for the benefit of his students, some others on the second floor and anyone in the car park as well. For obvious reasons, I was initially thankful for his soft hands, but the fervour with which he pressed and poked the gland caused me to squeak involuntarily as my eyes watered, and I was suitably grateful when the examination was finally over. With a flourish worthy of a magician conjuring a dove from thin air, he removed his glove, and ignoring my existence, proceeded to address his findings to the students while I lay at his side, bare bummed and slick with lubricant. It seemed to me that I was now as tiresome as the uneaten remains of a restaurant meal, waiting to be removed by the waitress.

I was lucky to overhear him report, "nothing of interest was discovered during my examination. This patient can be discharged, once he has been seen by the urologist."

An hour and two chapters of my book later, the urologist arrived with a pocket full of surgical gloves and his own tube of lubricant. He was a tall, elderly Irish man, with the serious air of someone who cared passionately about his speciality, despite his colleagues' constantly repeated jokes about whether he was serious about his diagnosis "or just taking the piss?" He listened attentively as I explained my initial medical history, carefully read through my notes and test results and then conducted yet another prostate exam.

After what seemed like an eternity, he washed his hands, reread my notes and then said rather seriously, "Well, I can't see anything wrong with your test results, you seem to be in excellent health; but I am a little worried. Your prostate seems to be strangely swollen and tender."

Through gritted teeth I barely contained my temper as I pointed out that his prostate too would be strangely swollen and tender, if it had been examined so enthusiastically and frequently, in such a short time. In the end we agreed that my medical needs would be best served if I was discharged immediately and treated at home with plenty of fluids and a nice hot bath!

Chapter 15 – In which we gain a new friend

The hot summer drew to an end with a succession of wildfires across the moor. Sometimes these conflagrations were caused by natural combustion in the peat, sometimes by a carelessly discarded cigarette, but some fires "spontaneously" started in a one hundred metre line, upwind of an area that had become too overgrown to graze cattle. In October, one such fire consumed hundreds of acres of the moorland just opposite the house, with flames jumping to a height of fifty feet as the gorse and heather ferociously burned. I was sitting at the top of our quarry watching the spectacle, whilst keeping a careful eye on the progress of the flames which were steadily working along the valley floor towards the west; suddenly I felt the wind change direction, blowing the fire towards the house. As a precaution, I ran indoors and called the fire brigade, taking a few minutes to ensure that they knew exactly where we were and then I went back outside. Within those few minutes, the smoke and burning embers were starting to blow over the top of the house and the flames had almost reached the road opposite our land. I was genuinely concerned that the fire would jump to the huge pine trees that lined the north end of our property, as I knew they would burn fiercely and carry the fire to the house. Luckily the flames started to die back naturally, so by the time the fire engine and a van full of council "beaters" arrived, the fire was much less intimidating. Armed only with shovels, the men quickly formed a line and expertly beat at the edges of the fire to stop it spreading further, effectively containing it until it burned itself out naturally. It was sad to see the beautiful moor reduced to a blackened wasteland, but the fire naturally cleared the old, inedible brush and gorse, making way for new growth. Within a matter of days, fresh green shoots were starting to break through, and by the following spring there was almost no sign of the damage. Given how far away we live from civilisation, I must admit to having felt some considerable trepidation and a dreadful sensation of helplessness, as I watched the flames march unimpeded towards our house. I had some appreciation for the plight of the poor people in California and parts of Australia who had lost their homes, and sometimes much more, in the annual wildfires. We are adequately insured, but no amount of money can replace the real value of a house that you have committed your heart and soul to turning into a home.

At that time power failures were quite common, partly because we are the last house on the line and therefore instantly plunged into darkness by the slightest fault twenty miles away. There was also a planned programme of line replacement, which for several months left us without power for up to eight hours on a weekly basis. For variety, the power would stop sporadically during periods of bad weather; at other times it would flicker and surge for a couple of hours, usually after some drunken driver had managed to demolish a pole and the power line. We hadn't experienced such blackouts since the oil shortages in England during the 1970s, so there was a mild sense of excitement when the power first went off – but the novelty value was short-lived. Luckily we were well prepared to cope without electricity; with the wood stove we were able to heat the house, we could boil water and cook meals with the gas cooker, and I even had a small generator as a backup in the event of a long period without mains electricity.

One windy night as we sat watching television, the power vanished, plunging us into sudden darkness. With a little assistance from the glow of the fire, I successfully groped my way to the kitchen cupboard where we kept candles and matches for just such an event. Just as we were lighting the last of the candles, the power came back on – so we went around blowing them out again. No sooner had Lesley and I extinguished the last of the candles than the power went off again; we got out the matches and lit them all once more. Moments later, the lights returned. This time, we waited to be sure things had settled down before blowing out the candles, only to be plunged into darkness again –just as I quenched the final flame. Out came the matches, now diminished in number, and we set about relighting the candles. The process was repeated with exquisite comedic timing – three more times. Eventually, we were both crying with laughter and decided to leave two candles burning until bed time.

Luckily most of these power outages were pre-planned and well-advertised, while for nature's interruptions, there was a recorded message available on the power company's emergency telephone line, predicting when the power would be restored. We try not to get too stressed about these power failures, being mindful that, while we sat in front of the fire, trying to read a book by candle-light, at that moment some poor devil was out in the cold lashing rain, trying to restore the power to my house. Being the last building on the line caused problems for us at the house whenever there was a thunderstorm, even if it was several miles away. If there was a lightning strike somewhere in the distance, the power surge would travel unimpeded along the electrical or telephone lines until it reached our house. Then, without any warning, any electrical item that was switched on, or even just plugged in, was likely to get its circuits fried – usually accompanied by a loud ominous popping sound and a big blue flash for cinematic effect. We now have electrical surge protectors sited throughout the house which have helped to some extent, but not before we had suffered several hundred euro's worth of damage.

The Christmas of 2007 arrived overnight, as stealthily as the fat man in a red suit, delivering a deep and soft blanket of snow, which hung heavy on the trees, creating a landscape of extravagant beauty, as the brightness of the morning sun was softened through the mist and snow. When we took our dogs for their morning walk, the usual quietness of Glenmadrie was reduced to an almost ghostly stillness, as the deep snow on the ground and the impossibly large flakes falling through the air muffled all sound – except for the eager panting of our little terrier, who was enthusiastically attempting to catch every falling snowflake. Both Lady and Kia were in full hunting mode, hastily running from side-to-side and burying their noses in the snow, in an attempt to sniff out their quarry. They always seem to be more excited when hunting in fresh snow; I presume that this is because the new scent trails are more distinct, as most of the usual background smells have been masked by the snow. For such a remote place, I am always enthralled by the number of fresh animal tracks there are when you encounter a blanket of fresh snow; it goes to prove just how prolific the wildlife is, if you know where to look. Poor Romany, our little white Lhasa Apsos, was getting old and finding it difficult to get around; although she still liked to go for walks in the woods, she was getting noticeably slower. To my mind she always seemed to be muttering quiet complaints to herself as she plodded along – like a diminutive hippopotamus in a white fur coat. Being so low to the ground and with fur that acted like Velcro, she periodically ground to a halt under the weight of enormous "clown feet" of snow and several under-body icicles, which had to be removed before she could get underway again. When she was a youngster, Romany was incredibly shy and would spend ages inspecting various trees and bushes, before choosing one that provided exactly the correct amount of privacy for her to conduct her doggy toilet. But as she became older she grew less picky, or just more tired, simply choosing instead to turn three tight circles in the snow, before assuming the position – regardless of the number of interested onlookers. Once the deed was done, a spring would return to her step, if only for a few minutes.

We were delighted to see so much snow, particularly because our daughter Joanne and her new boyfriend Mark were due to visit to help us see in the New Year. I knew they would both appreciate the beauty and romance of Glenmadrie at its most spectacular. We had first met Mark during the summer; he is a delightful gentleman, who seemed a perfect fit for Joanne, and we were starting to suspect that he might turn out to be "the one." Time would tell, but my first impression was that they were very much in love and got on so well that they already seemed like an old married couple.

Over the next few days, the overnight temperatures fell sharply, down towards minus fifteen degrees, and there was enough light snow each day to keep the roads well covered. In England we were used to the roads being cleared and gritted by the local councils whenever there was any hint of snow or ice; rural Ireland is a very different matter. Whereas the big cities like Dublin, Galway, Cork and Limerick may have the resources to clear and treat the metropolitan roads, we country folk have to cope with roads hard-packed with snow and sheet ice for weeks on end. I have fairly considerable experience of driving in bad weather, including snow and black ice and I am pleased to report that I have never had a crash nor even been stuck. So on the morning I was supposed to collect Joanne and Mark from Shannon Airport, I was embarrassed to discover that I couldn't even get the car out of the driveway. For almost a week, only a little farm traffic had braved the road at the front of the house, firmly compressing the snow which, after a slight thaw, refroze into an inch of solid ice – too slick to even stand on. I was confident that once I got going, I could safely drive to Shannon and back, with the careful use of my gears and cadence breaking, to overcome the lack of ABS on our old car – but only if I could get the damn thing onto the road. The problem was that our driveway went steeply downhill to where it met the road at an eighty-five degree angle, where you had to turn left and climb steeply uphill for about one hundred yards before the road levelled for the next two miles. After that it was downhill all the way to Shannon. Despite sprinkling grit, ash and sand on the road and even lowering the air pressure in the tyres, the car simply refused to make the left turn and change of elevation, either sliding across the road towards the ditch like a drunken duck, or spinning its wheels uselessly on the sheet ice. I wasted two fruitless hours trying different methods to coax the wallowing Skoda estate, with its plump tyres and soft suspension, to climb the slope. Finally I admitted defeat and decided to try defrosting my little Toyota Starlet, in the hope that the much thinner tyres might be better at providing grip. Although it is twenty years old, the brave little Toyota was in its element; it shot up the hill without a hint of slipping and made short work of the remaining miles of ice and slush on the road to Shannon. I was delighted to arrive safely, just four hours late, to collect Joanne and Mark. They were understanding and kind enough to forgive the delay, even though it resulted in them eating the worst breakfast on the planet. Incidentally, I visited the same restaurant recently and enjoyed an excellent breakfast in delightful surroundings – well done Shannon Airport! Over the next few days the weather was so bad and the roads so icy, that we barely ventured out in the car, preferring to sit in front of the fire, reading our Christmas books and playing board games, whilst leaving the youngsters to take long walks in the woods – where they could spend some romantic time alone.

In the UK, seeing in the New Year is quite a big thing, as it is in many countries, and although Lesley and I had not sampled such an event in Ireland, I assumed that it would be an excellent opportunity to show Joanne and Mark some Irish "Craic". A few days earlier I had telephoned the local pub to find out if there were any spaces left for the night of the thirty-first, and to ask if we needed to buy tickets. Initially the young lady that answered the telephone seemed a little confused by my enquiry, but after checking with the manager she assured me that there were plenty of places left. She even suggested that they would make an extra effort on our behalf – it sounded like we were in for a night to remember. On the night of the thirty-first, we arrived at the pub a little after ten o'clock to find the place almost deserted, except for the bar staff, a couple of local farmers and a buxom lady with peroxide blonde hair. In the corner, three schoolgirls armed with a flute, a fiddle and a guitar were playing Irish music and being roundly ignored by everyone. Fearing that we had arrived at the wrong pub, I asked the barmaid about the absence of the anticipated New Year's festivities. She gave me a slightly embarrassed shrug and explained that, although the Irish didn't really "do" New Year's Eve, as we had phoned they would be making a special effort on our behalf. She brightly assured me that things would soon "kick off" and pointed knowingly at the baskets on each table, which appeared to contain some dusty party poppers, streamers and a packet of paper hats – which might have been left over from the Millennium celebrations. Returning to our table, I disclosed my growing suspicion that the night's festivities would probably only exceed our expectations if we lowered them considerably – and then it was still going to be a close run thing. I apologised for our lack of experience in locating the local swinging hot spots, brought about by the fact that Lesley and I were usually at home and asleep by this time on New Year's Eve. So with nothing else to do, we sat in our quiet corner, listened to the "diddly-i" music, downed a few pints and had a pleasant enough evening just chatting and telling tall tales.

By eleven-thirty another three people had flooded into the pub, making the tiny room seem almost crowded – until the three schoolgirls decamped, presumably heading home for an early night. Perhaps sensing that they were losing the moment, someone put on a cd of more festive music, and enthused with alcohol, we got up to join in with the singing and dancing. A few minutes before midnight the music stopped, then Harry the pub landlord came over; to our surprise he then proceeded to introduce us to the other customers, as if we were visiting dignitaries. As each person in the bar stepped forward and formally shook hands with Joanne, Mark, Lesley and me, Harry respectfully explained who each of us were, where we lived and what we did with our time to make a living. Then, like members of some royal family, we exchanged some uncomfortable pleasantries until conversation petered out. The next person would then be waved forwards and the entire process would begin over again, completely ignoring the fact that, as we were standing in a room the size of a car parking space, they had already overheard the introductions to the previous people. As this bizarre ritual played out, I watched as the clock ticked on past midnight, completely ignored by our fellow patrons. When the last of the introductions were finally over and we were fully fifteen minutes into 2008, Harry led us through a mocking countdown towards the pseudo New Year, then we all gave a desultory cheer and, along with the usual hugs and kisses, set off a few party poppers. Finally there was a round of "Auld Lang Syne" followed by a rigorous, and somewhat violent, version of the "Hokey Cokey" – where Joanne had the pleasure of being repeatedly squished up against the wildly enthusiastic peroxide blonde. On the drive back to the house, we agreed that it was a night to remember and Mark commented that the previous New Year he had visited Edinburgh, where all of the festivities had been cancelled because of gale-force winds and snow. "It took a lot to top the disappointment of that night," he added ironically, "but you did it!"

As soon as spring had sprung I started ripping out the walls, floors and joists in the main part of the house. This was clearly going to be a mammoth task, but one that could not be avoided. There was so much wood rot that it would have been futile trying to do repairs without doing the whole lot. The boards of the first floor were so rotten and weak that even cautious walking lightly sprinkled everyone below with woodworm dust and caused the wardrobe doors to swing open. In retrospect, I have come to the opinion that when Lesley took a long bath, the only thing stopping her going through the floor were the woodworms desperately holding hands and hoping she hadn't chosen a long book.

Whilst rebuilding the centre of the house, I would take the opportunity to raise the ceiling height in the sitting room, gaining a few precious inches of additional headroom; at the same time, I could move the fuse box, replace the ancient electrical wiring and renew the plumbing for the new bathroom. Not wanting to reinvent the wheel, my approach would be similar to how I rebuilt the kitchen. First, I would strip out all of the upstairs floors and walls, rip out the dry-lining and any insulation, disconnect and remove the old electrical wiring and plumbing, remove the joists and then make good any holes in the stonework. Because the new floor level would be higher than before, the new joists needed to be hung on wall plates, which are attached to bolts, glued into the stonework using some special extra strength mastic. As I was dry-lining and insulating the sitting room, the framework for the new walls would be made from my favourite four by two inch timber. This would add some additional support to the floors above, leaving the whole structure solid and strong. The ripping out process was slow and incredibly dusty as we were removing wood that had been in place for almost one hundred years. I was horrified to discover quite how rotten some of the wood was; many of the floor boards just crumbled as we pulled them up, and some of the joists were only supported in the walls by half an inch of rotten wood. It was astounding that the whole thing hadn't fallen down under its own weight. On the positive side, it was clear that whatever I built, however bad, was always going to be much better than what we started with.

Living in and around such renovations would be beyond many people, but Lesley seemed to take it all in her stride, happily doing her bit to keep the house clean and maintain some illusion of normality, although she must sometimes have questioned if the work would ever be finished. One of these days I must buy her a "world's most patient wife" mug and tee-shirt. At the height of the renovations, every part of the house was being used either for storage or as working space; there was a bath in one bedroom, the kit for a new bannisters in another and a workbench in the sitting room. All the remaining pipes and wires were held up with string. For several weeks, our only bathroom was out in the wing and access to the bedrooms was by ladders – securely tied to ring bolts in the walls. Being of a certain age, I frequently had to make the nocturnal journey, climbing bare-footed down the ladder and out to the toilet, passing through the kitchen, the conservatory and the wing – and stepping over several sleeping dogs along the way. In retrospect, perhaps making this journey several times each night was good incentive to get the work completed.

The dogs seemed to take the structural chaos in their stride, except for poor Romany, our Lhasa Apsos, who was really starting to show signs of her age, getting progressively more frail and confused. Partly because of her failing eyesight, Romany found it very difficult to cope with simple obstructions like a length of wood lying in her path and would either set off in search of another route, or just sit and woof until rescued. Late one night after the upper floor was laid, but before I had installed the new bannisters, Romany took it into her head to explore the new upstairs layout. I was awoken by the sound of a loud thump and a pathetic squeal. Unable to see in the dark, Romany had stepped off the edge and dropped almost ten feet onto the sitting room floor below, possibly bouncing off the staircase on the way down. She was obviously shaken and very confused, though apart from a bloody nose and a few bruises, she was relatively unscathed – but we both recognised that she might be in her final years.

The other dogs were in great form, living the life of Riley, with long walks, lots of love and plenty of food. Lady, our foxhound, even managed to catch and kill another large hare, which she carried back to the garden and proceeded to consume in a single sitting, bones, fur and everything. It was an incredible sight; the hare was actually larger than our terrier, Amber, and must have weighed all of ten pounds. It was a very rotund and breathless foxhound that came proudly back into the house and collapsed prostrate in front of the fire, squeaking and rumbling as she noisily digested her catch. I have never before smelt anything quite as pungent and unpleasant as the odour Lady produced as that hare fermented in her stomach; it was so truly eye-watering that it left a stubborn taste on your tongue. Even the other dogs were begging to be let outside, for fear of suffocation, or perhaps because of the risk of an explosion, as Lady blissfully leaked toxic fumes near the fire. For a while we were undecided whether to kick Lady out and then try to decontaminate the room, or to give it up as a lost job and sit outside ourselves, while we burned the house down. In the end we evicted the guilty dog and opened all of the windows for several hours, until it was deemed safe to return indoors.

A few days later we observed the early indications of the developing recession, when someone dumped a puppy outside the house. I had heard a car pull up opposite the front gates, then a door slammed shut and the car swiftly drove away. This caught my attention, as it was unusual activity in such a remote area. Suspecting that someone had just dumped a rubbish bag, I walked down to the gates, but I could see nothing obvious when I looked around. However, the dogs clearly sensed that something was up, so, in response to their persistent and unusual barking, I went out to look again. After a short search I discovered a brown collie-cross puppy, pathetically huddled in the ditch opposite the house. The poor thing was obviously terrified and confused, alternating between seeking our reassurance and trying to hide from the excited yapping of four unfamiliar dogs. I locked our pooches indoors and, with a little coaxing in a soft voice, managed to encourage the painfully skinny and shivering puppy to approach the house. Over the next few days we checked with the dog pound several times, to see if anyone had reported her missing, but the lack of any enquiries supported our suspicion that she had been dumped. We had no intention of taking her to the pound and an untimely death and she showed no inclination to leave – so we named her Cassie and welcomed her into our lives. Cassie was probably less than six months old and likely to be a discarded Christmas present that had become uninteresting or unaffordable. She was already the same size as our foxhound and wore a soft light brown coat, a bright centre stripe on her nose and white boots on her enormous paws. Understandably, she was initially very unsure of herself, choosing to sleep in the outhouse, but although she never became truly confident, her hunger soon overcame her fear and she cautiously ate some dog food. The next day she allowed me to stroke her, cautiously licking my hand in return. After a week she ventured warily into the house and started to bond with the other dogs. I have found that the best way to start bonding dogs into a balanced group is to take them for walks together. Because they are then all facing in the same direction and doing the same thing, they soon seem to accept each other as being part of the same group. I have found this approach to be much more effective than introducing the new dog into the group when they are all barking excitedly nose-to-nose, and facing in opposite directions, a set-up which can be seen as confrontational by the existing group of dogs. I guess the same principle applies to people; it is far easier to negotiate with someone while you walk side-by-side, than it is when facing each other confrontationally across a desk.

Everything seemed to go very smoothly at first, but an unusual problem soon showed up. Lady, the foxhound, had always been the front-runner amongst the dogs, being the fittest and fastest, always leading the others in a chase against some imagined fox or hare. But now there was a new kid on the block. Although she was less experienced in the mystical ways of the mighty hunter, as Lady would have you believe, she was definitely younger and fitter. When Lady took Cassie off across the moor during our walks, initially everything was fine. Lady felt superior because she was teaching Cassie how to hunt, demonstrating her wisdom and experience. However, we soon noticed that their runs were taking longer and longer, as if Lady was unwilling to return until Cassie was tired out. The problem, of course, was that Cassie was younger and once she had put on a little weight, she had much more stamina than Lady, who was almost four years old. Just like many people, Lady was unwilling to admit that she was getting older and when confronted with the insurmountable energy of youth, our stubborn foxhound pushed herself harder and harder – to try and maintain the illusion of superiority. When they finally returned from their run, Cassie would be puffing and a little tired, but Lady would arrive so exhausted that she would shake uncontrollably, only finding enough energy to drink a couple of litres of water before collapsing to the floor, panting helplessly for the next half hour. At first we tried to call them back, but once Cassie started to run, Lady was totally unable to resist the challenge to prove that she was the fitter and faster dog. For a while, I was concerned that they may have been worrying livestock and if they were it would have been irresponsible to continue letting them off the lead, but we were a long way away from any sheep and most of the time we could see them distantly, running across the moor. Nevertheless, it was obvious that something had to be done because, regardless of the amount of food she was packing in, Lady was losing weight at an alarming rate. After three weeks of this relentless exercise, she had dropped almost half of her bodyweight, was as lean as a racing snake and seemed almost on the verge of burnout; Cassie, on the other hand, looked ever more fit and healthy. We tried keeping Lady indoors, or leaving her on a lead at walk times, but she just howled pitifully and as soon as she had the chance she would set off running with Cassie again – ignoring our calls to return.

It seems sometimes that our dogs are deaf to the words we say. Commands like "get down!" "sit!" and "stop it!" are roundly ignored, but others are not. On occasions, as Lady started to run away with Cassie, I had seen her break stride in doubt as she heard our calls to return, but then you could clearly see her thinking, "I know I am going to get in trouble for this, but sod it – I can't help myself!" and off she would go again. On the other hand, words like "walk," "chew," "dinner" and "biscuit" elicit an instant pavlovian response, regardless of how softly they are spoken. Our dogs also seem to have an uncanny ability to tell the time, presenting themselves without fail at exactly the correct moment for breakfast, mid-day snacks and their evening meal, even adjusting automatically when the clocks change for British summer time. If I were a more cynical fellow, I would suspect that our dogs understand every word that we say, but selfishly and deliberately choose to ignore certain words.

In a desperate attempt to stop Lady's physical decline, we bought an electronic "dog shocker," which is a little box that simply clips onto the dog's collar. An accompanying remote control sends a radio signal that causes the device to make a loud buzzing sound, before administering a mild shock, similar to a bee sting, to the back of the dog's neck. The idea is that you should identify when your dog is about to be disobedient and then trigger the device along with a loud confident command, thereby deflecting the animal's attention and bringing it back to obedience. Ideally, after just a couple of uses, the buzzing alone will become enough of a warning and the dog will desist before it is necessary to administer a shock. Lady quickly figured out what the device was and who was making it work. While she could see that you were holding the remote control, she would sit obediently, all angelic and well behaved, but as soon as you put it away, she was off. Once she was out of sight, you could buzz and shock as much as you liked, but Lady would ignore the little stabs on the back of her neck, in the sure knowledge that we would give up before she did.

After a while we stopped using the "shocker," partly because it was not having the desired effect, but mostly because Lady figured out that if she went and laid in the pond for long enough – she could drown the damn thing. I was also worried that I was beginning to experience a slightly sadistic pleasure out of seeing my unruly dog jerk spasmodically in response to the shock, as she yet again ignored my pleas to return. However, what comes around, goes around – or so they say. One day, whilst trying to fit a new electrical socket in the sitting room, I inadvertently zapped myself with the residual static charge in the cables. As I hopped around the room, sucking my thumb and swearing, I noticed that Lady was standing close behind me – and she almost seemed to be smiling. Suddenly one day and for no perceptible reason, Cassie and Lady tired of the chase and never ran off again; maybe Cassie had matured enough to see how exhausted Lady was getting and for her sake decided to quit the game, or perhaps Cassie was just getting tired herself. Whatever the cause, it was not a day too soon. Slowly Lady started to regain some of the weight she that had lost, with the help of some high protein food and a few unlucky hares. Cassie became a loving and obedient dog, although she still remained painfully shy and we were never able to get her to walk on a leash.

The other dogs seemed to take to Cassie very well and there was never any sign of animosity or jealousy, although sometimes it was a bit of a juggling act to try and fuss five dogs, all at the same time. Kia can also be a little unsure of herself, so we would make a special effort to ensure that she got her share of the attention. Mind you, she was very good at getting her share of other things. One day, Lesley was doing some baking for her friend's children's birthday party. She was taking a short coffee-break, and leaving her beautifully iced creations for a moment, she stepped outside to share a drink and chat with me while I cut some construction timber. As we stood together by the front door, talking about nothing in particular, Kia appeared from out of the kitchen, with a stolen cupcake clutched gently in her mouth. She carefully squeezed through the gap between Lesley and me, pausing as if to say, "excuse me please" before proceeded towards the lawn, where she could calmly lay down to eat her prize. Lesley and I both did an almost comedic double-take, and then I called out, "Hey, Kia! Where do you think you are going with that?"

Kia paused in midstride and then ever-so-slowly she turned her beautiful innocent brown eyes towards us, as if to say, "it's okay, I left you some in the kitchen and they are really very good!"

She thoroughly enjoyed her cake, as did the children the next day, unaware of our unique quality control manager.

Although we had taken the precaution of having all of our dogs inoculated and spayed, there was one obvious omission and we were of the opinion that Cassie was old enough to get pregnant if she encountered a stray dog, which was quite likely. Lesley was away visiting some friends in England, so it fell to me to take the lovely pup down to the vet for her operation. Although she was a little tentative at first, when we arrived at the surgery, Cassie showed just how much she had developed in confidence in the few months since she had been dumped on our doorstep. She was on her best behaviour, licking every proffered hand, enjoying each stroke of her soft brown coat and endearing herself to all of the staff who surrounded her and commented on what a lovely dog she was. Even the vet instantly fell in love with Cassie, asking almost jokingly, if she could keep her after the operation. So she was understandably tearful when she telephoned me three hours later, to report that poor Cassie had succumbed to a sudden heart attack during the procedure.

I brought Cassie's body back to the house and laid her in the conservatory for a while, so that the other dogs could appreciate that she was dead. Lady sat with Cassie for several minutes, watching carefully and giving her flank the occasional nudge with her muzzle; then she gave a huff and simply walked away, with her head and tail hung low. Later, the pouring rain hid my tears as I dug a grave and gently wrapped Cassie in a blanket, before placing her in the ground. Lesley was equally upset and shocked when I telephoned her that night with the awful news. She matched the earlier words of the vet when she said, "well at least we gave her a few additional months of happiness."

Lady seemed remarkably unaffected by the loss of such a close companion, quickly returning to her life, exactly as it was before Cassie arrived, or perhaps she just hid her sadness better than the rest of us.

Chapter 16 – In which Nick gets surprise

By mid-August 2008, the majority of the structural renovations to the middle section of the house were complete. Over the previous nine months, with Lesley's help, I had added new beams to raise the floor level, stripped and rebuilt the staircase and fully dry-lined and insulated all of the walls. Then I had built a new bathroom, bedroom and corridor on the first floor and completed all of the necessary plumbing and electrical upgrades –all while having my busiest year at work. There was still a lot of dust around, with bare floors and walls and we had yet to do any plastering, decorating or any of the other twiddly bits; but we felt that we were really making progress.

One day towards the end of the month, I was fettling away upstairs, cutting skirting for the bathroom and whistling tunelessly to myself, when a movement caught my eye and I looked out of the window. To my amazement, walking up the driveway with absurdly exaggerated "let's sneak up on them" steps, were Joanne and Mark, both dressed in party hats and carrying presents. Lesley had conspired to arrange a surprise for my fiftieth birthday! I did my best to play along with the plan to sneak them both into the house, by pretending I hadn't noticed anything, but within seconds the dogs gave the game away in a cacophony of barking – accompanied by some desperate shouts of "get down!" and "shut up!" In any event it was a lovely surprise, I couldn't have wished for a better gift. I was delighted to see our daughter again and happy for the excuse to take a few days off – if only to celebrate surviving my first half century. During that long Bank Holiday weekend, we took Joanne and Mark out for a couple of pub lunches: first to Bofey Quinns at Corofin, and on another day to the Old Ground Hotel in Ennis. We ate a magnificent meal in a section of the hotel restaurant called "Poets corner," which can be a little crowded, not dissimilar to trying to eat your lunch on the London underground at rush hour, but the food is excellent. On the Sunday we had a day-trip to County Offaly and the town of Birr (ironically the town that holds the record for being the coldest place in Ireland) and then we took a trip around the magnificent castle museum, grounds and gardens. It was well worth the visit, as there are some lovely walks through the grounds and along the river, which gave us ample opportunity for some family snaps. The museum also provided plenty of fascinating information about the preceding owner's interest in astronomy, photography, botany and engineering. Joanne and Mark spent a lot of the day walking ahead, holding hands and giggling like a couple of teenagers on a first date; it was lovely to see two people so much in love – particularly as one of them was our daughter. Lesley and I watched them from a distance, delighted to see our Joanne so very happy; clearly their relationship could soon be moving towards matrimony. Late on the Monday we gave them a tearful send-off at Shannon Airport, as they went back to working in the City and a seemingly endless round of corporate events, hen-nights, stag-dos, weddings and christenings. Then we quietly returned to our house, our dogs and our very pedestrian lives – happy and contented.

A few weeks later, we decided it was time to get some chickens. When we lived in England we had kept a few at the top of the garden and although those particular hens were vicious and moody, we enjoyed having them about the place, as well as eating delicious fresh eggs. However, if we were going to keep chickens successfully at Glenmadrie, I would have to build a secure pen and chicken house. From experience, we knew how much damage even a few chickens could do to a lawn or flower bed if allowed free rein. Chickens love to scrap the earth. In their quest to find juicy bugs and worms they are relentless, hardly ever stopping to rest, and they will show no respect for potted plants, flower beds, or a freshly planted vegetable garden. I did a little research and came up with a workable design for a movable chicken hutch that we could bump up and down the lawn so that the chickens could have access to a fresh area of grass each day, as well as protection from predators and the elements. I used some scrap wood, roofing felt and chicken wire to make an eight by six foot cage, with sloping sides that rose to a five foot apex housing the nesting boxes. This nesting area was accessed from below by the chickens climbing a drawbridge ladder and by a door at the top – so we could collect the eggs and refresh the straw. I had seen similar arrangements on sale in Ennis for about three hundred euro, but they were so lightweight that they would have blown away or disintegrated during the first winter storms. My manly construction may not have looked as twee, but it was almost free to manufacture and would not resemble a wooden kite by the first week of November. That Saturday, I visited the Ennis farmers market and purchased three healthy "point of lay" chickens for just €18. Early the following morning, I watched a sly fox carefully inspecting my handiwork as he circled the chicken coop and tried to work out how to get to his breakfast. In an effort to discourage any further visits, I wound up the dogs and encouraged them to "chase the fox!" Inevitably they burst out of the front door, barking and yelping excitedly – and then ran off in entirely the wrong direction. The shrewd fox sat by the chicken coop and calmly waited until the dogs were out of sight and the noise had died down before ambling off in the other direction. I was pleased that my defences had worked, and we were delighted with our three friendly chickens that we named "Little," "Nugget" and "Drumstick"; we were equally thrilled by the delicious eggs that they produced every morning.

Although I moved the cage each day, the damage to the lawn was substantial and the chickens were clearly frustrated by the limited space. Lesley had recently started using a lot of eggs, by baking cakes to sell at the local market, and she said she could probably sell any extra eggs we happened to have – if only we had more chickens. Consequently, a few months later, we decided to create a much larger pen and expand the flock; I chose a flat area just beyond the vegetable garden and got to work. At the front of the chicken coop, I hammered in a series of angle-iron posts to create the frame and then used cable ties to secure the chicken wire fencing, which was buried at the bottom for extra security against rats, pine martens and such-like. I hadn't quite finished the enclosure by market day, so when I added our seven new chickens to the existing stock, I kept them locked in for a couple of days. This gave them a chance to settle down and learn were the roosts were, while I finished work on their new home. The chickens watched me carefully as I put the finishing touches to the six foot fence and stepped back to proudly inspect my handiwork. I told my attentive audience, "that'll keep you in – ladies," and then I opened the door to the coop and called them out.

They didn't need much encouragement to start exploring, but despite their much publicised inability to fly, four chickens showed that they hadn't read the relevant memo and immediately took to the air. Two chickens flew twenty feet up, into a nearby tree, one just hopped over the fence and the fourth flew three graceful circles around the cage before landing gently onto my head. Eventually I managed to coax them back to safety, where they busied themselves scraping the surface, digging for worms, and generally doing their best to turn their pen into a mud bath.

Around tea-time I went out into the rain to check on the chickens, carefully counting them to make sure that none had escaped. Then right before dusk, I went back again to lock them into the coop for the night. Most of them had now settled onto perches, but three stragglers were resolutely refusing to go in –just squatting miserably in the mud at one side of the cage. If they were left out overnight, they would be fully exposed to the elements and at the mercy of all kind of nocturnal predators, so I entered the cage and making full use of my talents as a professional trainer, I attempted to guide them into the coop. At first I tried some simple verbal directions, accompanied with pointed fingers as a visual aid, but the chickens just looked at me blankly. Secondly I experimented with some basic corralling techniques, by gently flapping my arms and taking slow sideways steps, to place myself on the opposite side to where I wanted the chickens to go. This was marginally more successful as the chickens started to move around a bit – but sadly not towards the open door of the coop. I am a patient man, so I was unperturbed to spend the next ten minutes, quietly but unsuccessfully sloshing through the mud and gently waving my arms like some wellington clad Frankenstein monster as the chickens dashed hither and thither around me – like naughty children refusing to go to bed. To make matters worse, several of the other chickens had now come out of the coop to investigate what all of the fuss was about, and they were standing on the side lines, clearly enjoying the show. Finally I decided that the only way I was going to get these three chickens back into the coop, was if I caught them and shoved them through the door myself. So I chased my disappointed audience back indoors, firmly closed the coop door and then set about trying to grab the three remaining feathered fugitives. Chickens can run surprisingly quickly, even on wet sloppy mud; unfortunately I cannot – particularly when I am wearing wellington boots and attempting to run in my patented "chicken catching" crouch. I managed to snag and box the first two within a couple of minutes, mostly because they had become tired of the game and probably wanted to go to bed anyway. But the last chicken was full of wiles, cunning and damned fast, repeatedly darting away from my outstretched fingers at the last second. By the time it was almost fully dark, I was becoming weary and my back was aching from constantly running around like some demented hunchback. The knees on my jeans were muddy, because I had already slipped over twice and I was covered in chicken poo and midge bites. So I was delighted when my quick thinking turned a third slip into a heroic rugby tackle and I snagged the final chicken, as I slid face down into the mud. My dear wife was typically unsympathetic when I wearily trudged back indoors, still caked in feathers, poop and mud; in fact, for some reason, as I recounted my attempts to catch the chickens, she couldn't stop laughing.

Amber, our little terrier, considers that she is the biggest of our dogs, as well as being a fearless and mighty hunter; so she was quick to follow me into the chicken pen the next morning, to check out the new arrivals. All of the dogs consider the chickens to be part of our family and have never shown any sign of relating these noisy balls of feathers beaks and claws with the meat in their favourite brand of dog food. They will, however, happily eat the carcase of a dead chicken, or steal any eggs that are left unguarded. Because chickens are such excellent runners, Amber has been known on occasion to give chase. The little dog displays no intention of ill will or aggression during the pursuit; she is merely seeking to demonstrate her superiority, and the chickens seem to enjoy the exercise. Typically she will run faster and faster in response to the speed of the chickens, stopping only when they flap and squawk, or we shout an admonishing "AMBER!!! Stop it!"

On this day, as I was pottering about changing the water and collecting the eggs, Amber was dawdling along checking out the newbies, and sniffing for any tasty poo to eat. On a whim, she suddenly decided that it would be fun to chase a chicken. They all did the usual bit of running around for a few seconds, before I called time and Amber dutifully desisted. However, previously we had just three chickens – and now we had ten. As soon as Amber turned her back, the new chickens, perhaps intrigued by what appeared to be an oversized rat, started to follow the little dog and were quickly joined by the remainder of the flock, along with a curious sparrow. For a while everything was fine in this harmless game of "follow the leader," but once Amber noticed she was being shadowed, by what appeared to be ten descendants of the dinosaurs and an audience of sparrows, she started to walk a little faster. The chickens responded in kind, and alarmed by this turn of events, Amber immediately upped her pace – only to discover that the chickens were matching her stride-for-stride. Moments later, little Amber was frantically running up and down the cage, failing completely to look brave and confident as she was chased by ten large and determined chickens, watched from a safe distance by a crowd of noisy wild birds. Whilst watching this pursuit, I was reminded of my first game of rugby at "big school," when as a skinny first year, I stupidly caught the ball and was immediately confronted by the sight of several muscle-bound sixth-formers charging towards me. Common sense and logic told me to pass the ball, but my survival instincts took over and I turned tail and ran – all the way back to the changing room! In her blind panic, Amber completely ignored my attempts to direct her to safety, preferring to run a serpentine path in an attempt to shake her irate pursuers. This flawed strategy caused her to run into a corner, where she was assaulted with surprising ferocity by all ten chickens and a passing finch with a score to settle. I quickly shooed the chickens away and again rescued our little dog, fortuitously unharmed, but rather embarrassed. Of course, once she was safely outside the wire, Amber puffed herself up and indignantly ran around the cage, barking furiously, challenging the chickens to a rematch, whilst all the while carefully watching my whereabouts to ensure that I could still come to the rescue, if needed.

Although I seemed to be busier than ever at work, I was acutely aware of the risk of economic recession and mindful that this particular bubble was about to burst. As the economy continued its downward spiral, it looked like the renovations might be finished just before the money ran out – but it was going to be a close run thing. To promote my business locally and make a few bob as well, I had started to write a weekly newspaper column and begun work on a book about training. I enjoy writing. I find it cathartic and beneficial. Writing instructional material is also an excellent way to test and consolidate your understanding of your own specialist subject. But writing can be a thankless task. Apart from the challenge of convincing a publisher to take on your work, all your family will see is endless hours at the computer, liberally sprinkled with fear, doubt and self-loathing, while you create, edit and re-edit your work, without the guarantee of anything positive to show for it. To make any substantial progress, the writing guides tell us a writer is supposed to work regular hours, as in any proper job; some even suggest putting on a suit and driving around the block, before beginning work. Once seated, the writer should type diligently for several hours, focusing on volume, rather than content or quality, as that element will be corrected during the editing stage. I fail miserably on all of these points – and many others. Personally, I can only write when the mood takes me, or as a print deadline looms and I will frequently become distracted or spend endless minutes staring out of the window in search of an elusive word or sentence. Whenever I am at home, whether I am writing or just working on the house, I have embraced the Irish tradition of taking a decent break for lunch at one o'clock. Initially I found the practice rather funny and endearing – particularly when I first saw a notice boldly declaring "closed for lunch" on the door of a local restaurant – but now I see the value. My mind is more relaxed, even if I can't see my belt buckle anymore. Sometimes my writing progress is painfully slow, but on other occasions the words seem to flow from my head faster than I can type. Perhaps the biggest difficulty is that there are always several other things that I could be doing instead of writing; but I know that if I relent, the writing will remain unfinished – probably forever. Thankfully Lesley is incredibly patient and understanding; she has generously given me sufficient space and time to get the job completed, whilst not always moaning about the other jobs that are left undone.

Of course with such an old property, there always seem to be so many jobs that need to be done. For many years there were the obvious renovations – and anything that didn't need renovating probably required maintenance. Lesley has a huge task just looking after the planted parts of the garden, along with digging, weeding and harvesting. Every autumn she disappears for hours, picking the masses of free fruit that grows in the hedges around the house, ready for making jam and delicious crumbles. I do my best to keep our wide expanse of lawn under some sort of control; from August through to the end of October, most of my spare time is consumed by cutting, splitting and stacking firewood, ready for the winter. One problem caused by living in such a remote area is the risk of "cabin fever," caused by being in and around the same house for days, or even weeks, without seeing another soul and then having ever more complicated discussions with our idiot dogs. Because we are relatively self-sufficient, several weeks can go by between shopping trips to town, making it is easy to end up becoming depressed and lethargic. So it is important to make an extra effort to get out and mix with other people, even if it is just through a grocery shopping trip, a visit to a friend's house or window shopping around Ennis. On the other hand, when Lesley is away, I love to sit at the top of the quarry in the late evening and enjoy the solitude and silence while I watch the sun set. This idyllic reverie is usually interrupted by a cloud of midges buzzing around my face, or a crowd of dogs all trying to sit on my lap at the same time; but the beauty of the moment remains untarnished.

By the end of the year, Lesley was baking every week for the local market and enjoying the positive feedback she was getting about her delicious cakes, scones, awesome chutneys and jams. The downside is that the house is usually filled with the delicious smells of a farmhouse kitchen, and there are always plenty of extra cakes to brighten my mood and widen my waist-line. With so much gardening to do, along with baking almost non-stop from Thursday until the early hours of Saturday morning, I was worried that Lesley was taking on too much and would again become ill. Sure enough, a few weeks later she was back at A&E again, even though it was only for a badly twisted ankle. However, the moment she was in front of the doctor, she developed chest pains and was immediately admitted for cardiac observation. As a routine precaution the hospital put Lesley on blood thinners. Initially they were given by injection, which left her with dramatic multi-coloured bruises, but after a few days they changed to tablets. Because of the holiday weekend, it was several days before Lesley even started to undergo any tests. Being cooped up in hospital when there was so much gardening that she could be doing, she naturally became annoyed and frustrated; more distressingly, she was also finding it increasingly difficult to breathe. Within a few days, even the short slow walk along the corridor to the coffee machine would leave her blue lipped and panting. We were getting very worried by her deteriorating health and the lack of any definitive medical information. Several times I cornered the doctor on duty to try and get a diagnosis and the response was often less than comforting....

"Oh, excuse me, doctor, I am sorry to trouble you." I said on one such occasion, body blocking his path along the corridor. "Could you please tell me how my wife is doing?"

"Yes, of course," the doctor replied, juggling an arm full of charts. "Who is your wife?"

"It's Lesley, this lady here," I said, pointing to the person who he had been examining just thirty seconds earlier.

"Ah yes, Lesley. Now let me see." He found the chart and started to flick through the pages, making "Um" and "Er" and "Ah, yes" noises. Finally he looked up from the chart and fixed me with a confused stare. "What was wrong with her?"

"What do you mean, what was wrong with her? Don't you know what's wrong with her?" I asked incredulously.

"Ha!" He snorted at my stupidity, "Of course we know what's wrong with her – NOW." He rolled his eyes dramatically to the ceiling. "I was asking what was wrong with her when she came in!"

On each occasion that I spoke with a nurse or doctor, I asked if the blood thinners could be the cause of the breathing difficulties, pointing out repeatedly that Lesley had seemed to be in good health when she came into the hospital with a simple twisted ankle. Over and over the doctors assured us that there was no chance of the breathlessness being caused by the blood thinners, so they pressed on with the cardiac investigations. After two weeks they had examined, tested, poked and prodded my wife in every conceivable way, without finding anything of interest; they discontinued the blood thinners – and Lesley's breathing magically started to improve. Within a week she was back to normal, digging the garden and baking at all hours of the night. It turned out to be an extremely expensive and time consuming sprained ankle. In future I imagine if Lesley broke her leg, she would just grit her teeth and walk it off!

Chapter 17 – In which our family grows again

Throughout 2009, there seemed to be little chance to sit and rest. Although most of the structural renovations were now completed, almost two thirds of the house needed to be decorated. I still had to attach new light fittings, curtain rails, radiators and skirting boards, fit the doors and carpets and do all the other fiddly things that seem to take forever. Lesley is our chief decorator and she was also doing sterling work altering and making up curtains; this helped considerably to protect our meagre savings. All of these little extras seemed to cost an incredible amount of money and took a lot of time to source and fit. For a while, we were spending almost every other weekend in Limerick, looking for bargains in the DIY and soft furnishing sales. The up-side of the ever deepening recession was that prices were starting to fall and there were some genuine bargains to be had if you were patient and prepared to haggle.

As the autumn rains started to set in, we took a delivery of wood for the fire. The previous year I had discovered a local sawmill that will deliver a lorry load of off-cut timber for just a few hundred euro; all I had to do was cut it into logs. The wood was mostly pine and not of particularly good quality, being largely the slabs of bark and wood that are created when a round tree trunk is trimmed to become a square. But it is cheap fire wood and it will burn, although not with the heat you would get from better quality woods like cedar or oak. I managed to lash down a large blue gazebo, to keep me and the wood reasonably dry while I set about turning thirty foot tree trunks into tidy logs that would fit into the stove. I did my best to keep everything watertight, covering the wood pile with plastic and working under the gazebo, but with the rain and high humidity, the wood was soon covered in mould and smelly black slime. This was our second delivery of these "slabs," but unlike the first delivery, this wood was already quite damp and, thanks to the nonstop rain, getting wetter by the day. To get any heat efficiency out of wood, it needs to be cut, stacked and air dried for about a year before it is burned. It was becoming obvious that this load of wood was going to do little to heat the house and we were going to have to buy a lot of coal or peat if we were going to keep warm that winter.

The winter rain set in during October and carried on falling relentlessly for what seemed like weeks. Soon the lane at the back of the house was running like a small river. The pond had overflowed, the meadow was flooded and puddled into six inch deep mud by the cattle and the chicken pen looked like a mud bath. However, we are fortunate; we live at the top of the hill. Down below, the effects of the worst autumn rain on record was horrific to behold. The Shannon basin is low lying and the gradient to the sea is slight, making the rivers slow to clear any excess water. Add to this the uncontrolled increase in houses and industrial estates which, through lax or corrupt planning through the boom years, have been built on flood plains. The flooding that followed was a disaster waiting to happen. Although insignificant when compared to the Haiti earthquake and the Asian Japanese tsunami, the flooding throughout the west of Ireland at the end of 2009 was a local disaster. Coming on top of an already deep recession and high unemployment, it hit the local area hard. The rain fell unrelentingly, day after dreadful day, drenching the soil until the water gradually ran out of places to go. Soon the fields, roads and towns began to flood, so much so that several towns and small villages became completely cut off. We heard numerous heart-breaking stories of families and businesses that had lost everything they owned to the encroaching water. Many of these poor people remained uninsured since the previous incidence of flooding and were relying on charity or friends for food, clothing and accommodation. Hundreds of farmers were unable to save their stocks of winter feed and many tragically also lost much of their livestock to the merciless water. In mid-December, the rain finally stopped and the water gradually receded, giving way to recriminations and the inevitable public enquiry. Then, just as we began to think that perhaps the worst was over for the winter, a high pressure weather system stalled over Ireland, pulling icy Artic air in from the North, dragging the temperature down and turning the flooded roads and fields into ice. At the house, the thermometer stayed below freezing for several weeks and overnight fell to as low as minus eighteen degrees centigrade, freezing several of our water pipes, until I positioned some heat lamps to maintain the overnight temperature. Outside, even wrapped in insulation, the regulator on the butane gas cylinders froze up and needed to be warmed with liberal amounts of hot water before we could cook any breakfast. During the days, thick fog and cloud blocked out any heat from the weak winter sun, and then rolled away to expose a stunning star-filled sky each night, which sucked any remaining warmth from the air. For several days, the cold became so intense that even the antifreeze in Lesley's car froze solid. Eventually the warm and wet westerly airstreams returned, driving the cold weather back towards Siberia and Ireland returned to a more normal run of humid sunshine and showers, heralding the welcome onset of another spring.

As we progressed nearer to the end of the renovations of the house and garden, life became more predictable and even a little ordinary. For many days and even weeks, it would be fair to say that nothing really happened, at least not anything particularly interesting or exciting. After all of the hectic years leading up to, and following, the move to Ireland, it was nice to sample some of the "simpler life" that we had previously dreamed of. Of course the reality of this life, without pressure from the corporate monster, without the constant stress of living under a burden of debt and with the freedom to more or less do as we pleased, was that it could easily become quite boring and uninteresting. Unless we found some ways of productively filling our time, we could both become sluggish and depressed, drifting through life, rudderless, until we became hateful of the dream we had sought and the new life we had achieved. Conversely, we had to be cautious that, in an effort to keep our lives interesting and challenging, we didn't recreate the very things that had motivated us to seek a new life in the first place. I think that everybody needs some challenge and achievement in their lives to maintain some sense of self-worth, but in our modern society, where our appreciation of value is blunted by instant consumer satisfaction, yesterday's challenge can quickly become today's boring routine – and then the search for a bigger challenge begins over again. In the end we can find ourselves becoming addicted to this cycle of challenge and gratification, which ultimately leaves us discontented and heading towards depression. Whether we are chasing advancement at work, striving to accumulate more wealth and possessions, or just endeavouring to build a better mousetrap, the cycle is continuous and ultimately unsatisfying. I am sometimes reminded of the disappointed faces of children, just two days after the Christmas present "glut," saddened because life now has so little to offer and they feel that they have nothing to look forward to until next year. Yet the happiest children I have ever met lived in a mud hut in Nigeria and only had a rusty bicycle wheel to play with. I suppose that what Lesley and I needed to do at that stage was to develop a sense of perspective, focusing our minds on what we had and being contented with what we had achieved; after all, so many people would covet the life we now had – and so should we. I am not a religious person, being educated in a convent school quite literally beat any religion out of me at an early age, but I can see the sense in what the Buddhists call "the second noble truth". This says something along the lines of "rather than struggling for what you think you want, modify your wanting," or, to paraphrase, "be happy with what you've got – you twat!" I suppose the trick is to find some insignificant but interesting things that you would like to do, do them well and then sit back and enjoy them. I do my best but I haven't mastered the art yet, and Lesley still has the capacity to turn the smallest project into a life consuming monster that can leave her angry, frustrated and unable to sleep. We both know what we need to do to be happier, but sometimes being stupid keeps getting in the way.

Sometimes, something getting in the way can help me remember why we decided to move to Ireland in the first place, particularly when I get held up on the road. The stress of living and commuting in England often seems to manifest itself through various forms of road rage, from mild impatience, to oral and visual insults and extending right through to the extremes of tailgating and excessive and unwarranted violence. During the early morning commute in England, I have seen some of these apoplectic, blue-faced drivers, screaming and ranting at some other driver's minor indiscretion and then lurching their car dangerously towards the terrified and confused subject of their hatred, while splattering the inside of the windscreen with obscenities and spittle. I always wondered how bad their day was going to turn out to be, if they started out feeling so stressed, angry and uncompromising. So now, each time my commute is interrupted or delayed by loose cows, slow farm machinery, or perhaps two cars that have blocked the road while the occupants have a chat, I use the opportunity to enjoy a few moments of relaxation by looking out over the fields and listening to the birds. Sometimes the obstruction can provide its own entertainment, lifting the spirits and brightening your whole day.

One warm spring afternoon, I was driving back to our house from Ennis, when what little traffic there was ground to a halt outside the gates of a local school. I checked the time and then mentally kicked myself. I usually try to avoid passing the schools during dropping off and picking up times, as the adjacent roads become a minefield of haphazardly triple-parked cars and buses, chatting parents and wildly running children. However, on this glorious sunny day, fate conspired to deliver a coordinated coincidence of events, with such exquisite comedic timing that I still laugh each time I pass that spot. All of the traffic in both directions was stationary and the pavements outside the school were crowded with dozens of primary school children. The youngsters were all laughing and pointing, despite being held back by the hapless teachers and some parents who were desperately trying to block their view of two dogs fornicating in the centre of the road. The female dog, a pretty black collie cross, had her head hung low and turned away, as if in shame. Meanwhile, the male dog – a scruffy beige wire-haired mongrel, tongue lolling and cross-eyed in ecstasy – proudly went about his business, perhaps encouraged by the presence of an unplanned audience and an elderly nun, who was indignantly beating his rump with an umbrella, as if she was engaged in some outlandish ménage à trois!

As 2009 drew to a close, with the beginning of another bitterly cold and snowy winter, we were finally far enough ahead with the decorating that we could consider putting on a truly festive Christmas. For the better part of six years we had been living in what amounted to a building site. What would have been the point of sticking a Christmas tree up beside the stacked rolls of insulation, or hanging decorations on the exposed electrical wiring and plumbing, merely to satisfy some elements of society and the retailers? However, this year the bulk of the renovations and decorations were completed and Joanne and Mark were coming to stay during part of the festive period, but only on the understanding that we would "do a proper Christmas". So we took a trip to Limerick and splashed out on a nice plastic Christmas tree, along with a few boxes of decorations and in no time the living room resembled Santa's grotto. A few days later, I delicately picked my way along the ice-packed roads to Shannon Airport, to collect our daughter and her boyfriend, and then with equal care, I brought them home for a proper Glenmadrie Christmas. Keeping to the strict traditions of the festive period, we ate too much, imbibed alcoholic beverages, wore our loosest clothing, watched old movies on television, exchanged silly gifts, played board games and argued about the rules and generally ignored the religious significance of the holiday. Most days we had a late breakfast of French toast with lashings of maple syrup, which is strangely satisfying, but leaves one stricken with guilt for the remainder of the day. After breakfast we would take the dogs for a long walk through the forest and then snack on satsumas, chocolates, mince pies and crisps until it was time to attack our evening meal. This was usually chicken for the carnivores, with a vegetarian alternative for me, lashings of roasted potatoes, parsnips, sweet potato, carrot and delicious boiled vegetables like kale or cabbage, along with cranberry jelly, bread sauce and gravy. For "afters" I had prepared an American style cheese cake, from my mother's secret recipe, made with enough cream cheese, sugar, egg white and sour cream to weigh in at almost one thousand calories a portion – pure indulgence! After two days of such slothfulness, we became bored, bloated and restless, so we decided to get active. Mark did sterling work filling a couple of empty barrels with chopped kindling for the fire; then he helped me clear up the last of the rubbish that had been generated during the renovations. Indoors, Lesley and Joanne sat by a roaring fire doing some mother and daughter crafts. On the third day the fog and low cloud gave way to a hard frost and crystal clear skies, which gave Mark and Joanne the opportunity to take some long romantic walks, accompanied by our decidedly unromantic dogs. As they ambled along the wooded hillside, they took some stunning photographs of the misty snow-covered valley below, glinting in the brilliant sunlight. On the last night we had great fun, a few beers and many laughs, playing a family game of darts out in the wing, where I had set up the board. For a while the competition was fierce and the atmosphere lovingly acrimonious, as we battled uncompromisingly to become champions. Despite the fun, our interest slowly began to wane, perhaps distracted by our inability to hit the required double – or even the dartboard. As the newly painted wall became peppered with indentations, proving that alcohol did not compensate for a lack of skill and practice, we called it a draw and gladly returned to the welcoming warmth of the sitting room.

Sadly the break was over all too soon and yet again, Joanne and Mark were off back to the daily grind of commuting to work in London. Although the company had been warm and friendly during our darts match, we had noticed that the wing resisted any attempts to raise the temperature above a dank sixty degrees, and in places the tiled floor had even become slick with condensation. Clearly I needed to undertake some remedial work to improve the situation. Although all of the walls and ceilings that I had built were well insulated, feeling dry and warm to the touch, the original stone and concrete walls were constantly cold and damp. During the five years since the wing was built, we had only really made regular use of the utility room and the shower; the office and reading room were utilized for nothing more than storing furniture and boxes of ornaments, homeless until the renovations in the main part of the house were completed. Although the building had remained apparently dry whilst unoccupied, now that it was in more regular use and being heated, the damp was being pulled through the old walls and evaporated away, sucking any heat from the air. I decided that the only reasonable alternative to knocking the whole thing down and starting again, was to dry-line the cold areas. I could add a vapour barrier along with additional insulation, and then lay a warm wooden floor over the cold tiles.

It took me several weeks to build the new framework for the false walls and vapour barriers, before I was able to start adding the dry-lining. There were some complicated twiddly bits around the arched windows and in several places I had to move the electrical sockets. I also took the opportunity to correct a mistake that I had made when reinstalling the central heating. Being a naive fool, I had assumed that the original heating system had been installed by a competent professional and that I would be safe to copy the layout when I replaced and extended the plumbing; I was mistaken.

Although my design worked when I tested it, we noticed that the radiators warmed up one after another, when they should all heat at once; as a result the heat never adequately reached the far end of the system. Although it was a silly little mistake to make and demonstrated my inexperience, it would be relatively easy to rectify, provided I could locate the correct pipes and connections – without demolishing the entire house in the process. But by now all of the plumbing had been concealed in the walls and behind the dry-lining, some of it up to five years previously. Accordingly I spent several hours sitting with my eyes shut, trying to map the various pipes and junctions, before I was confident and ready to proceed. However, it took several frustrating attempts to explain the problem and my proposed cure before Lesley gave her reluctant authorisation for me to knock some holes in her beautifully decorated walls. Finally, armed with the correct work order, I set about carefully removing the skirting boards, cutting some square holes in the plasterboard and stripping away the insulation, until I could access the pipes and reroute the plumbing. Happily my mind mapping proved to be unerringly accurate, or just extraordinarily lucky. The three small holes that I made were spot on target, exactly where I needed to alter the plumbing and once the system was drained, it was a straightforward job to make the corrections. When we were confident that the heating was definitely working correctly, I was able to cut some new plasterboard and make good the damage. With the dry-lining completed, the floors and walls protected with a vapour barrier and a new laminate floor fitted over the cold stone tiles, the wing was now largely free from damp and a good deal warmer; I could finally get on with some other things.

Although the chickens were housed in a large pen, their constant scrapping for worms and bugs, combined with another wet summer, soon turned the surface into a sea of deep mud. So we decided to let them range freely and took the risk of letting them out of the pen whenever possible. Chickens are quick learners, for such stupid birds, and they were soon ranging far and wide around the land in search of the juiciest bugs. There is something very calming about having loose chickens quietly pecking and scratching about the place – unless you happen to be trying to dig in the vegetable garden. Within seconds of Lesley pushing a spade into the earth, you will see the chickens sprinting across the lawn towards her, followed by a flurry of swearing and kicking. As far as the chickens are concerned, my wife is just a very large chicken who is capable of uncovering worms on an industrial scale and unaware of her desire to make progress with the gardening, they attempt to outdo each other, making ever more death defying dives for worms, outwardly oblivious to the angry gardener and her plunging spade. Thankfully no chickens have ever been accidentally decapitated and I learned to let them out only on non-digging days. Each evening at around dusk, I walk up towards the chicken pen, rattling a plastic bucket containing some wild bird seed and shouting "Here chick-chick-chiiickens!" Within seconds they will appear, running comically, but with enthusiasm, as they follow me back towards their pen. Usually one chicken will be missing, only to be found after a search around the land, stubbornly digging under some bush in an effort to get just one more worm before bed time.

For a while we were lucky that no predators found our friendly and well-fed flock, but one evening while searching for a missing chicken, I found a scattering of bloody feathers. There had been a murder! Most likely we had been visited by a fox or a pine marten, although during my forensic investigation I never found any footprints or other indications of what did the deed; it may even have been a stray dog. In any event, the procedure following such a crime is to keep the chickens inside the pen for a few days, in the hope that the predator has moved on to an easier feeding ground. You might imagine that our four dogs would take the initiative, stationing themselves around the land in strategically advantageous positions, where they could protect the flock and ward off any foxes that exhibit a bad attitude. In reality the chickens are only protected from predatory postmen and passing cyclists; our dogs spend most of their days lying prostrate in the conservatory, only rising to remind Lesley that it is long past time for their mid-day biscuit.

Dear old Romany seemed to be getting more blind, deaf and immobile every day. She was not unlike a very small but fat sheep, or a legged version of one of those white fluffy things, that some people feel it is appropriate or fashionable to put over toilet rolls. She had become so stiff that her little legs stuck out from her cylindrical body, at ten and two o'clock, making her squirm and wiggle for several seconds before she could rise from a sleeping position – like a furry tortoise that had inadvertently rolled onto its back. Romany now slept so deeply that it was not unusual to consider that she had quietly passed away, so reluctant was she to being roused by anything but the most determined prodding. And yet somehow, whenever I stepped over her recumbent form, she would look up at the wrong moment and receive a sharp kick in the head from my trailing foot. Despite the accidental nature of this assault and my immediate apology, Romany would always look at me in confused accusation, clearly mouthing the words, "what the fu....!" You would have expected her to learn one of life's little lessons from these repeated incidents, but no! Undaunted, she continued to lie in doorways or across the corridor, presumably to avail of a refreshing breeze. And inevitably, whenever I had to step over this pink bellied sausage in a shabby fur coat, up she would look, and there would be a "clonk," followed by further profuse apologies and another incriminatory stare.

Over the next few weeks we lost a further two chickens to the unseen predators and sad as it was, financially we would have been about even, because the chickens ate hardly any pellets when they had access to so many bugs and worms; still, the egg yield was down. One day, I had just arrived back from work and was climbing out of the car, when I heard an almighty cacophony of squawks from the meadow. Correctly suspecting that the chickens were under sustained attack and even though I was wearing new shoes and my best pair of trousers, I heroically ran to try and intervene, but without success; the field was strewn with chicken feathers and the bloodied remains of one lone wing. Once I had rounded up the remainder of the terrified chickens, the count revealed that we had lost four. We decided then that we would probably need to keep the flock permanently penned. During the next few days I bought more chicken wire and angle iron posts and extended the pen considerably, more than doubling the surface area. The following weekend, I met with the "chicken lady" in the market car park in the centre of Gort and restocked our diminished flock. Lesley had been out shopping that morning, so when she returned she excitedly walked up to the chicken pen, to inspect our new arrivals.

"Those aren't chickens," she said knowingly, pointing to two snow white, six inch tall, yellow beaked individuals that were quacking loudly at each other.

"Eah, no," I admitted, "They're ducks." I shrugged. "I saw them – and I couldn't resist!"

"What type are they?"

"I think they are called Aylesbury ducks. They grow quite big," I explained. "They were going cheap – or quack.," I quipped.

Lesley thumped me lovingly. "What do they do?" she asked.

"Well the lady had laying ducks and eating ducks. These are "eating ducks," so I don't expect they will lay many eggs."

"So what will we do with them?"

"Just keep them as pets – I suppose. They can live in with the chickens," I suggested. "Perhaps they will go in the pond eventually," I added hopefully.

The ducks, who we named "Jemima" and "Puddle," after the Beatrix Potter book, grew at an alarming rate, almost doubling in size every few days. Within weeks they were the size of swans, and despite being "eating ducks" they both started laying large white eggs every day. Even for a duck, Jemima was cantankerous and argumentative, always quacking loudly and irritably and running away with her huge wings flapping whenever we went near her; it was as if she had been horribly mistreated in a previous life and was never going to let it happen again. "Puddle," was the complete opposite, incredibly friendly and welcoming. She would run over whenever she saw me, fluttering her wings in silent ecstasy if I consented to stroke her broad, white back. Contrary to popular belief, ducks do not need to swim in vast lakes to be happy. They only require a few inches of water to remain clean and contented and "good weather for ducks" is actually warm and sunny. Nevertheless, as I had dug the pond a few years earlier and it was regularly visited by some local wild ducks, I thought it would be nice to give our two Aylesburys the same privilege. Accordingly, when they were about two months old and a good bit bigger than a chicken, I let them out of the pen and led the way up to the pond. The fifty yard walk took about fifteen minutes, as they were excited by their new environment and became easily distracted, stopping to inspect every flower and bug along the way. After much cajoling, encouragement and quite a bit of chasing, we finally arrived at the pond – which Jemima and Puddle viewed with suspicion. Thinking that perhaps they needed some instruction in the art of being duck-like, I waded in until the water was almost lapping at the top of my wellies, and splashed gently with my hands. This seemed to do the trick and both ducks waddled a few inches into the water and started to feed, by sieving the rich mud with their beaks. Everything went swimmingly for a while (so to speak), until Jemima decided to take a shortcut to the other side of the pond. She walked out until the shelf fell away and then started to flap and quack loudly in panic. I could almost imagine her shouting, "Holy crap! I can't touch the bottom!" In seconds, both ducks were out of the water and running back to the chicken pen, where they hid in the coop for the rest of the afternoon. After two further embarrassingly unsuccessful attempts to introduce our ducks to the pond, I relented and purchased a hefty child's sand box made of bright blue plastic, which would hold a few inches of water and was large enough for the ducks to bathe in safety. That afternoon I set the makeshift pool into an indentation in the ground within the chicken pen and filled it with water from a hosepipe. Both ducks were bathing in their new pool, even before I had finished filling it; in fact, their playful dives and splashes were so exuberant that I had to top up the water twice within the first hour. It was a beautiful warm evening and at dusk, when I went to close up the animals for the night, both ducks were still paddling happily in their pond. Disregarding my orders to go to bed, it seemed as if they were a couple of school children playing with a new toy. As they looked at me with pleading eyes, I imagined them saying, "Please Dad, can we play a little longer? Ple-e-ease?"

Although Jemima and Puddle would continue to visit the pond fairly regularly, they only ever stood in an inch of water whilst filter-feeding and never again attempted to swim – unless they were in the safety of their blue plastic pond.

Chapter 18 – In which our numbers increase again

As the dry and unseasonably warm autumn of 2010 drew to a close, there were many heather fires on the moors dotted around the county, started accidentally by casually discarded cigarettes, or perhaps deliberately to clear the old growth and make room for young fresh shoots. Locally there were two: one about a mile away to the west which lit up the night sky like the London blitz and a second that again consumed the moor opposite the house. This second fire was so large and fast moving that I called out the fire brigade as soon as I noticed the writhing smoke and flames. Once I had given the telephone operator detailed directions, I hurriedly drove my car down the hill to warn the occupants of a house that seemed to be directly in the path of the advancing flames. The house was unoccupied and my trip now seemed a little unnecessary as the flames were clearly not going to pass as close to the house as had first appeared. However, the wind was strengthening and I could see that the fire was closing in on the road that would take me back to the house, so I jumped back into my car and swiftly set off for home. As I climbed the hill a few hundred yards from my front gates, smoke started to pour through the hedge to my right and I could see the flames leaping above the trees; within seconds the road ahead disappeared in a wall of flame, smoke and flying sparks. My instincts told me that attempting to stop and backup could be disastrous, so I jammed my right foot hard on the loud pedal, gripped the wheel tightly and prayed to the blessed angels of acceleration and internal combustion to deliver me from a fiery death. For a few seconds the car was engulfed in a cauldron of flame and the heat on the side window was so intense that I had to turn my face away. Then, just when I was starting to suspect that I had made the last bad mistake of my life, the car burst into daylight and roared away from the fire. By the time I had parked the car and checked it over for damage, my heartbeat had slowed to a mild gallop and I figured that I deserved a nice cup of tea. It was, after that, slightly surreal to go indoors and discover one's loved one, with her feet up watching television, completely oblivious to what had just occurred.

"I just heard a car. Have you been out?" Lesley asked, looking up as she sipped her coffee.

"Yea," I said, "I just went down the road to that old cottage to warn them about the fire."

"I think it's empty, isn't it?" she offered helpfully, glancing back at the television.

"Yes. Bit of a wasted trip, as it turned out. The fire was a bit close on the way back, though," I offered.

"Mm, sorry? What did you say?" She asked, glancing briefly away from the horticultural delights of "Gardeners World."

"I said, I think I can hear the fire engine now. I'll go out and look."

"Okay," she said, nodding to herself.

As always the firemen did a grand job of watching the main fire carefully and sneaking up on any stray bits that tried to make a break for freedom – and then bashing them over the head with a spade, until there was nothing left but a sooty mark on the ground. However, I was mildly amused to see one brave fireman, who was taking a break for a cup of tea and a cigarette, casually flick his dog end over the hedge after he had finished his smoke. Perhaps he was hoping for some overtime!

Apart from the susceptibility to stress, which encouraged us to move to Ireland in the first place, and an irritable stomach, I have been fortunate enough to remain in pretty good health for most of my life. Over the previous ten years I'd had several small skin lesions removed, purely as a precaution and without incident. This usually requires a little local anaesthetic, a small cut, a quick inspection of the offending lump under the microscope and ten days later, a visit to the G.P. to have the stiches removed – if I can't reach to do it myself. More recently, perhaps because of the damper climate, my old karate injuries had started to ache, so the doctor had prescribed some magic jollup to lubricate my old joints. It worked miracles and has helped me to feel a lot better, if you can ignore the unfortunate side effect of periodic bouts of violent and uncontrolled flatulence – which is hard to do if you have just frightened the dog, or blown the duvet off the bed for the third time that night. The wags that are empowered with inventing names for such medical conditions must have been especially pleased when they came up with "meteorism" for this particular malaise. At my age I try to avoid looking in the mirror, but my memory is going, so I have to relent when it comes to shaving. One morning I noticed a small lump on the side of my nose, which had tripled in size within a fortnight and become painful to the touch. I assumed it was a small infected spot, but my doctor said it was another lesion and should be removed; and so a few weeks later I was back at the hospital, in the day surgery waiting area – waiting. Perhaps in an effort to be interesting, the medical staff called our dank little room "chairs"; it was slightly larger than a broom cupboard, but not nearly as nice. Would a rose by any other name, smell as sweetly? This particular rose had the sour smell of fearful sweat and disinfectant. There were several patients waiting along with me, sitting quietly, watching a fuzzy picture on the small television and trying not to be nervous. Periodically a nurse would take a patient from the room to pre-op interrogation, where they would be stripped of their dignity and clothing. A junior doctor would use a blue felt pen to draw a circle around their offending lump and then add a large arrow for humorous effect – or to assist the myopic surgeon to find the circle. A little while later they would sheepishly return to the waiting area, wearing a stiff smile and an equally stiff blue cotton gown that refused to close at the back, carelessly displaying their baggy underpants or pimply buttocks for all to see. When it was my turn, the junior doctor spent some time reviewing my charts and may even have used his smart phone to sneak a quick look at the internet before he successfully located my nose – but I may have helped by pointing to the spot with my finger. Then with his tongue out, he carefully drew a circle on my nose with his pen; but, presumably quite confident that the surgeon could find my nose without additional assistance, he decided against adding the usual arrow. However, suddenly stricken with self-doubt and perhaps fearing the wrath of the terrifying senior surgeon, the young doctor then asked if I minded that he was not adding an arrow.

"It's no skin off my nose." I replied with a broad smile, wiggling my eyebrows in a forlorn attempt to lighten the mood.

But my jocularity was wasted on him, "I had better ask a nurse – to be on the safe side," he mumbled as he wandered off.

So with only a blue circle to indicate the whereabouts of my nose, I paid a quick visit to the gents to ease my nerves and then returned to "chairs" to wait along with the other unfortunates. I felt slightly embarrassed because I had been allowed to keep my clothes on, but it later transpired that I had left my flies undone, so perhaps the others didn't feel quite so uncomfortable after all. Certainly a couple of them had pointed discreetly at my crotch and given me a knowing nod, presumably appreciative of my inadvertent gesture of solidarity. We were all a little apprehensive, and in an effort to alleviate the tension, I started to tell a few witty anecdotes; then one of the other patients added some of his amusing stories and I responded with a further joke or two. Like refugees in a bomb shelter, motivated by mild fear and the desire to raise our collective spirits, everyone in the room joined in the entertainment. Before long we were all laughing loudly, mopping at our tears and holding our aching sides. Suddenly the door burst open, as a stern looking nurse came in and demanded to know what all the laughing was about; I explained that we were all a little nervous and were using some collective witticisms to keep our spirits up.

The nurse slowly turned in my direction and gave me the full force of her fiery stare.

"Jokes is it?" she asked incredulously. "Well stop it at once! I could hear you right at the other end of the corridor; I will not permit laughing in my ward!" And with that she spun on her heel and marched out of the room.

We sat in stunned silence for a few seconds and then, like a group of naughty schoolchildren after the teacher had left the classroom, we burst out laughing. With our spirits lifted by humour and our fear dissolved through our camaraderie, we sat back and waited in contemplative silence for whatever was to follow. Soon the nurse came to summon the first patient to the theatre, and ten minutes later she returned for a second and then a third. Was I the only one to notice that the patients went out –but never came back? Finally, it was my turn and after waving farewell to my remaining compatriots, I followed the nurse to another set of chairs outside the operating room, where I was given blue paper booties to cover my shoes and an elasticated hat for my balding head. Finally I was escorted into the operating theatre, which seemed to have been fitted into an unused alcove in the corridor that, in other circumstances, would have been used for storing surplus sports equipment. The surgeon greeted me in a thick Pakistani accent, and then proceeded to examine my nose, which he seemed to find quite easily – without the assistance of a junior doctor or a blue circle. I was beginning to feel quite optimistic, until he started to disparage my lump.

"Is that it?" he asked in a tone of voice that reminded me of an old girlfriend. "I expected something bigger."

"Well I'm sorry," I said indignantly. "I thought size didn't matter."

"Ha!" snorted one of the nurses, safely hidden behind her mask. "You were misinformed."

The surgeon ignored the nurse's jibe. "I meant that this lump is hardly worth removing."

"Well that's as maybe," I explained. "But I am here now and my doctor is quite insistent – it has to come off."

"Oh well, okay then," he sighed. "Hop up on the table and we will cut it out."

Once I was settled, he told a nurse to hold my hands, either for comfort, or to ensure that I didn't attempt to steal his wallet. Then somebody liberally painted my face with cold yellow water that smelled like cheap lavatory cleaner and placed some thick gauze over my mouth to prevent me from breathing – or perhaps to stop me from cracking more jokes.

Although members of the medical profession always describe an impending injection as "a slight scratch" or warn that it "may sting a little," I can assure you that having a local anaesthetic injection into the end of your nose is eye-wateringly painful, particularly when one is unable to flinch or pull a face in compensation. After a few moments the surgeon tapped the side of my nose with his finger and asked if it was numb.

"I think so," I said, "It's a bit hard to tell without touching it myself."

Then a few seconds later I yelled, "Owwww!!" as he sliced into my definitely un-numbed nose.

There was a flurry of quiet swearing, along with some fumbling for instruments, syringes, and gauze, to mop up the blood that was now running freely down my face, before a second attempt could be made to numb my rapidly swelling nose. In his haste to put things right, the surgeon even managed to stick the needle completely through my nose and squirt local anaesthetic across my chin. Nevertheless, once my proboscis was correctly numbed, the remainder of the operation went swimmingly – with everyone pretending that nothing was ever amiss. Fifteen minutes and three stiches later, I was sent home clutching some gauze, with instructions to return in ten days for a wound check.

The outpatients department of the Hospital was crammed into a building that resembles an old Georgian farmhouse, cunningly hidden in a forgotten corner of the grounds between the car park and what may have been a morgue. The clinic is always chaotically packed and it is not unusual to be seen three hours after your stated appointment time – as I was when I returned for my post operation wound check. In due course I was ushered into a small room with three connecting doors. Against one wall there was an antique examination table and a vanity screen, possibly left over from the Boar War, the walls were painted institutional bland and the floor was lovingly fitted with cracked and faded linoleum. An army surplus steel desk sat in the centre of the room, piled high with papers and charts that just failed to hide the same doctor that had performed my surgery ten days earlier. He was slouched comfortably into a sumptuous leather office chair, while I was expected to perch precariously on a rickety white bathroom stool. The room seemed to be in chaos as an endless parade of nurses, cleaners and kitchen staff appeared to be using the office as a shortcut to wherever they needed to be, only stopping momentarily to deliver or collect charts from the desk and chat with the doctor. After looking briefly at my wound, the doctor needed three attempts to locate the correct chart before he began to review my case. In between discussions with other members of the medical staff, who happened to pass through the room, and several telephone calls, he delivered my histology results.

"Now I see that we …. A cheese sandwich with pickle and a scotch egg… removed a lesion… tomorrow at three… ten days ago and… No, I'll see him tomorrow… tell my wife not to worry… got all of the cancer…fine for golf on Sunday at two …wound is healing well…excellent film but a little long…see your G.P. to have the stitches removed next week…ask him to wait for a while…coffee with two sugars…follow up in six months – good day." He slapped my chart shut and started hunting for his next case.

I remained seated, resolutely ignoring the nurse who was hovering nearby, ready to whisk me away at the first opportunity. In response, the doctor ignored my continued presence, ostensibly enthralled by something that he had just spotted in the chart he was holding. I coughed lightly, like a man unsure if his recent attack of diarrhoea had passed; the doctor looked at me over his glasses, like a headmaster considering a disobedient student.

"Are you still here?" He asked, as if noticing me for the first time. "What do you want?"

"Er… Sorry. Can you just repeat the middle bit again?"

He huffed and rolled his eyes, in a perfect parody of a disgruntled teenager, then pulled my chart and read slowly, "The wound is healing well, go and see your G.P. next week to have the stitches removed."

"Er…Actually I think there was a bit before that."

He flipped back a page and mumbled something incomprehensible.

"Sorry can you say that again?"

"I said…cancer fully excised." He looked up and smiled.

"Cancer?… Really?" I croaked.

"Yes, but fully excised," he said proudly.

"What cancer? What does this mean? What do I do now? Should I write a bucket list and stop reading long books?" I squeaked bravely.

In response he checked his watch in a deliberate and obvious gesture of boredom, then scribbled the name of my cancer on a post-it-note and suggested that I look it up on the internet if I wanted more information. After that, the nurse took me firmly by the arm and quickly guided me out through the back door and left me standing alone in the car park. I drove home with my head spinning and set about doing some internet research, which provided a little more clarity and reduced my stress level – slightly. My G.P. was more helpful and confided that there was little to worry about as long as I continued to use a high factor sunscreen, wear a hat and check regularly for any new lumps. He explained that I only had a squamous cell carcinoma; it had been detected at an early stage and removed promptly with minimal damage. He pointed out that it was unlikely to reoccur and that in any event, only 10% of cases were fatal. I turned the event to my advantage by using it as an excuse to start wearing smart trilby hats to ensure that my ears and neck are protected, and I even treated myself to a brown fedora "Indiana Jones" hat. Any hope that I might start to resemble Harrison Ford were scuppered when Lesley pointed out that I just looked like a fat bloke in a fedora. On a positive note, every lump I have now has to be surgically removed; personally, I see it as a useful weight loss programme.

As winter approached I decided it was time to begin work on the last remaining room in the house that had yet to be renovated. The studio sits at the south end of the house, underneath the master bedroom. It is about the size of a double garage, with small windows, two doors opening to the outside and a low ceiling supported in the centre by a two foot wide tree trunk running the length of the room. Because we had no other use for the room at the time, and the doors on the west side gave easy access for deliveries, we had used the studio for storage ever since we had moved in. We had christened the room the "studio," because the previous owner, a musician, had used it for band practice; now the room was empty, it was just wasted space, and would remain that way until I had repaired the leaks and water damage. Lesley and I spent a good deal of time discussing how the room could best be used, before coming to a decision that was mutually acceptable. We agreed that we would get most benefit from the space if I created three connecting rooms: a walk-in larder for storing bulk purchases of canned and tinned food as well as cleaning materials; a sewing and crafts room for Lesley; and a workshop for me, with a sturdy bench and some cupboards. This layout would allow me to remove the tree trunk that was supporting the ceiling and replace it with a dividing wall, and to discard the old rotten wooden garage doors for some smart waterproof windows. As a final touch, I would install several bookcases so we could display some of our large collection of books – which were currently still stacked in boxes in the bedroom above.

Once I started to remove the water damaged areas of wall and floor, it soon became clear that the damage was so extensive, and the build quality so poor, that the whole lot needed to be ripped out. So out came the pry bar and the sledge hammer again, and I set about removing the wooden floors and plasterboard walls. Within a couple of weeks, all that was left of the studio was the bare stone and concrete, a couple of light fixings and some temporary supports for the floor above, ready for when I removed the beam, or tree trunk, that currently held up the ceiling. Given the amount of weight in boxes of books and craft materials that were stored in the bedroom above, I was truly horrified to discover that the roof beams were only supported at each end by a bare half inch of wood! Terrified that the entire edifice could collapse at any moment, my first job was to use a stack of my favourite four by two inch timbers to create some solid walls that would add much needed support to the ceiling. The rafter on the exposed south facing wall had suffered most when the water had been leaking into the house, and it was now so rotten that it literally fell apart under my pry bar. The replacement was a fifteen foot length of pressure treated, six by three inch timber that had to be wiggled into place from below. I was grateful that Lesley was available to help lift and steady the beam while I attached the new bolts. After a good bit of shoving, pushing and swearing, we managed to get the beam successfully into place. I was just attaching the first bolt when the other end of the beam slipped from its bracket and fell... I could see the beam falling towards the window and desperately tried to hold it from my end – but without success. Fortunately the beam missed the window. This was primarily because it hit Lesley squarely on the top of the head and was then gently lowered to the ground, as her knees buckled – what a piece of luck! Some of the old flooring was still in reasonable condition and I didn't want to waste it, so I took a few days out from the renovations to make a new, much larger, chicken coop. The result was a six by eight foot shed, fully lined with plastic and covered in roofing felt, with individual nesting boxes and roosting perches. Even though it was built in several easy to handle sections, it still took two of us to carry the bits up the garden and assemble it, but the chickens were grateful for the extra space and, like most of my creations, I was confident that it would not blow away. Although the old tree trunk roof support was riddled with wood worm, it was clearly very heavy and I suspected that it would need two strong men to shift it safely. Luckily Mark and Joanne were coming over for Christmas.

It was lovely to see them both again and while Mark and I bashed, levered and sawed until all of the heavy work was done, Lesley and Joanne cooked dinners, chatted, did jigsaws and generally bonded together as mother and daughter. That year we were having another bitterly cold winter, with thick snow and temperatures as low as minus fifteen degrees. It was so cold at night that I had even fitted up one heat lamp to keep the chickens warm and a second to stop our water pump from freezing. At about seven o'clock on the second evening, there was a sudden hullabaloo outside, with the dogs barking wildly; clearly they were disturbed by something. Believing that there was a fox about, or perhaps some deer, Mark and Joanne took a torch and went out to investigate. They returned to report that there was a stray dog in the driveway. They had managed to get our loopy dogs back indoors, but the stray was clearly very scared and unsure of itself, refusing to leave, but unwilling to come any nearer. I immediately put on my coat and went outside, where they used the torch to show me a beautiful rough collie, the breed made famous by the "Lassie" films. He was clearly very thin and so afraid, or cold, that he was visibly shivering. We tried to get nearer, using kind, calm and gentle voices, and offering him biscuits, but without any success. We were all getting cold and frustrated, so in desperation I gave the two-tone whistle that I use to summon our dogs; amazingly he immediately trotted over and sat obediently at my feet, looking at me as if to say, "okay, you are my owner now!" As I had done before, with Cassie, even though it was dark and snowing, I immediately walked all of the dogs together, to ensure that they bonded and understood that the new arrival was now part of our pack. Although he was clearly an "outdoors dog," that had lived in an outhouse and was never allowed into the house, because it was so cold, he needed little encouragement to come in and take pride of place by the fire. As he had nominated me to be the boss and I was heady with my newfound power, I decided that we would call him "Jack". When I tried out the name on our new friend, his ears pricked up and he looked at me quizzically for a moment before giving an almost imperceptible nod of agreement, as if to say, "that will do" – and so Jack came into our lives.

The poor dog was in a bad state. He was underweight and undernourished, very unsure of himself and his coat was filthy and matted. Over the next ten days, we gave Jack a good bath to remove some of the muck and smell, and Lesley brushed him for at least an hour every day. Although Jack soon looked much cleaner and happier and smelled a good deal better, with most of the loose hair removed from his coat, it was painfully obvious just how underweight he was. There were also signs of joint problems in his hips and knees, which the vet put down to the canine equivalent of rickets, probably caused by a bad diet when he was a puppy. In an effort to improve his overall conditioning and build up his muscles a bit, we encouraged him to eat a little more food than perhaps he had been used to. Soon he was showing promising signs of being able to walk a bit further, and sometimes he even ran a little along with the other dogs. He is a delightfully good natured dog, although still dreadfully unsure of himself, which makes him appear to be rather shy. For such a large dog, he is pathetically scared of any loud noises, particularly running water, heavy rain and, his greatest fear, thunderstorms combined with hail drumming on the conservatory roof. The first such event was painfully disturbing to watch. As the hail gradually started to fall, Jack instantly jumped to his feet, circling and whining, as if he was desperate to escape from the noise, but unsure of where to go. Then he began salivating uncontrollably, dribbling on the carpet in agitation and orbiting the room in pathetic anxiety as the storm built. With a mighty crash of thunder the squall reached its peak, mercilessly pounding the house with hail and vivid flashes of lightning, prompting poor Jack to bury his head in Lesley's lap and repeatedly howl in terror, oblivious to her attempts to provide any comfort. We have theorised that being locked in a shed as a lonely puppy, newly separated from his mother, where thunderstorms and the beating of torrential rain on a tin roof created a cacophony of terror, had left him mentally scarred for life – or perhaps he is just a big scaredy-cat. He is also completely unable to climb stairs, cross water, or traverse any kind of tiled floor, either because he had been punished previously for entering a tiled area, or perhaps because poor eyesight makes such obstructions appear impassable. This second problem has caused us quite a bit of inconvenience because, although all of the other dogs will walk through the kitchen to get from the conservatory to the lounge, Jack has to go outside and back indoors through the French windows. To add to the entertainment, he is so polite that he refuses to go through any door before a human, consequently I have to go out in the pissing rain and lead him from the conservatory and around to the other door. We have tried all of the conventional strategies to encourage Jack to walk through the kitchen and climb the stairs, but without success. We still have to walk him out of the conservatory when it is raining and carry him upstairs and back down again at bath times. With the help of Joanne and Mark, we finally managed to get Jack to cross the small stream at the bottom of the hill, so we can now go on longer walks. It was an amusing thing to see when he finally got across the water for the first time; Jack was so proud of himself that he positively danced along for the next half-mile, with a huge grin on his face.

Because he is so shy, he will not take an offered biscuit from your hand, unlike Lady, who will happily take most of your hand as well. Jack's biscuit must be laid on the ground where it can be sniffed and examined, before being eaten and savoured ever so slowly. Although he has become rather partial to having his head patted and his ears rubbed, he is slow to ask, shyly edging towards you, as you sit on the couch, but backing off immediately if another dog pushes in. Once in position, he will place his chin on your knee and wait patiently, until he can roll his eyes and hum with pleasure should you honour him with a tickle behind the ear. On the other hand, once you have started, he would rather you didn't stop, and he will continue to demand further attention, giving your knee little bumps with his chin and staring at you pleadingly, until he is forcefully pushed away. When he is certain that no more attention is forthcoming, Jack will wander off to the corner of the sitting room, where he will slump down on the carpet, giving out a long contented rumble of satisfaction, like distant thunder echoing from deep within his chest.

If excited by the other dogs, Jack has a curious habit of woofing into his own ears, by turning his head alternately left and right with each bark. For some reason he has never learned to play with dog toys and resists any instruction, proving that you really can't teach old dogs new tricks! Whenever Kia and Amber engage in a game of tug, or I throw a ball for them to chase, Jack just barks loudly with excited confusion. I have tried throwing a ball for Jack to chase, but all he does is watch it roll away. Once when I threw the ball for him to catch, he sat still until it bounced off his head and then he walked away and hid under a bush, staring at me accusingly. His only vice is ripping up plastic, which he may have learned through being around farms where silage bales and the associated plastic were common. We have discouraged him from simply destroying any and every bit of plastic he finds whenever the mood takes him, but not before he had stripped all of the plastic from the chicken coop and uncovered several rolls of loft insulation. Luckily he has never set about dismantling the polytunnel, and he now has his own large sheet of plastic, which he likes to play with on windy days. Outside of the occasional game of chase with Lady, the only time I have seen Jack play was when he found a chicken feather on the lawn. He carefully picked it up in his mouth and then ran wildly around the lawn with such enthusiasm that I honestly believe he thought he might fly!

Some six weeks after he had arrived, I returned home from work to discover that Jack had gone. Lesley tearfully told me that during the afternoon someone had turned up at the house to claim their dog back. I understand that they had been aware of his location for some time, along with our concerted attempts to find his owners in the fortnight after his arrival. However, they had only now found the time and enthusiasm to make the one-mile journey to reclaim their dog. We were very sad, and naturally a little annoyed, to see Jack go, but they had a prior claim and there was little else we could do. The house and our lives seemed emptier without him. Two days later I arrived back from work to find Jack sitting patiently outside the French windows. When I opened the door, he marched in, lay down in front of the fireplace and with a deep rumbling sigh, went off to sleep until dinner time. Later that week, I met with the previous owners and they agreed that Jack had made his views abundantly clear and should be allowed to stay for as long as he wanted.

Just before Joanne and Mark were due to return to England at the end of their Christmas holiday, the girls went out walking the dogs while Mark and I remained behind to wash the breakfast dishes. As the last plates were being put away, Mark announced that he wanted to ask me something of great importance. In a fearful voice he very formally asked my permission to propose marriage to my daughter. I was very impressed that Mark should uphold the tradition of first asking the father for permission, but not surprised – as I knew he was such a well-grounded young man. At the same time I was naturally delighted for Joanne, as it was abundantly clear that they were both very much in love and likely to have a long and happy marriage. I had no hesitation in saying yes immediately, although as a part of his "husband training," I added the caveat that we should check with my wife first. For once, Lesley was fully in agreement with me, and the only problem remaining was that of suppressing our wide grins in front of Joanne until their flight home later that day. We succeeded and the secret remained intact until a planned weekend at a romantic hotel in England two weeks hence, where Mark would pop the question – and our family would grow again.

Chapter 19 – In which we go on holiday

Mark's plans for a romantic proposal almost fell at the first hurdle. He had ordered a delightful engagement ring from a swanky Hatton Garden jeweller, but to negate the risk of accidental loss or discovery, he had planned to collect it at the very last minute. Unfortunately, on that day, London was gridlocked after a sudden snow storm slowed most of the traffic had to a crawl. Faced with the prospect of trying to make a romantic proposal with a plastic curtain ring, Mark, had no choice but to carry out his plan. So he fibbed to Joanne about why he needed to make such an obviously irresponsible journey and then, like a knight undertaking a final quest before winning the hand of his princess, our future son-in-law bravely set off into the teeth of the blizzard. The 180 mile round trip took most of the day, but it was worth the effort, as the following night she accepted his proposal. The news quickly spread across their social media networks, touching hundreds of friends and the members of our extended families; leaving everyone rightfully delighted. Within days of the formal announcement, the planning got underway for a September wedding. After seeing and attending so many weddings themselves, both Mark and Joanne had come to the opinion that a big wedding would be an unnecessary and wasteful extravagance – particularly as they had been living together for some time; the original plan, therefore, was for something small and quiet. However, over the next few months some degree of "wedding fever" took over; the plans slowly became more elaborate and the strict budget more flexible. I wish I could have funded the whole enterprise, but that commitment was one of the casualties of our move to Ireland; Joanne and Mark understood this and I love them even more for how understanding they were. While we did what we could financially (which wasn't a lot, given how dreadfully our local economy had been hit by the recession), our main assistance was in providing support, by phone and by email. Lesley committed to travelling over to England for a week before the wedding, to help with the preparations and use her prodigious baking skills to produce the wedding cake and hundreds of cupcakes. Mark's parents, a lovely couple that we had only recently had the pleasure of meeting, also gave considerable help and support in arranging the festivities. In the end, the bulk of the planning and arranging fell to Mark and Joanne. Luckily, after helping with so many of their friends' weddings, they were practically expert wedding planners – so much so that Joanne had recently started a bridal business of her own. Furthermore, they wanted to have an exceptionally bespoke wedding, with a retro theme loosely based around the "rock n roll years." Over the next six months they spent hours dreaming up ideas and searching internet auction sites for anything suitable to support the overall theme. Soon they had a spare room crammed with old advertising posters, flashing neon signs, photographs of famous musicians, 45rpm single vinyl records and many other clever little touches to create the correct atmosphere perfectly. As a final elegant touch, Joanne came up with her own design for a beautiful period wedding dress, which we managed to get hand made by a company in China for a fraction of the usual cost. I sometime think that Mark and Joanne got almost as much pleasure out of the planning process as they did out of the event itself, although I can testify that the wedding was thoroughly enjoyed by all.

While all of the wedding planning was going on in England, back in Ireland it was still "business as usual." Lesley was working almost flat-out tending to our garden and vegetable plot, cooking, baking and producing jams for the market, while I was trying to earn as much money as I could to help with the wedding. Inevitably, and with viciously exquisite timing, the recession had worsened considerably and my business was now very quiet – although still vaguely profitable. On the up-side, this gave me extra time to put the finishing touches to the rebuilt studio. It was quite a moment when I applied the last lick of paint and declared that, after eight years of hard grafting, numerous mistakes, hundreds of cuts and bruises, tens of thousands of euro's worth of materials and immense patience from my wife, the renovations were finally finished. Although there will always be lots of maintenance to keep me busy around the house and garden, it was with a considerable sense of satisfaction and achievement that I stood back and admired my work. Considering that I am not a builder, plumber or electrician, or even particularly skilled mechanically – by patiently and carefully following the instructions in a DIY manual, applying a little common sense and a lot of money, we had transformed a run-down old farmhouse into a delightful family home.

Perhaps a celebration was in order.

So that we could both leave the country together to attend the wedding, Lesley had arranged for Danny, the student son of a friend, to "house-sit" for us while we were away. With so many dogs and chickens to be looked after, it was the most practical option. I also liked the added security of having someone staying at the house – particularly since the economic downturn had triggered a spate of local burglaries. By way of a test run, I asked Danny to look after the house for a few days during August, so that I could take Lesley away for a much needed rest and to celebrate the end of the renovation project, along with our thirtieth wedding anniversary. Incredibly, for the first time in the eight years of our house renovations, apart from shopping trips, the occasional pub lunches on birthdays, and four trips to the theatre, we were both going to be away from the house together. We had little experience or knowledge of Ireland, outside of County Clare and some bits of Limerick and Galway, but after some research we chose to visit Killarney, because it was easily accessible by road, had several famous walks and gardens for us to explore – and we found a hotel that was within our meagre budget. So, on a lovely sunny day in mid-August, we gave our house-sitter a list of telephone numbers and hotel addresses, along with a list of instructions regarding the care and welfare of our animals, worthy of parents leaving children with a teenage babysitter for the first time. Then with a jolly wave, we set off towards Killarney – as excited as newlyweds on a honeymoon trip.

We had only been on the road for around an hour when we entered the village of Adare in County Limerick and immediately decided to break our journey. Although I had visited Adare once before, my trip had only taken me as far as the scrumptious Adare Manor Golf and Country Club, to meet with some clients. So neither of us had ever been to the village and had no idea that it is recognised as being Ireland's prettiest and most picturesque. Driving south from Limerick, we had passed the impressive wrought iron gates of Adare Manor, before noticing Desmond Castle on our left as we drove over the ancient stone bridge that straddles the River Maigue, a tributary of the mighty Shannon. A mile later we entered the village, where the main street is punctuated with stone buildings, brightly painted thatched cottages, medieval monasteries and tree lined parks; we decided that we must stop and explore. Compared to sleepy County Clare, Adare seemed to be teaming with tourists, shoppers, buskers and beggars dressed as unidentifiable historic figures or silver painted statues. We easily found a free parking place in the main street and, armed with our cameras, a packed lunch and jackets in case of rain, we set off to explore the village. Many of the cottages turned out to be nothing other than cramped but pretty tea shops, art galleries and so on, selling Irish or Adare village souvenirs and craft to the tourists. These shops held little interest for us, so we navigated our way through the throngs of visitors towards the Adare centre. There we immersed ourselves in the history and heritage of the area as we walked, almost alone, through the interactive historical exhibition. The village site can be dated back to 1200 ad and has been the subject of many rebellions, wars and conquests, leaving behind a legacy of historical monuments – along with the usual and understandable distrust of anything British. In the early nineteenth century, the Earl of Desmond drew up the plans for the current layout of most streets and houses in the village. The farms and cottages were then rented to local tenants under various agreements, some of which are still in force today. As we had a little time in hand, we decided to join the other tourists on a short coach trip around the sights of Adare village, followed by a guided tour of Desmond Castle, which was expertly delivered with humour and passion by a friendly and knowledgeable Irish tour guide. We ate our packed lunch sitting in the sun in the tree lined park that dominates the centre of the village. Then, after a pot of tea in the heritage centre, we continued our journey towards Killarney.

The remainder of our drive was largely uneventful, although our little Satnav seemed to disagree strongly with the actual geography of the area. After we ignored its instruction to "turn right now," which would have stranded us in a ploughed field, it spent long periods repeating the mantra, "recalculating – recalculating – recalculating," ever more desperately, before finally lapsing into a lengthy, depressed silence, emerging only to announce brightly, "arriving at destination, on the right," just as we found the hotel on our own. The long downhill run as we approached Killarney is reminiscent of parts of the drive from Bristol towards Devon, but the view is much more spectacular and considerably less industrial. On the N22 about fifteen miles or so before Killarney, as you drive over the top of the hill after the long climb since passing into Kerry, you are presented with a magnificent view down the hill towards the valley enclosing the beautiful lakes and mountains that surround the town. Even from this distance, it was easy to see why Killarney and the surrounding 20,000 acres of National Park are such a popular tourist destination. Centre stage sat Lough Leane, glistening in the afternoon sunshine; to the right we could see Tomies Mountain and the aptly named Purple Mountain. Away to the left, behind the town, we could make out Torc Mountain just ahead of the sinister looking Devils Punchbowl, which was just visible through the mist.

Once we had checked into our hotel room and had a refreshing beverage, we jumped back into the car and drove a mile further to the base of Torc Mountain, where the Torc upper car park gives "convenient and easy" access to the walking trail. The walk only takes a couple of hours along a well-maintained path that climbs up past the impressive Torc waterfalls. The path then loops steeply up through the high forest, providing delightful views over the lake, before crossing above the head of the falls and looping gradually back to the road; this is the point at which you will discover you have completely lost your bearings and are unable to find your car. Fear not however, because there are plenty of enterprising "jaunting car" drivers who "for a small fee" will take you back to your car – or you can walk, as we did. These horse-drawn open carriages are either two-wheeled types, which seat two passengers facing forwards, or larger four-wheeled carts that carry around a dozen people – precariously balanced on bench seats, facing sideways. There are literally hundreds of jaunting cars around Killarney. It seems that, wherever you go, you can hear the steady "clop, clop,

clop" of the horseshoes as they plod along and the lilting commentary of the official drivers, enthusiastically relating stories of witches, fairies and the like to their appreciative audience. Just before our trip, there had been considerable complaints from the drivers and even threats of strikes and blockades, because of a new rule requiring all of the horses to wear a sort of equine nappy to collect their poo. After much negotiation, both in the press and behind closed doors, they reached a consensus with the authorities, which may have resulted in some local councillors having particularly well fertilised rose bushes – but I can't be sure. In any event, given the sheer number of horses parading around the area, it was not surprising that something had to be done, before Killarney disappeared under a mountain of horse manure.

After our walk and a quick dip in the hotel pool, we were both ravenous, so we strolled the short distance up the Muckross road into Killarney town in search of an eatery that met with our approval. We had already looked at the menus for the two restaurants in our hotel and decided against eating in house – partly because we wanted to see the town, but also because the two vegetarian dishes on offer didn't appeal to me. Although we didn't set the bar particularly high with regard to our culinary desires, we continued to be disappointed as we walked around the town in a fruitless search for some variety – which was odd considering the brilliant spread on offer when you eat out around our native County Clare. Lesley was fairly easy going about her meal, saying only that she "quite fancied a roast dinner". Consequently, being the only vegetarian in the household, I got the blame for our inability to find something interesting to eat. The best range of vegetarian meal choices are usually found in Indian and Chinese restaurants, but we had agreed that we would stick with European fare during our holiday. For some reason every place we looked at had the same two vegetarian options on offer that were available in our hotel. In fact, either by accident or design, every restaurant and pub in Killarney rotated their menus in perfect harmony, minimising the choice for vegetarians for every night of our trip. After an hour of fruitless searching, interlaced with window shopping, I suggested that we picked someplace where Lesley could eat what she wanted, and I would choose one of Killarney's Monday night vegetarian specials of "sweet and sour vegetables" or "stuffed field mushroom with rice." Once we were seated at our table and after Lesley had ordered her roast beef dinner, the waitress, perhaps sensing my dissatisfaction with the unimaginative menu, suggested that the chef would be happy to prepare something especially for me. I was delighted, and after scanning my mental database of vegetarian dishes, I chose something both exotic and challenging.

"Two fried eggs, chips and peas – please." I said with a big smile. The waitress rolled her eyes dramatically and Lesley gave me a swift kick.

Despite my bruised shins, I thoroughly enjoyed my expertly prepared meal and I was relieved to see that Lesley was happy with her roast dinner. At the end of our meal, my wife of thirty years even smiled coyly when I saluted her coffee cup with my Guinness glass and wished her a "Happy Anniversary!"

The planned highlight of our short trip, which took up all of the second day, was a visit to see Muckross House and its gardens, which sits below Mangerton Mountain on the banks of beautiful Muckross Lake. Built in 1843 and designed by William Burn, Muckross House is a spectacular Victorian country house, similar to many that I had seen in Scotland during my childhood. Originally owned by Henry Herbert and his wife Mary, who was an excellent amateur artist, the house was used for entertaining the rich and famous – including Queen Victoria. Unfortunately Mr Herbert's entertaining skills far out-shone his earning potential, particularly with regard to the Queen's visit. To cover his enormous debts, in 1899 he sold the house and surrounding estate to Lord Ardilaun, of the Guinness brewing family. For the next twelve years the house was used as a holiday let, so that wealthy people had somewhere to stay when they were shooting deer and game. Then in 1911, the wealthy American, William Bourn, bought Muckross as a wedding gift for his daughter Maud – as I would have liked to have done for my daughter Joanne. Sadly, Maud died just a few years later and, in 1932, her husband Arthur Vincent and her parents donated the house and estate to the Irish Nation, a gift which allowed the creation of Ireland's first National Park.

The weather was dull and overcast, with bouts of light rain, but it failed to dampen our enjoyment of the day. At ten o'clock we started with a walk along a long winding lane that meandered its way through a series of traditional Irish farms. Some were just small cottages with a bit of land and a few chickens – rather like home, while others were grander affairs with antique farm machinery, heavy horses and delightfully energetic sheepdog puppies. When we were buying our tickets for the farm tour at the gift shop, we were offered the chance to ride around on the little bus, which we politely declined, despite the stern warning that it was "quite hard going." After several years of walking our dogs up steep rocky forest paths and along muddy tracks across the moor at Glenmadrie, we thoroughly enjoyed the easy walk of a mile or so along well maintained tarmac lanes set on gentle slopes. We were happy to take our time, pausing to chat with the staff and carefully read the information posters along the way. By comparison, we were passed by several busloads of overweight and red-faced tourists, evidently on a mission to complete the tour in record time; an hour or so later, we overtook them at the café, where they had stopped to refuel with the help of trays heaving with cakes and sweets.

At the end of the sixteenth century, much of Ireland was still heavily wooded, mostly with oak and alder. The south west was particularly rich in woodland, which provided natural concealment and protection for the Irish armies in their on-going battle with the English forces of Queen Elizabeth. However, through a combination of deliberate deforestation for industrial use and shipbuilding, along with land clearance by the new settlers, much of the forest soon disappeared. There are few places in Ireland where the majesty and splendour of these ancient native woodlands can still be seen, but Killarney is one. With 3,500 acres of woodland, a trip to Muckross House would not be complete without visiting the exhibition about the Oakwoods of Killarney National Park. Much was made of the on-going battle that Coillte Teoranta, the State Forestry Service, was waging against the rhododendron and bamboo that are gradually taking over the park. These invasive species grow so vigorously that they will starve most other plants of food and sunlight and if left unchecked, they will quickly cover the land. On our walks around Killarney, the sheer scale of the problem was depressingly obvious. Many of the mountains are now completely covered in a solid mass of rhododendron, and there are also many thousands of bushes covering the ground between the trees throughout the woodlands. Beautiful as these plants can be when they are in bloom, they sour the land and gradually exclude all other plants. In some places along the river banks and lakesides, thick bamboo plants, up to ten feet high, form an impenetrable barrier that can be hundreds of yards deep. I have no idea how these plants will ever be cleared, or even if they can; rather like the Irish sovereign debt, the growth far exceeds that which we can cut down. Perhaps there is an opportunity to solve two problems at once; surely there is money to be made here – if only someone could find a market for Irish bamboo.

The guided tour of Muckross House visited most of the beautifully maintained rooms and lasted around an hour. Starting with the huge entrance hall, our journey took us across the dining room with its scrumptious red velvet wall covering, through the library, along the awesome main hall, leading up the hand carved oak staircase to the billiard room, which is hung with exquisitely hand painted Chinese silk wall coverings. Every room seemed to be filled with beautiful furniture, carpets and fittings, and our guide was enthusiastic, knowledgeable and interesting as she enthralled us with the history and story behind each piece. We were particularly impressed with the beautiful examples we saw of locally made Killarney furniture, which is of the highest quality, intricately inlaid with arbutus, yew and holly – yet I have never seen or heard mention of this spectacular work on "The Antiques Road Show," or any other similar television programmes. I have since discovered that this exquisitely attractive work is greatly prized by collectors, commanding high prices and sometimes called "a forgotten industry." After a delicious lunch of thick vegetable soup with fresh wholemeal bread, we walked around the walled garden centre and the gift shop. Sadly, the once spectacular walled garden, which at one time would have produced fruit and vegetables in sufficient quantities to feed the household and guests all year round, has been changed into a pretty, but somewhat pointless, flower garden. The remainder of the day was whiled away in dappled sunshine, with a gentle stroll around the thirty-five hectares of well laid-out and beautifully maintained gardens that surround Muckross House. The associated guide book helped us to navigate our way along the well-trodden paths, ensuring that we saw most of the attractions, without either getting hopelessly lost or walking in circles, which was otherwise entirely possible.

We returned to the hotel, and after a swim and sauna to ease our aching feet, we ate an early supper in the bar and then, around seven in the evening, walked back into town to do some window shopping – or at least that was our intention. In Ennis, most of the town centre shops are shut by six o'clock, when the shoppers give way to those seeking company and sustenance in the busy pubs and restaurants. So we were pleasantly surprised to find Killarney town centre was crowded with tourists and shoppers, with most shops remaining open until nine o'clock. We thoroughly enjoyed our slow walk through the teaming crowds on this lovely, warm summer evening, stopping occasionally to chat with other tourists when they asked for directions and then engaged us in easy conversation. After browsing for books, looking around an antique shop and buying several bags of sticky treats in a retro sweet shop, we made one final stop before heading back to the hotel. The gift shop was a standard affair, with a fairly typical range of tourist gifts advertising Ireland, Killarney or Guinness, along with a few pieces of Waterford crystal that had caught Lesley's eye. When we entered the shop I had said "hello" to the lady behind the counter, who I assumed was the owner or manager, and she had smiled sweetly in return. After a few minutes, bored with watching the back of Lesley's head while she looked at the crystal, I tried to engage the manageress in some sociable conversation.

"Working late tonight," I commented, "You must be looking forward to having your tea."

The grey haired manageress was around sixty years old, but slim, with a healthy pink complexion and smoky eyes. She slowly turned her head in my direction, as if noticing me for the first time, and as she spoke her eyes looked a little out of focus, as though she was looking at something far away and a long time ago.

"I had me tay already," she said, breathing a wall of peppermint and alcohol in my direction.

"Have you been at work all day?" I asked, speculating that perhaps she had been called away from a party to cover for a sick member of staff, "you must be tired."

"No, I only started at six," she replied, trying to focus on me, but missing with both eyes.

"Oh, right then," I said uncertainly. "Well, I'd better be getting back to my wife."

Clearly surprised that she had failed to notice a second customer, she quickly turned her head and then grabbed the counter for support, as her eyes bounced around in their sockets uncontrollably and her legs wobbled.

"Yesh," she slurred carefully and gave me a stiff smile. "Happy to help."

When I turned away she was valiantly trying to prop her bottom onto a stool that was behind the counter. I slowly walked over to Lesley, who was holding up an ornament and squinting, in an attempt to make out the price without the aid of her glasses.

I whispered in her ear, "I think the woman behind the counter is drunk."

"Really?" she asked, still squinting at the tag. "How much is this?" She held the ornament up for me to see. "I wanted to get something for Lucy."

"Jesus Christ! It's €80 – you're not going to buy it are you?" I hissed. "She's completely sloshed! It looks like she can hardly stand up!"

"Who is?" Lesley asked, putting the ornament back on the shelf and looking at me for the first time.

"The woman behind the counter." I whispered again, "She stank of booze and mints."

Lesley looked over her shoulder, "What woman?"

I looked and the counter was unmanned, "Perhaps she went out the back," I offered.

"Who did?" Lesley asked in a distracted voice as she drifted towards the exit.

"That woman who was behind the counter. You know – the drunk one."

"I can't believe she'd be drunk, and at work. You probably just imagined it," Lesley said as she walked outside.

Meekly I followed behind, chastised for my overactive imagination, but grateful that we had avoided an unnecessarily extravagant purchase. In passing, I glanced over the counter. There, laid on the floor, soundly sleeping in a visible fog of brandy fumes, was the manageress.

As we walked through the town, taking in the sights and enjoying the unaccustomed bustle and affluence, we spotted a young, disabled man, with crutches, weaving his way uncertainly along the pavement, on a journey between two pubs.

I thought to myself. "Poor fellow – well at least he seems happy."

Around an hour later, as dusk fell, we were walking back along the busy Muckross road, towards our hotel, when I spied an electric invalid carriage, without lights, driving erratically along the centre of the road. I recognised the driver as the same young disabled man I had seen earlier.

"Hey, look at that," I said to Lesley, pointing at the invalid carriage as it weaved unpredictably through the slowly moving traffic.

As we watched in disbelief, the obviously intoxicated driver approached a red light with almost suicidal determination. Then, with only the sound of his diminutive horn as a warning, he drove at alarming speed, straight through the intersection, scattering several cars and their startled drivers in his wake. The little invalid carriage continued off into the darkness of the Muckross road, detectable only by the lights of the swerving cars and their tooting horns. Some two hundred yards later the petite electric buggy slowly rolled to a stop, sideways to the oncoming traffic, as the driver slipped from his seat and onto the road. In the amber glow of the street lights we could just make out the concerned tourists who had jumped from their hire cars and were attempting to help the young disabled lad back onto his seat. I could almost sense their disbelief, as clinging desperately to the steering wheel for support, he performed a ragged "K turn," gave them a merry toot from his horn, and set off uncertainly towards home.

"Perhaps he isn't disabled after all," I speculated. "Just very drunk."

Chapter 20 – In which we reach the end of the tale

The following morning, as I was contemplating my choices at the breakfast bar, I happened into a conversation with an affable American tourist. I was on nodding terms with this distinguished looking gentleman from the previous morning, so I took a moment to ask if he and his wife had enjoyed their tour around the "Ring of Kerry". This spectacularly scenic drive loops along the mountains, cliffs and beaches for 179 kilometres of the Iveragh Peninsula, and is popular with tourists. He reported that the weather had been kind and the views were spectacular, but the journey had taken a long time because the traffic had been so very heavy.

"These Irish roads are so narrow that you have to pull over each time you meet any oncoming traffic," he said in a distinguished Boston accent, "and we seemed to meet a lot of oncoming traffic. We had to pull over almost every hundred yards or so." Then he gave me a tooth perfect smile. "But everyone was very friendly – they all seemed to be waving at us."

Somewhere in my head, a bell was ringing. I asked, "Which way around the loop did you go? Clock-wise or anti-clockwise?"

"Well, we just followed the sat-nav. I guess we were going clock-wise," he answered, sensing my suspicion.

"Well, there's your problem then!" I laughed. "Because the road is so narrow and busy, you are only supposed to drive the Ring in an anti-clockwise direction." I gently patted his shoulder in sympathy, "I expect that the people were waving to warn you that you were heading in the wrong direction."

"But it can't be one-way," he complained. "We would have seen the road signs."

"Ah... Yes. Well, this is Ireland – it's a sort of unofficial one-way system. It's mentioned somewhere in the brochures and on some web pages; other than that, you are just expected to know."

He thanked me for the information, added another sausage to his breakfast plate and walked away, shaking his head and mumbling, "Nutty country!"

As we were not due back home until the evening, after we had checked out of the hotel, we walked into town, hoping to find somewhere else to visit. Because we were only planning to stay for a while, Lesley wore her sensible heels and I changed into regular street shoes, leaving my walking boots in the car, but we took a couple of light jackets in case of rain. Quite soon we saw a sign for Killarney house and garden where we took a left turn and began to explore. Sadly, the magnificent French Chateau style house, although scheduled for renovation as soon as the money becomes available, has fallen into a wretched state of disrepair, and is now only a shadow of its former glory. After a quick look around, we decided to walk on a bit further and strolled off along the cherry-tree lined buggy track that leads away from the town. After half an hour the well maintained path crossed a little foot bridge, where we reached a junction. The tourist finger posts showed that one path would take us to the town and the other went to Ross Castle and the lake – around two miles away. Figuring that we could always turn back if necessary, we decided to walk a while further. It was a pleasantly warm day, the walking was easy and enjoyable across level land, but I was glad to be wearing my latest trilby hat for protection from the sun. There were plenty of other walkers, as well as whole families of cyclists on rented mountain bikes, who gave a friendly wave as they rode past. Every few minutes we had to stand aside as another horse drawn jaunting car trundled by. For a while we were enclosed by trees and unable to see much scenery, but as we approached the naturally flooded land along the shoreline, we began walking through a huge forest of tall bamboo plants which seemed to stretch as far as the eye could see. It was like stepping out of rural Ireland and, in an instant, finding that we had been transported into deepest China; I almost expected to see a Giant

Panda leap out at any moment. Although we were happy to do so, we had no choice but to stick to the path for the next half mile. The mud flats and marshes, that had once been a haven for all types of wading birds and a dazzling variety of plants, were now just an impenetrable wall of monotonous bamboo. After an hour we arrived at Ross Castle, which sat impressively on the boat lined lake front and was surrounded by grassy embankments. The picnic area was alive with gaggles of tourists and wildly running children, clearly intent on consuming all of the crisps, sandwiches and ice-creams in the garden shed tuck shop. Walking on past the castle towards the Bronze Age copper mines, we encountered a tall and slightly eccentric looking Englishman, who was chasing the dog that had just thrown itself at us – as if desperately begging for rescue. We got chatting to this amiable fellow, who lived nearby and introduced himself as Derek. We must have accepted his invitation to show us "some parts of Ross Island that most people miss," because he continued to walk alongside us, even when the dog ran off again. As we strolled along admiring the scenery, he regaled us with tales of how his expertise in local geography and history had made him a much sought after tour guide. He winked knowingly when he mentioned how fortunate we were that he was on a rare day off. A few hundred yards later, our ad hoc guide stopped at the entrance to the copper mine and, after taking a theatrical stance, he launched into his spiel.

"Many artefacts have been discovered during archaeological excavations of the Copper Mines at Ross Island, proving strong links with the Bronze Age. Copper mined from this island provided the very first metal to be used in Ireland over 4000 years ago, and again during the early Christian period in Ireland."

As he stumbled through his presentation, like an inexperienced air hostess reciting the pre-fight safety instructions, I nodded politely; then I noticed that he was actually reading surreptitiously from a tourist information panel which was placed conveniently close to where he was standing.

"Substantial shipments of copper ore were also delivered to British smelters during the eighteenth and nineteenth centuries to meet the demands of the Industrial Revolution," he continued, oblivious to the fact that we were also reading from the same board, only a little faster.

As we walked along a little farther down the path, Lesley conversationally commented on how beautiful the trees were looking and as she pointed to a particularly large example, Derek enthusiastically asked if she knew what species they were.

"Yes" she said. "That's a pine tree."

Derek nodded slowly and repeated, "P-i-n-e T-r-e-e," as if to commit this nugget of information to memory, for later use.

Further up the trail we reached Governor's Rock, which provides a spectacular view across Loch Leane. Again our guide stood directly in front of the information panel, openly reciting the words, but pretending that they were from his own encyclopaedic memory. We were both starting to become a little fed up with the charade, particularly as we had intended to have a romantic walk together, but in typically British fashion we were unable to bring ourselves to confront the problem, for fear of being thought rude. Luckily, a timely mobile phone call from our daughter in England gave us a good excuse to move away for some privacy. We sat on a rock overlooking the lake and bathed in glorious sunshine while we chatted to Joanne, who was at work in London, where for once it was raining. She was delighted to hear Lesley so happy and enthusiastic, and correctly commented that we would both benefit from getting out and about more often. After the call ended, I remarked that Derek seemed to have wandered off, ending our unplanned tour. I took Lesley's hand, happy that we could enjoy our time together in such a beautiful location.

She said, "I reckon that he latches on to unsuspecting tourists who are passing by, gives them a little spiel and then hopes to get paid."

"I think you're right. Did you notice he was just reading from the signs?" Lesley smiled and nodded.

We started to walk back towards the castle, as I added, "Next week he'll probably be pointing out all of the pine trees!"

Just then we rounded a bend in the path and there was Derek, patiently waiting for us while he studied a nearby tree. Clearly this fellow was as persistent as a leech and he was not intending to go away while he still had some prospect of getting paid; there was nothing left to do but pry him off. Fortunately he reacted quite well to my polite admission that it was our anniversary, and that we were hoping for a romantic walk in the woods – alone. A plan that would be better served if he went away. Thankfully this time he did.

By the time we arrived back at Ross Castle, we were hot, hungry, desperate for a nice cup of tea and looking for any excuse to rest our aching feet. We paid a small king's ransom for cheese and pickle sandwiches, which we gratefully consumed with our beverages whilst sitting on a bench overlooking the lake. We were about to start walking back towards town when we noticed a guide boat that was about to begin a tour of the lake. Hand-in-hand and giggling like teenagers; we ran down the pier and jumped on as it was pulling out. The boat journey lasted for around an hour, which gave us ample time to relax while we were shown Library Point, Governor's Rock (again), the Devil's Punchbowl, Lover's Rock and several hotels that were considerably beyond our budget. The highlight of the trip was the chance to see, up close, the recently reintroduced white-tailed sea eagles, as they nested and fed along the shoreline. As the guide boat pulled up to its mooring at the end of the tour, Lesley pointed out one further attraction; Derek, our erstwhile guide had latched onto two other tourists and was pointing out the interesting features of Ross Castle, whilst standing conveniently in front of the information panel.

Back in Killarney, we rested our sore feet again, this time cocooned in sublime luxury, while we consumed afternoon tea and biscuits in an up-market hotel, which was very much beyond our meagre budget – for anything other than light refreshments and using the sumptuous toilet facilities. Refreshed for our journey, we recovered our car and set off for County Clare, sad to be leaving, but happy to be heading home. Two hours later, almost as if we had been away for a year, we were being mobbed and licked by five frantic dogs. Our trainee house sitter had done a decent job of keeping the home safe and the animals happy and well-fed, so we were reasonably relaxed when we set off to our daughter's wedding three weeks later.

Lesley went over to England a week ahead of the ceremony, taking her car on the ferry, so she could transport the promised wedding cake along with several boxes of baking supplies containing the ingredients for hundreds of cupcakes in support of the festivities. My presence was not required in the preparation process; I finally flew over just two days before the wedding and then flew back again the night after. Ironically work was quite busy at the time, so I was still able to look after the house and see enough clients to top up our dwindling coffers. The wedding was a marvellous affair, themed loosely around oldies music and many of the female guests dressed accordingly. Mark and Joanne, with the help of friends and family, had done a magnificent job preparing the hall and ceremonial room at the hotel. By mid-morning on the day of the wedding, the tables were arranged and beautifully decorated with flowers, old fashioned "favourite and forgotten" sweets and other retro touches. The walls were hung with bunting, disco lights and old posters of advertisements and music stars, while the garden was charmingly bordered with ribbons and outdoor candles – ready for the inevitable photographs. In pride of place, the wedding cake was resplendent in white icing with a navy-blue ribbon to match the flowers. The side tables were laden with cupcakes, wedding cheeses and every conceivable sweet treat from the last three decades. Overall the effect was one of a very personal, but totally professional wedding. Mark had put his prodigious organisational skills to good use, creating a well-planned and widely distributed running order, ensuring everyone knew where they were expected to be – and when. Our bride and groom had decided to forgo the usual speeches, choosing instead to have a reading by Mark's father before the ceremony, with an entertaining table quiz prior to the serving of the meal and a short toast from me to congratulate the newlyweds. Perhaps fearing that I would say something inappropriate, accompanied by a PowerPoint presentation, Mark and Joanne were adamant that they did not want the usual speech that would be expected from the father of the bride, and because of my inexperience in such matters, Mark kindly gave me some detailed instructions on what to say and how to prepare. After several hours and much head scratching, I was able to put together some sweet words and a few light witticisms that would acceptably fill the couple of minutes allocated, before I was to propose the toast.

Finally the time arrived for the wedding to get under way and, dressed like James Bond at a casino, I made my way to the bridal suite to collect Joanne, so I could escort her safely to where I would have the honour of giving her away. The day was sunny and warm, and as we had a little time in hand, we stood in the side garden while everyone with a camera took some pre-wedding photos. Despite being a beautiful woman, Lesley hates having her picture taken and will usually look away or close her eyes at the wrong moment. For once, she was unable to avoid being photographed and I was delighted, particularly as she looked so elegant in her new dress. As Joanne was almost the last of her group of friends to get married, most of her lovely bridesmaids had recently given birth or were heavily pregnant, so the official photographer had to break out the wide angle lens for a few of the group shots. Soon we were fashionably late and it was time to begin the ceremony. A kind friend of the bride and groom had loaned a beautifully restored yellow 1960s VW camper, to be used as our transport around the car park and back to the front of the hotel. It was a lovely gesture, for which we were most grateful.

Although I am naturally biased, I looked at my daughter, resplendent in her white silk wedding dress, with her hair in a side bun and her makeup exquisitely applied to mimic the fashion of the period, and I thought that she had never looked more beautiful than she did at that moment. As we stood outside the room where the wedding was to take place, surrounded by her bridesmaids and waiting for our cue to enter, the tension level began to rise and I was suddenly struck with a choking fear that Mark would say "no" and run screaming from the hotel, or that some other disaster would overshadow the day. Perhaps sensing my concerns, or more likely projecting those of her own, Joanne squeezed my hand and smiled at me, and my racing heart began to slow a little. Moments later, to the sound of Jimmy Durante singing, "It's so important to make someone happy," we walked arm-in-arm to the head of the room and the wedding got under way. The civil ceremony was a touching and romantic affair, with the usual exchanging of oaths and rings to the soundtrack of tears and repeated nose-blowing from the delighted friends and relatives. As the exchange of vows began, Joanne took Mark's hand and squeezed it gently, as if to say, "We can get through this together" – although she may actually have whispered, "Screw this up and I will kill you!" After the legal formalities were completed, David (Mark's father) was invited to say a few words. After hesitantly making his way to the front of the room, he shyly cleared his throat and then in a powerful and confident voice, recited a beautifully written poem. As I listened to his soaring oratory about love and commitment, I imagined that Laurence Olivier or Anthony Hopkins could not have done a better job. Then I remembered the scrap of paper in my pocket carrying my notes for the upcoming toast, pictured how my reading glasses were still on my desk back in Ireland, and I realised how London Mayor Boris Johnson may have felt as he watched the opening ceremony of the Beijing 2008 Olympic Games – gamely, I fought back the tears.

While the newlyweds went off in the VW camper for some scene setting photographs, the wedding party moved to the reception garden where we could chat and quench our thirst with some fruit punch. I was particularly thirsty and had consumed several glasses on an empty stomach, before I realised that the punch was extremely alcoholic and that I was starting to feel rather too merry. Conscious that I was many years past being a regular drinker, I cautiously sidled away from the punch bowl in search of some water. As I circumnavigated the room, chatting with the guests, thanking them for coming and agreeing how lovely Joanne looked, I noticed that somehow I had acquired a glass of beer. Once the happy couple had returned and everyone was seated, the wine was served and the table quiz began. The best man compered an excellent and keenly fought competition, and as the shouting and laughter continued, cross-eyed with alcohol and without my reading glasses, I surreptitiously tried to read my notes for the impending toast. In the end I need not have worried, as most people were too kind, or too drunk, to recollect what was said – including me. I can only remember starting nervously, by calling David "Alan" by mistake, and finishing by advising Mark to remember that, "No wife ever shot her husband while he was washing the dishes!"

After the meal, everyone went outside into the warm twilight to get a "99" from a rented ice-cream van in the car park. Then we watched the terrifying sight of twenty unmarried girls, grappling like New Zealand rugby players, in an effort to catch the bouquet. The wedding band called "Anthem" was truly excellent and added substantially to the festivities. The newlyweds shuffled around slowly for a minute of their first dance, before the band upped the tempo and the dance floor was invaded by all of the young lovelies, bursting with alcohol and enthusiasm. Their gyrations were happy and unrestrained, staying that way into the early hours of the morning, with the dancers pausing only to refill their glasses, or replenish their blood glucose with stacks of Lesley's delicious cupcakes. As the dancing got ever more frenzied, the room became hotter and more humid than a tropical rainforest. The bride, rather than changing into something more appropriate for such vigorous gyrations, came up with the practical alternative of giving away several of her petticoats and turning her wedding dress into a miniskirt, with the aid of some borrowed cummerbunds and a pair of scissors. With so many young, energetic and enthusiastic sales people on the guest list, the reception was always going to be an exhilarating affair – and it was. At four o'clock, even the band commented that it was the best night they had ever had. After a late breakfast the following morning, bleary eyed and tousle haired, we all waved the newly-weds off to Italy for their honeymoon, before setting off home ourselves.

Back in Ireland our lives seemed to have a sense of completion. The renovations to the house were over, we had a lovely garden, my business was established and surviving the recession, Lesley was busy at the market and our daughter had embarked on her new life.

One afternoon a few weeks later, we were enjoying a chat over coffee with one of our closest friends, when our oldest dog suddenly let out a pitiful squeal and went into a seizure. Over the previous thirty-six months poor old Romany had suffered a few similar events, probably because of minor strokes associated with her great age. Normally she would bounce back quickly, but this time she remained lame, confused and unable to eat. Gamely she fought on for two days, but the outcome was inescapable and it was with heavy hearts that we had to arrange for her to be put to sleep. The next morning our little white Lhasa Apsos, our constant companion of so many years, the tiny puppy that fell in a stream on her first walk, the hilarious young dog that changed colour by "mud surfing" on a beach in Devon, the mature dog that gladly came with us to Ireland and enthusiastically embraced our new lifestyle, the old dog that had been so central to our lives for so long and the real owner of our house, quietly went to sleep for the last time. We left her body in the conservatory for a while, so the other dogs could say goodbye. Lesley and I hugged and cried, sad for our loss but relieved that Romany's pain was over. Later that day I buried our little dog under her favourite spot on the front lawn. For a few days, Lesley was beside herself with grief and the rest of the dogs remained strangely subdued for quite a while, particularly Lady – who seems to miss little Romany the most. Although deeply saddened by her passing, whenever I am mowing the lawn near the hazelnut tree that marks the spot where she lies, it pleases me to remember her sitting there and barking at her own voice, echoing from the cliffs across the moor. I like to imagine that she is still there, watching over our new life, in our new home – in Ireland.

Chapter 21 – And another thing....

So what of the move to Ireland – was it worth it?

We moved to Ireland to get away from the stresses of modern living and to begin a new life debt-free, without pressure, where the air is clean, the people are friendly and we would have the freedom to do as we please. Like Darwin's finches, we have adapted to our new environment. It is cooler here, so we wear warmer clothes and enjoy the simple pleasures of sitting by a warm fire on cool evenings, and warming our insides with delicious homemade vegetable soup. When I visit England, I find the weather to be rather too warm for my liking, and I don't always notice the rain in Ireland – although Lesley has yet to achieve this level of evolution! As I am writing, it is a beautiful and warm, early autumn day here in County Clare. From the window of my office I can see the hill behind our house, where the trees are changing colour as the leaves begin to wilt and the heather, as if in compensation, is blooming a glorious violet. Early this morning I saw a fox, boldly making his way across the lawn, and last night some deer passed behind the house, mercifully unnoticed by the dogs. Today there is barely a breath of wind and I expect that the midges will rise later, perhaps to help feed the hundreds of wild birds that now live within sight of our bird table. Every so often the silence is broken by a passing tractor, as the local farmers race the approaching storms, to harvest the sweet meadow grass for conversion to silage that will feed the cattle during the winter. Occasionally I can hear "Bruce," our mighty Orpington cockerel, announcing his mastery over our flock of 21 chickens and two ducks. At the moment they are eating a pound of chicken feed each day, along with two pints of porridge and a bucket of fresh greens, and in return they are providing just three eggs a day; they should be grateful that I am a vegetarian, because they seem to be eating better than we are.

Of all of the sacrifices we have made by moving to Ireland, being away from family is by far the greatest, particularly now that both of our mothers are becoming frail and experiencing more frequent bouts of ill health. Now that our only daughter has married, we could soon find ourselves 800 miles away from our first grandchild. It is dangerous to play the "What if" and "If only" games, to speculate how things might have worked out differently. We thought through our plan to start a new life in Ireland carefully and consulted with our families before coming to a decision. Now that the renovations are complete, we have enough space to accommodate one or both of our surviving parents, should the need arise, but they are equally insistent on staying in their own homes for the time being. It is also worth remembering that it took as long to drive to visit either mother from our old house in England as it does to fly from Ireland, although the flight takes a little more organisation. When I recently talked to Mark about how we may miss out on seeing as much of our future grandchildren as we may hope, he was quick to point out that he could think of no nicer place for his children to holiday, than our little corner of Ireland.

As we intended, Lesley and I are still living debt free and comfortably within our budget, but in a country that is now burdened with such immense sovereign and personal debt that it can never realistically pay it back. The crippling austerity measures forced on Ireland by Europe and the IMF have caused great hardship for the citizens of this great little nation. Locally unemployment is well above the national average – and there are more cuts and tax rises to come. The people of Ireland have taken this economic blitz with commendably quiet reserve, a reserve which I find astonishing, given that most of the sovereign debt arose because the country was hoodwinked into guaranteeing a debt that was not of our own creation. It is sickening that a country which fought so long and hard for its freedom has so quickly been sold into economic slavery, while the very people that have let us down so badly are now forcing further austerity upon the people of this island – whilst maintaining obscenely generous pay and pension packages to go along with their undocumented expenses.

Even though we are both retired, I still try and work every day and Lesley bakes for the local market – turning our kitchen into a little factory for at least two days of every week. My business is still operating, although more quietly than before – but at least I have more time for writing. I sometimes fear that we are doomed to repeat the mistakes of the past: judging our worth by the quantity of our possessions and our successes at work, rather than for the quality of our lives, the love of our friends and family, and the simple joy of being together – free to enjoy this spectacular place. I wonder if we are already making the same errors all over again. Is my job and the desire to work what defines me now? If I have a bad day at work, does that really make me a bad person? If Lesley has a week off from the grind of baking for the market or tending the garden, should she feel such shame? There is still some work to do before we can get the balance right. Perhaps we need to be reminded of why we initially found Ireland so endearing; luckily things regularly pop up to remind us....

Last week I saw a man unloading beer from a heavily laden car; several barrels of Guinness were lovingly tied in place on the seats and in the boot, to ensure that no alcohol was damaged in the event of a sudden stop, but the small child on the back seat was left to whatever fate that God, gravity and physics had in store.

For over a year, on the road to Ennis, there have been road works with traffic lights. The work to bypass a dangerous bend with just three hundred metres of new road seems to have ground to a halt, because electricity cables are blocking the way. At each end of the road works there is a large orange sign bearing the words, "Slow Excavation". Recently someone added the word "Very". This witticism was not casually applied with spray paint, or a felt pen, as one may see in other countries, but with the application of a carefully constructed addition, attached to the top of the sign. For variety and additional entertainment, the following week the sign was substituted with "Particularly" – an equally well made replacement, and ten days later the third example of local handicrafts said "Painfully". Perhaps embarrassed by this onslaught of quiet stoic humour, a few days later the offending cables were moved and the work on the new road crept slowly forwards.

The white tailed sea eagles, which were reintroduced to County Kerry at such huge expense, have decided to follow us to County Clare; they are now happily nesting on nearby Loch Derg – obviously these rare birds are blest with good taste!

Finally, a recent conversation with an English chap exquisitely summed up the reason why many people leave modern rural England for the relaxed countryside of beautiful County Clare. A few years ago he lived alongside a quiet country lane outside a pretty village in southern England where, along with a few chickens, he also kept a cow. In exchange for being allowed to eat the grass on the lawn and hedgerows, his cow provided a few pints of milk each day. He decided to move to Ireland on the day that an irritatingly posh woman banged on his door to complain. Apparently she had just driven through a cowpat in the road and had poo on the wheels of her new four wheel drive BMW. She then went on to demand that he should pay to have it cleaned!

So what of the move to Ireland – was it worth it?

My answer is yes.

Despite all of the work renovating the house and garden, the pain of being away from family and putting up with the wretched economy, the unrelenting rain, the endless weeks of dull overcast skies and vicious midge bites as soon as the sun emerges – it has all been worth it. We have transformed a derelict farmhouse into a beautiful home and we have a wonderful life with four delightful dogs, clean air to breathe, a little money to spare and the freedom to do as we wish. On those occasions when we have both become blind to the extraordinary beauty that surrounds us each day, when we start to feel sick of our "awful lives" or become melancholy and frustrated because we are geographically separated from our relatives, on those dark days we are grateful when someone, or something, reminds us of how lucky we really are to be "living the dream".

14413554R00150

Printed in Great Britain
by Amazon.co.uk, Ltd.,
Marston Gate.